Corporate Reputation and Competitiveness

Reputation is at the heart of a company's success. This unique book, from four of the world leaders in reputation research, reveals the very latest thinking about how organizations can improve, whether they are in the public, commercial or not-for-profit sector. The philosophy is to match the external (customer) perception of the organization and what they value, to the internal (customer-facing employee) perception and their organizational values. Only when these are 'harmonized' can the firm be truly competitive.

Corporate Reputation and Competitiveness takes the subject of Reputation Management further than any previous text. It covers some familiar ground: dealing with the media, crisis management, the use of logos and other aspects of corporate identity. But it also argues for Reputation Management to be seen as a way of managing the long-term strategy of an organization. It presents a new approach to measuring reputation, one that relies on surveying customers and employees on their view of the corporate character. It carries detailed results of studies showing the interaction of customer–employee perspectives and how and why customer views influence commercial performance.

The book introduces the Corporate Reputation Chain – the potential to link staff and customer satisfaction via the organization's reputation, and to the Corporate Personality Scale – a way of measuring what customers and staff feel about the organization itself. Detailed case studies from a variety of different companies and sectors reveal the practice of Reputation Management. *Corporate Reputation and Competitiveness* is intended to be useful to both managers and students on postgraduate courses.

Gary Davies is Professor of Corporate Reputation at Manchester Business School where he heads the Corporate Reputation Institute.

Rosa Chun is Fellow in Reputation Management at Manchester Business School and a member of the Corporate Reputation Institute. She teaches Reputation Management and Business Strategy.

Rui Vinhas da Silva is Lecturer in Marketing at Manchester Business School and a member of their Corporate Reputation Institute. He teaches Reputation Management and Marketing.

Stuart Roper is Senior Lecturer in Marketing at Manchester Metropolitan University.

Corporate Reputation and Competitiveness

Gary Davies

with

Rosa Chun, Rui Vinhas da Silva and Stuart Roper

London and New York

First published 2003
by Routledge
11 New Fetter Lane, London EC4P 4EE

Simultaneously published in the USA and Canada
by Routledge
29 West 35th Street, New York, NY 10001

Routledge is an imprint of the Taylor & Francis Group

Typeset in Baskerville by Wearset Ltd, Boldon, Tyne and Wear
Printed and bound in Great Britain by The Cromwell Press,
Trowbridge, Wiltshire

British Library Cataloguing in Publication Data
A catalogue record for this book is available from the British Library

Library of Congress Cataloging in Publication Data
A catalog record for this book has been requested

ISBN 0-415-28743-X

Contents

Figures

Tables

Foreword

What drives competitiveness? This is the central question that animates most discussions about strategic positioning. As a researcher, how can I explain one company's ability to sustain higher margins than its rivals over long periods of time? As a manager, how do I create a strategic advantage for my company that other cannot easily duplicate?

To these questions, one of three answers is typically given: (1) companies build competitiveness from owning better stocks of physical assets – they invest in their infrastructures; (2) companies build competitiveness by gaining better and lower cost access to financial resources – they lower their cost of capital; and (3) companies build competitiveness by attracting better human resources – they create proprietary intellectual assets. Competitive advantage is therefore achieved when managers succeed in stockpiling the very best physical, financial, and human resources. This creates very high barriers that rivals cannot easily jump over, and so enables them to charge higher prices and sustain better margins.

A fourth answer has gained prominence in recent years: that companies achieve competitiveness from being better regarded than their peers – from *reputation*. In this view, managers build strategic advantage by generating favourable perceptions about the company in the minds of key stakeholders. These favourable perceptions become visible in the attractiveness of the company's products, services, trademarks, and brands, and constitute a company's *reputational capital*.

The focus on perceptions invites managers to take a more active, focused, and scientific approach to communicating with key stakeholders – an approach that is rapidly gaining currency under the label of 'Reputation Management' in companies around the world. As pragmatic interest in Reputation Management has grown, so too have academics begun incorporating 'corporate reputation' into the conceptual models. In the last six years, the Reputation Institute that I direct has conducted over seven research conferences on the topic of reputation and competitiveness. We have screened over 450 academic and practitioner papers, the best of which have been published in the Institute's quarterly journal – the *Corporate Reputation Review*. Quite significantly, contributions have been multi-disciplinary, and showcase work done by a wide-ranging group of economists, strategists, accountants, marketers, and organization theorists. To economists, reputations are traits that signal a company's likely behaviours to rivals. To strategists, a company's reputation is a barrier to the mobility of rivals in an industry. To accountants, reputations are an intangible asset, a form of goodwill whose value fluctuates in the marketplace and is tied to the company's market value. To marketers, reputations are perceptual assets with the power to attract repeat customers. To students of organization, reputations are an outgrowth of a company's identity, a crystallization of beliefs held by stakeholders about what the company is, what the company does, and how it does it.

In part, academic and practitioner interest in corporate reputations can be traced to the widespread visibility given to the topic by the development of various corporate rating schemes. *Fortune*'s annual empirical survey of 'America's Most Admired Companies', begun in 1982, is probably the most visible of these – and the one used by most academics, for lack of a better measure. Since its inception, the survey has spawned a small industry of followers in publications such as the *Financial Times, Asian Business,* and the *Far Eastern Economic Review* (Gardberg 2002). Social ratings agencies like the *Council on Economic Priorities* and investment funds like *Kinder, Lydenberg, and Domini* (KLD) also rate companies on various aspects of their social performance and academics often use their ratings as surrogate measures of corporate reputation. These have been criticized on various grounds, not least of which their lack of theoretical grounding. To overcome these weaknesses, in 1999, the Reputation Institute and Harris Interactive proposed the Reputation Quotient® (RQ) as a standard measure of corporate reputation. Since then, RQ studies in the USA, Australia, South Africa, and across Europe have been conducted, with over 300,000 people surveyed and hundreds of companies measured. The results demonstrate that the measure is a valid tool for gauging and analysing how stakeholders think about companies.

It is to this developing field that Gary Davies and his colleagues bring their research on the 'Corporate Personality Scale'. Those of us who know Gary have followed with great interest the theoretical and empirical analysis that has been done at Manchester Business School under his leadership over the last few years. In the research they describe, the focus is put squarely on two pivotal stakeholder groups: employees and customers. Perceptions of companies by both of these groups are clustered into dimensions that describe various corporate personalities. The detailed empirical work of Gary Davies's Manchester-based research programme is that these 'corporate personalities' are central in generating both employee and customer satisfaction and loyalty. In turn – and most importantly – they show us that these attitudes are directly linked to key financial outcomes like turnover and sales – the holy grail indeed!

By developing a conceptual framework that ties employees' internal to customers' external views of the company, and by tying these cognitions to results, the book makes an appealing contribution to the our understanding of corporate reputation. It shows us that a company's image and identity are related, that Reputation Management involves harmonizing the two, and that harmony produces financial value. Surely this is the aim of strategic management, which makes this book's contribution very much worth reading by all practitioners and academics interested in improving their understanding of how stakeholder perceptions build competitive advantage.

Charles J. Fombrun
Professor of Management, Stern School of Business, New York University
Executive Director, The Reputation Institute
March 2002

Introduction

If you believe passionately that the best way to create a strong corporate reputation is to advertise, then return this book from where you purchased it and try to obtain a refund.

Advertising has many possible roles: the recruitment of new staff, the announcement of some important changes and the creation of an image. The advent of television advertising in the latter part of the twentieth century and to some extent that of cinema advertising slightly before then, opened up a new era for corporate communication. At the same time the consumer economy in most developed societies was booming. People wanted to spend money and to demonstrate to themselves and to others that they had the ability to do so. Advertising to create an image around a physical product was one of the ways that manufacturers could link the two potent ingredients of sales growth together, consumer demand for products and their demand for imagery.

Advertising can be used to create an image. But is this what corporate reputation should be about or even can be about? Is the reputation that an organization has with its stakeholders (customers, employees, suppliers, investors) something that can be created in their minds, despite the daily reality that they experience? Can a glitzy advert be more than a dangerous waste of money if the imagery that the advert proclaims is totally different from the reality that the customer or employee experiences?

Certainly a corporate name can also be a brand name and this is something that we address in our book. However ours is a new approach to managing a company as a brand, something that depends more upon the emotional attachment that customer facing employees have with their organization and less upon the creativity of an advertising agency. Even having employees who are fanatical about their corporate brand is not enough. What they value about their organization should harmonize with what the most important stakeholder group, customers, value in the corporate brand.

Today's brands are not just those of the fast moving consumer products industry. *Every* name that identifies an organization is potentially a brand name. Managing a corporate brand, a corporate reputation, is not the same challenge as managing the brand associated with a box of detergent. It is a more fundamental and therefore a more difficult task. Because it involves the whole organization, and not just the marketing or corporate communications functions when managed properly, reputation is not yet a business function. Because reputation relates to long-term commercial performance, involves many of the line functions of an organization and addresses issues that are at the core of a business, reputation is a strategic matter and not something that can, any longer, be delegated or relegated to any existing functional area. We argue that for many organizations, and particularly for those whose business relies upon serving the customer as well as providing them with products, that reputation can be a useful way of looking at the entire business. We argue that the reputation perspective or paradigm is likely to be useful to the majority of organizations, not just to commercial organizations but to government departments, to not-for-profit organizations such as charities, to schools, to political parties in fact to any organization which needs to maintain a positive image with its main stakeholders.

We have worked closely with a number of organizations and researched others from a distance. We cannot reveal their names, but we would like to record our thanks to them for their support and for their enthusiasm. While many of the ideas in the first part of our book are drawn from the work of those who constitute the reputation community, the core thinking and data in the second part of the book are quite new. Our first survey using the approach we detail was in 1999. The first draft of the Reputation Chain model followed in 2000. The first evidence that employee identity and customer image co-vary and that these link to satisfaction and then on to financial performance emerged in that same year.

Who are the 'we'? Gary Davies is the main author of the book and is Professor of Corporate Reputation at Manchester Business School, (MBS). Rosa Chun, Rui da Silva and Stuart Roper were the first researchers on the project and most of the data in the book is theirs. Rui is currently a Lecturer in Marketing at MBS, Rosa is Fellow in Corporate Reputation there and Stuart is a Senior Lecturer at Manchester Metropolitan University. Individual chapters draw heavily on research papers written by two or more of us. One chapter also contains insights from a study by Louella Miles a freelance marketing writer and Gary Davies. Chapters 6, 7 and 8 draw substantially from Rosa Chun's doctoral dissertation. Other material reflects the investment into research made by MBS and previously by other universities employing the main author over the last twenty years. Extensive reference is also made to the work of other academics, practitioners and consultants in the reputation field over the last thirty years. We hope we do them justice.

The book is in two parts. The first makes the case for reputation as a strategic focus, pointing out that reputation for many organizations affects too many aspects of the business including long-term financial performance to be seen as a tactical or functional matter. The second part outlines the approach to Reputation Management that we have developed and used with a number of different types and sizes of organization. The first chapter places reputation as a strategic approach in the historical context of the way thinking about business strategy has developed and has had to evolve in response to a changing environment.

Part 1

Reputation as a strategic approach

1 A brief history of strategic thought

What strategy is about, what ideas have been most influential in strategic management and why the need for a new approach, where this book makes its contribution.

Before explaining what we mean by reputation and its management it is worth stepping back to see where our thinking stands in the short history of formalized thinking about the strategy of organizations. A brief history of strategic thought will help to explain the need for a constant evolution of thinking as to how organizations should be managed and where gaps are appearing between the nature and needs of business and such thinking. We believe that a reputation perspective is a timely addition to existing approaches to strategic management.

An organization is by definition something that has form. A business organization is something that also has a specific purpose, to achieve something in its business environment, a goal. It pursues its goal in the interests of its owners, often its shareholders, or on behalf of a wider and more diverse group, its stakeholders. How a business plans to achieve its goals has become known as its strategy, a military metaphor that implies that business is about conquest, battles that are won or lost, about campaigns and resources. This, rather dramatic, view of business management is not quite how strategy works within a real business. Strategy is often more subtle.

It is not always clear to managers how their business should be managed over the longer term. What to do day to day is clear enough (if there was only the time to do it all), but what of the long-term survival of the organization? A useful point to emphasize here is the word 'long'; the word 'strategy' has become abused somewhat and used to decorate anything associated with business, to any short-term initiative so as to make it appear more important. In this book the word 'strategy' is always used to refer to something that will take time to evolve, something that will guide a business over a time period measured in years rather than months and something that will lead a commercial organization towards improving its financial performance. We do not limit ourselves to such organizations and recognize throughout that many organizations are not profit maximizers or even profit seekers.

Early books on business strategy aimed to structure and codify the many company histories and memoirs of business leaders. They contained precious little theory or models drawn from economics or other social sciences. They did contain many good ideas but few frameworks in which to place them. There was limited guidance as to when and where any one idea would or would not work. Just because an idea was useful in one company at one moment in time does not mean it will always work. Gradually ideas and models emerged that provided the necessary structure to the chaos of anecdotal memories.

What is strategy in a business context?

First we need to distinguish between corporate and business level strategy. At the corporate level businesses need to ask themselves fundamental questions such as 'Which business should we be in?' At the business level a business needs to ask itself, 'How do we compete?' It is at this latter level that we position our thinking. The organization has decided that it will compete in a certain market and is seeking ways to optimize what it does in pursuit of its goals, in other words what its strategy should be.

How we think about business strategy has evolved and changed as new and better ideas have become more widely known and accepted and as the needs of business have changed. Business strategy has had many definitions but these are two that give a sense of what is involved irrespective of where we are in time: 'Strategy is about matching the competencies of the organization to its environment. A strategy describes how an organization aims to meet its objectives'.

The changing environment for any business can be understood by assessing the main factors that create change in a marketplace: political (including legislative), economic, social and, technological trends. If strategy is about matching your business to the opportunities and challenges of the environment then it pays to understand what that means and how the environment is changing and likely to change in the future.

A company's ability to match itself to its environment can be assessed in turn by listing its main strengths, weaknesses, opportunities and threats, the now familiar SWOT analysis. PEST and SWOT analyses have become the logical starting points for any business looking to appraise itself and to define or redefine its strategy. How a company matches itself to its environment is left to its management to decide. We believe that it is time to identify better ways in which any organization can identify how to match itself to the changing needs and views of the most important part of its environment, its customers. We also believe that management needs to look more inside their organizations to find the answers to the challenges presented by their environment.

A third definition of strategy explains why commercial organizations should invest time and money in creating a strategy: 'A successful strategy is one that achieves an above average profitability in its sector'.

We also believe that any approach to strategy must be capable of demonstrating that it can guide a business organization to above average profitability or at least to an increase in profitability. For not-for-profit organizations the performance measures will be very different. A business school might aim merely to break even but measure itself by the number of students it educates. A charity might measure its total giving or a ratio of donations to income. A church might measure itself by the size of its congregation. In this book we tend to use performance measures that are relevant to commercial business but the same logic can be applied to any type or style of organization.

Gap analysis

While companies still use SWOT and PEST analyses, other strategic tools have become dated as business has changed in its nature. A century ago the multinational was the exception on the corporate landscape. Most businesses were small and local and this is still true in many countries and in many sectors to this day. In markets where competition is fragmented and the main competitors are small, a relatively unsophisticated business plan, one that concerns itself solely with the business itself and its immediate market, is likely to be more than adequate. Gap analysis is still a relevant technique that can focus the management of such organizations into thinking about the main issues they face, specifically how to bridge the gap between their existing financial performance and where they would like the business to be in the future. If the gap is wide (Figure 1.1) and if the recent performance has been poor it is likely that the company will have to reinvent itself and to find a different answer to the question 'What business are we in?' Used in conjunction with a PEST and SWOT analysis a firm can construct a clear sense of direction. By identifying and costing various projects that will help to fill the strategic planning gap, it can create a strategic plan.

The value of gap analysis lies in its simplicity, but it has one key weakness. It ignores competition. It also lacks any model to help management decide what to do or how to appraise their ideas as to how to fill the planning gap. But first there is a question on the way strategies actually evolve. Is it via the purposive analysis implied by Gap, SWOT and PEST analyses?

Are strategies always deliberate?

There has been a lively debate as to whether 'strategy' is something that senior management can decide upon and impose upon an organization or whether

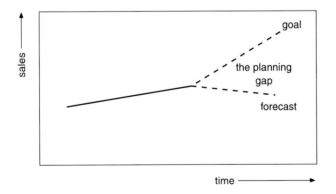

Figure 1.1 Gap analysis.

strategies emerge from within an organization, guided by managers rather than decided by them, Mintzberg (1987). Many argue that specific strategies tend to emerge, rather than be created, in larger organizations because many new and different strategies are constantly being created and acted upon routinely through the interaction between the firm and its customers or even suppliers. An order might arrive from another country and before it knows it the firm is in the export business. An existing customer, impressed by what the firm has done in the past in supplying one product or service, asks it to provide another outside its normal scope of operation. It does so successfully and finds itself in a new business. This idea of a business almost lurching from one opportunity to another may appal, but the analogy of strategy as evolution where a series of often random events occur, a tiny minority of which change the business because they produce sustained sales or profit, is not too far from reality. Indeed some have argued that you can apply this thinking outside of the firm, one business species thrives as it adapts to a changing environment while another is wiped out when its main source of nourishment declines.

In reality businesses do, indeed must, try to formalize their strategies, to take control of their own destiny. The problem is how? The best answer will probably be a combination of direction and evolution. From the top or centre will come an analysis and formal plan. This will include the financial objectives of the firm, as there is no sense in delegating those. The contribution from lower down the organization, the bottom up component can include the source of options to be analysed. The role of the planner is to select the best options so that the firm has a clear direction to follow. The worst possible situation is where the company is actively trying to pursue more than one competing strategy at the same time. It does not work.

The problem with such thinking is that it leaves the role of strategy formulation somewhat in limbo. On the one hand we are saying that strategy is about having a clear understanding of how the organization is planning to meet its objectives. On the other we are arguing the value of allowing radical ideas to emerge from the customer interface, somewhere not always regarded as the place where strategy is formed. So just where do we stand on the issue of who are responsible for strategic management?

What is best left to the senior team in our view are decisions about which markets to be in, whether to enter country X this year or next, whether to acquire Company Y or to divest Division A, what we labelled earlier as corporate level strategy. Our focus is on market strategy, what organizations should do to manage their way in markets they are already in and intend to stay in. For the first type of decision we concede the need for a centralized function that makes decisions. For the second type of role we will argue that managers should create a framework and set objectives and then let the organization get on with meeting those objectives.

Two flows of ideas

The strategy process is about flows of ideas and instructions up and down the organization. There will be two distinct flows in any business, the financial planning flow and the strategic planning flow. They interact (Figure 1.2) and often

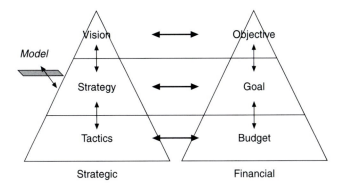

Figure 1.2 The two planning flows.

conflict. A typical financial objective might be to achieve a 24 per cent return on assets employed each year. A typical vision statement is more qualitative and more long-term, to be market leader in a specific field. Underpinning the company vision will be a strategy that gives practical form to that vision. At the same time it explains how the company expects to achieve its financial goals and objectives. All too often it is far from clear in written plans how the strategy will deliver the required financial performance.

Tactics are the shorter term, day-to-day matters that will be of relevance to many employees, for example a sales target of four customer calls a day, a production plan for 50 tonnes of product. Money is required to fund the business and to meet day-to-day expenditure. Typically a financial budget is prepared for every part of an organization. Individual budgets are totalled and compared with the revenue forecasts to judge the viability of the plan.

Those reading this who have prepared budgets and forecasts know only too well that preparing them is an art as well as a science. The art comes in not leaving yourself with too little fat, in slightly over forecasting a budget and under forecasting a revenue stream. Those reading this who manage those who prepare budgets and forecasts recognize that managers 'suffice' rather than maximize profit, and probably have a number of ways of ensuring that both forecasts and budgets appear challenging while still being feasible. There is a danger in our experience of believing one's own forecasts. Senior managers spend time and effort making sure that the next year's plan looks sound because revenue and expenditure balance. But what appears on paper is no more than a wish list. If the organization is in a stable environment then a simple extrapolation from last year is adequate. In such a case the financial flow will dominate management thinking. In situations where the environment is more fluid and less predictable then rigidity creates myopia. Organizations in the service sector have to be prepared to change, often on a daily basis to respond to shifts in what their customers want or in what their competition are doing. Visionary companies often out perform financially driven ones because there is not a reliance upon budgeting and forecasting, there is often not enough time to do such things as the business is too concerned with how it can cope with the opportunities that are there in the market and that can never be predicted. Having a rigid top down approach can stifle the very essence of an organization's ability to succeed. Senior management's role is to set targets and let middle and junior managers decide or at least influence how to meet them. As organizations become more complex and physically larger, it becomes more and more impossible for one person at the top to be able to manage 'top down'. Education standards have risen but companies can ignore the potential they recruit, trying to control what they should be letting free, lacking the framework that will guide employees to achieve without detailed manuals on what to do and how to do it.

In this book we aim to present an approach that is not budget driven in the sense that the firm relies upon replicating what it did last year, but not so free and easy so that senior management lose all control over what is happening.

The balance between the two flows in terms of the relative power they have in the organization is interesting to observe. Some companies have such a good strategy that they use the right hand side of Figure 1.2 just to keep score. Profitability is almost taken for granted. The debate is more about how much profit to return to shareholders, how much to invest, and what the staff bonus scheme should pay out this year. In other companies financial management is all powerful. It needs to be, as the business has not discovered a position in its market that it can use to achieve above average profitability, most probably because it lacks an effective strategy. It lurches from one financial crisis to another. Many businesses survive in this way for years, but the better employees leave for better paid and more satisfying jobs elsewhere. Even among some apparently better performing organizations employee turnover can be an issue. Here financial performance has been gained at the expense of employees, the ruthless organization that we will describe in a later chapter. Employees leave, disliking the uncaring attitude to both staff and to customers that means they care little for their employer.

Over the years a number of models have been produced largely from academic research that companies can use to improve their chances of achieving above average profitability. Figure 1.2 suggests that the strategic decision making in an organization is guided by a model, a simplified picture of what makes for success in business. So what are these models and how useful have they proven to be?

Strategic models

By the 1980s businesses realized that they needed more sophisticated tools to help them construct valid strategies. The main problems to be faced in their markets were not so much the trends identified by their trend analyses but by the, less predictable, actions of their competitors. Take the retail sector as a good example. In the 1950s there were few countries in the world where concentration levels in the retail sector were high. By the 1990s most developed nations had food retail sectors that were dominated by a small number of players. At the same time such companies owned more than one retail business and strategies were needed for each market.

To help make sense of the new complexity and to make the process of strategizing easier, a number of competing models of how to evolve a successful strategy came into being. Figure 1.3 is the most famous of its genre, the five forces model of Michael Porter introduced in the late 1980s (Porter 1998).

It is useful to think of the five forces as sources of pressure on the firm that can reduce its overall profitability. Within the central box are the existing players in the market. Higher levels of concentration usually mean more pressure on any one player. Other factors such as ease of exit and differences between capacity and demand will affect the potential of all players to make money from the market. If the market is profitable then other players will be attracted to join. Existing competitors can raise entry barriers to defend themselves from the increased competition that would result. More dramatically a new answer to the customers' needs, a substitute, may emerge, a fuel cell to replace the internal combustion engine. This could have a devastating effect on existing players, or they could adopt the innovation or focus on sectors that prefer the established technology.

Thinking of customers and suppliers as threats to overall profitability is a useful idea in that it emphasizes the negotiating strength of both compared with that of players inside the middle box. If the concentration level in either of the two adjacent boxes is higher than that inside the middle box then the power of companies to resist price negotiation is reduced. A large food retailer will find it easier to negotiate with a fragmented farming sector than with the more concentrated supplier group offering detergents. If the customers for a manufacturer of detergents become fewer as the retail sector concentrates, then price pressures on them as suppliers will grow. Customers are not without their own pressures either from their own customers in a supply chain if they are agents or distributors, but also if they are say shoppers buying on behalf of other consumers, as will be the case in many consumer product markets. These indirect pressures will impact on the relationship a firm has with its own direct customers.

The Five Forces Model is the least controversial aspect of Michael Porter's extensive work. It provides a useful framework to analyse virtually any market as a starting point for strategic planning. There is less agreement on the three generic strategies that he proposed for developing the options for the business strategy itself: cost leadership, focus and differentiation. The term generic strategy means a strategy that can be applied in any market situation. Porter argued that a business unit must adopt one or more of the three generic strategies to

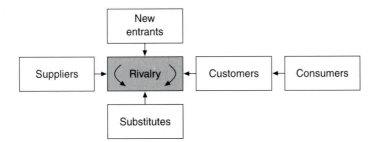

Figure 1.3 The Five Forces Model.

achieve above average profitability. Essentially this means choosing one of four options, cost leadership or differentiation, applied market wide or focused on one part of the market. Cost leadership is the easiest to understand, the company has the lowest costs among its competitors. It has an economy of scale that cannot be matched by competitors with lower volumes or who are further up the experience curve. However even here it is difficult in our experience to extrapolate the observation that a company has low cost to how it should use such an advantage in the marketplace. Should it sell at a low price, in which case its cost advantage can be negated? Or should it maintain an average price and make more margin due to having lower than average costs?

Differentiation means having a unique offer in the market, something that is easy to understand and difficult to achieve.

Focus is also easy to understand, being similar to the idea of market segmentation, and the company focuses on one part of the market. A product focus strategy is easier to operationalize than one based on a customer focus. Becoming the specialist in heart drugs or small electrical motors is easier to envisage than focusing on a group of consumers with a coherent attitude. Customers tend not to stay in neat boxes.

Critics of the three generic strategies have suggested other combinations of price, focus, and differentiation or very different lists, but all share the same problem of turning analysis into action.

A number of competing models have been proposed. The originators of one, the PIMS approach, Buzzel and Gale (1987), provide data on actual business unit performance from their panel of collaborating companies that suggests that Porter's three generic strategy approach is not totally reliable, because business units with a clear generic strategy do not achieve above average profitability. Instead Buzzel and Gale's data show co-relations between relative market share and profitability and between relative perceived quality and profitability.

They argue that companies should strive first to achieve a reputation for better quality as this will drive increased sales, creating higher market share, which in turn means better economies of scale which leads to superior profitability, the PIMS paradigm, summarized in Figure 1.4. Certain market factors can govern sector profitability such as the level of perceived differentiation between competing products, market growth rate, and the importance of the product to the typical customer's overall business. How a quality advantage is developed is less clear, particularly as Buzzel and Gale rightly point out that perceived quality is more important than actual quality.

PIMS is a very different approach to understanding how companies achieve above average profitability. Apart from the emphasis on relative perceived quality as a starting point, the approach is empirically driven, relying upon comparing data provided by member companies. Therein lies one of the potential weaknesses of the approach in that what correlated with profitability last year may not be the best idea in the next. Porter's approach is based on economic theory and therefore more likely to be valid irrespective of the environment. The problem is whether any economic and therefore high-level model of business is good enough to be useful in all contexts. What we aim to do here is to provide a framework for management thinking and strategic planning that is

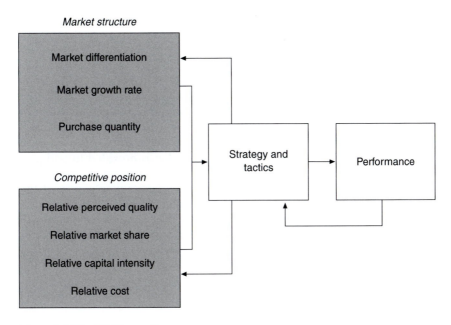

Figure 1.4 The PIMS paradigm.
Source: Adapted from Buzzel and Gale (1987).

not so prescriptive as either of these two models. We do not take the view that relative perceived quality or focus or cost leadership are strategies that companies must choose between. We assume that such possibilities will be embedded in the minds of business managers and that they are capable of being pragmatic about the use of such ideas, realizing that the advice of competing models conflicts, and that they need to apply their own judgement as to what is relevant in their own context. We aim to add to existing models and not to replace them.

Both approaches present a very rationalistic view of the customer. Even when they depart from this perspective, by mentioning perceived quality in the case of PIMS and differentiation in the case of Porter's generic strategies, how either is assessed at a strategic level is unclear. We will offer an approach to assessing the relevant aspects of both such that an organization will know whether it needs to emphasize perceived quality. How any organization is perceived will be important, and an image for quality is only one dimension of that perception.

The new economy

The Porter and PIMS models are two of the most widely taught for use by strategic planners in their assessment of the potential for use by managers in their decision making on the most appropriate strategy for a business unit. One problem with them is that they offer conflicting advice to practitioners. One draws from economic theory and the other from empirical data and so perhaps it is naïve to expect them to be totally compatible. But they share a weakness in that they both encourage a top down approach to the long-term management of a business. Implied in both is the idea that a specialist function within a business can produce a strategic plan that will change the direction of a business unit and lead it towards greater profitability.

Two trends make the top down approach less easy to believe in for the management of contemporary business. First the modern business is often too complex to manage top down. No one person has the intellectual ability to grasp the totality and detail of the modern corporation. The first statement is likely to be controversial, the second less so. The value added in a modern society is coming more and more from the service that is provided to and purchased by customers and less and less from the physical product that is provided. McDonald's sells products but we regard the company as a part of the service sector. Ford sell cars but we require assurance about the aftercare that goes with the vehicle. Not only is the service sector now the dominant sector in most developed economies but companies who might have regarded themselves as manufacturers a decade ago now argue that service to customers is more important to business success than product. Product has become part of the cost of entry into many markets and not the reason why people patronize a particular firm. 'Anyone can make product' has become a valid maxim and more and more of 'making' is being out sourced to specialists in low cost economies. Unless the technical content of the product is significantly different or there is some other aspect of it that is patentable or registerable then product alone is not enough to compete.

Service and the service sector

In a service company one issue with the PIMS paradigm is that the concept of quality is less easy to define for a service than for a physical product. The customer's actions form part of the service process, the product is created in the interaction between the supplier and buyer and the quality that is perceived will be shaped in part by the actions of the customer.

Service quality has been defined as: 'meeting or exceeding customer expectations'.

Customer expectations and the service experience cannot be managed with the precision that can be expected in a manufacturing process. Because of the differences between a product and a service business, different models have been devised to guide strategy in the service sector.

The SERVQUAL model was introduced in the 1980s (Zeithaml *et al.* 1990), to offer a structured way to measure service quality and to explain the gaps that can exist between what customers expect and what senior management try to provide, summarized in Figure 1.5. Its authors identified a number of dimensions to service quality but the task of deciding how to interpret them in the context of a specific business is left to the user. We believe strongly in the relevance of a gap between the internal and external view, but we will challenge the way such gaps are assessed.

Zeithaml *et al.* (1990) also argue that there are a number of dimensions of service quality, *access* (Can the customer obtain the service easily?); *credibility*

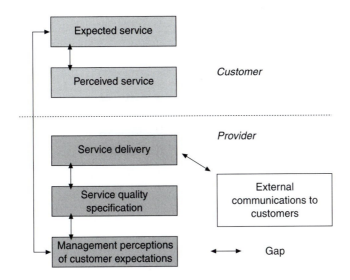

Figure 1.5 The SERVQUAL model and gaps.

(Can you trust the company?); *knowledge* (Does the supplier understand the customer's needs?); *reliability* (Is the service dependable and consistent?); *security* (Is the service free from risk?); *competence* (How knowledgeable and skilled are staff?); *communication* (Is the service well explained?); *courtesy* (Are staff considerate and polite?); *responsiveness* (Are staff quick to respond?); and the *tangibles* associated with the service (buildings, uniforms). The first five relate to outcomes from the service provided and the second five to the delivery process. (Dimensions such as trust, reliability, and competence are reflected in studies of reputation.)

The service profit chain

Reflecting again the growth in both the services sector and the need to evolve new models to support the strategic analysis of service dominated organizations, a number of similar ideas have emerged connecting profitability to the satisfaction of customers. Many see employee satisfaction as making a critical contribution to customer satisfaction. Prominent among these is the service profit chain, Heskett *et al.* (1994). Here the links between what managers do inside the organization in developing internal service quality (workplace design, job design, rewards and recognition) are argued to drive employee satisfaction. Satisfied employees are retained longer and are more productive. This in turn drives an external view of satisfaction, in other words customers get served better. This being so customers are more satisfied, more loyal, patronize more often and so sales and profits rise. Similar ideas can be found in other models, Barber *et al.* (1999), Rucci *et al.* (1998). The common idea is that management can drive performance by ensuring that certain links in a chain are in place. Empirical tests of the service profit chain effect as a whole or even the

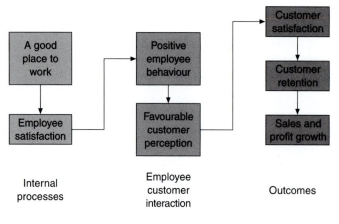

Figure 1.6 The chain effect in a service business.

Source: Adapted from Heskett *et al.* (1994).

individual links therein are not easy to find but the ideas that external and internal satisfaction are positively co-related and that one causes the other are intuitively attractive. The overall concept is summarized in Figure 1.6. However this is one of the aspects of contemporary strategic thought that we will challenge.

The Business Excellence Model

The European Foundation for Quality Management and the British Quality Foundation subscribe to the Business Excellence Model, summarized in Figure 1.7. Yet again there is an emphasis on the linkages between employee (people) satisfaction and customer satisfaction and business performance.

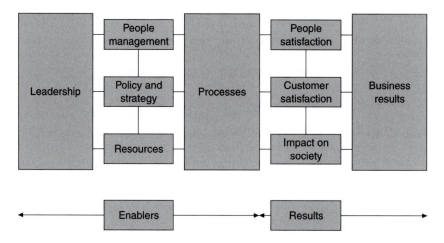

Figure 1.7 The Business Excellence Model.

One other element of the model worth noting in the context of this book is the inclusion of the box labelled 'impact on society'. The concepts of business ethics and social responsibility have been much debated and by the 1990s were appearing as key issues on the corporate agenda.

Business, ethics, and social responsibility

Companies now issue social, environmental, and other reports auditing their performance over the previous year as a corporate citizen. Such actions are relevant to any work on corporate reputation and so it is worth noting the debate around the issue of business ethics, as this has been a controversial one. Some argue that the primary role of a firm is to return profit to its shareholders; that it has no business being a corporate citizen other than staying within the law. We have strong evidence that companies cannot now afford to take such a view.

Free market economists still argue that any suggestions that business should do more than comply with the letter of the law are flawed, because they run counter to the economic role of business in society, that of producing goods and services at a profit and under competition. Others argue that business needs to look beyond profit and towards its responsibilities as a member of society (Beauchamp and Bowie 1993). In between are the views of those who suggest that business should identify those social issues that have the most impact upon them and manage these so as to improve their market image (Frederick 1997). We believe quite simply that firms cannot afford to ignore their roles as corporate citizens and we offer evidence that shareholders should insist for their own financial benefit that their companies become seen as good corporate citizens.

Achieving differentiation for a service business

Books on marketing and business strategy tend to have a number of ideas in common. The most important is that being different in a positive way in a market can be good for business. Where the customer cannot see any points of difference, then he or she has little option but to compare prices. Many customers will do this anyway, but it is more difficult to make a comparison if products and services appear to be different. If the customer cannot compare prices and performance clinically, then some value judgement must occur where the customer tries to balance less objective factors against differences in price, but the customer will be less sensitive to price. Creating positive points of difference in the product or in the mind of the customer is one way of achieving above average profitability.

For business units aiming for niche markets differentiation involves targeting the needs and wants of a relatively small group of customers. In strategy books this is called focus and in marketing books, segmentation. One feature of segmentation is that the majority of potential customers in a marketplace will probably dislike or see as irrelevant an offering that appears highly relevant to others. Mass-market products have to appeal more widely, but they need to appear to differ from any other similar mass-market competitors. In many mass consumer product markets the accepted way to differentiate is to advertise. One brand of cigarette, beer, washing powder or chocolate bar appears distinctive, not because any objective test can demonstrate difference but because advertisements create a different image. Differentiation can be a key to success in services marketing but we will challenge the relevance of advertising to a service business as the best way to create difference in the way a service is perceived.

There are only two ways to ensure that price competition is not a danger to the firm. Either the business unit can maintain a position of cost leadership or it can maintain a position of non-price differentiation. Cost leadership is one of the easier of strategies to follow as it can be measured, but there can only be one cost leader in any market segment. Other competitors will need to adopt one or more non-price dimensions on which to create a unique point of difference. Once this is achieved, the business unit can also look to reduce the costs of its operations to lower price or increase profitability, but the price/differentiation choice is a fundamental one for any business unit. Sometimes costs will reduce through experience, sometimes through finding different ways of achieving the same end. This does not alter the fact that unless the business unit can reduce its costs to below those of its competitors, then its strategy cannot be one of cost leadership. As there can be only one winner in each sector for this strategic game, it follows that most companies will be trying to discover a non-price point of difference.

In a service organization the nature of a service makes it more difficult to achieve differentiation. Services can be copied more easily than can products. They are then difficult to defend through patenting or through claims of intellectual property rights. One method to achieving differentiation, without necessarily creating a real difference in the product or service on offer, is by creating an image for being different, and the most common way of doing this is by branding. Branding is a highly relevant topic and will be covered later as having an important influence on our approach. It is possible to achieve cost leadership in a service business, but again only a minority can expect to use this approach successfully. This book is for the majority of companies that have to find another way; however we do not believe that service businesses can manage their image through advertising. We believe that there has to be something more tangible than that, in short that the service experience has to be really different.

Top down or bottom up?

As we indicated earlier, one of the implications of the strategy models that were introduced into business practice in the 1980s was that strategy was something that could indeed be thought of as a management function. Hire yourself some bright MBA graduates and create a strategic planning department. The role of such a department would be to analyse the markets of each business unit and write an appropriate corporate strategy for each and every one.

Those of us who have tried this approach know only too well that there is a difference between a strategy and strategizing, the process of managing strategy. There are two phases in any planning process, the first involves analysis and the creation of options. The second involves the selection of an option and its implementation. In a hierarchical culture, one where employees are looking to be told what to do, this two stage process will work well. In business cultures that are more democratic or more participative, the implementation of a strategy feels more like the imposition of a strategy. Mintzberg's idea of an emergent strategy, where successful strategizing involves a strategy that is often not imposed from on high but which emerges from within the organization is, in the authors' experience, closer to reality in many firms. You cannot as a senior manager delegate responsibility for strategic planning to something as amorphous as an organization, but you can usefully combine the analysis and implementation stages by involving the organization, the employees that have to make the strategy work, in its creation. At worst this takes time, at best you eliminate the implementation phase as employees start changing what they are doing almost before the ink can dry on any formal plan.

A 'bottom up' approach is particularly valuable in a service organization. The roles of management differ markedly in firms that are top down and bottom up in their management style (Figure 1.8). In the organization typified by the left-hand diagram, the role of management is to 'decide what is to be done and find someone else to do it'. The managers in one such company were asked what other careers they would have pursued if they had not joined the industry they worked in. The top two answers were the police and the armed services. Now both the last two mentioned organizations have changed a great deal in the last twenty years and have moved away from a hierarchical approach to management, but the response gave an indication that the managers we put the question to wanted to work in a structured environment, one where there was a clear sense of direction, an acceptance of the rights of managers to determine what employees do and how they do it, both for them and for those they manage. This is fine when senior management *can* decide what should be done and quickly enough such that the market has not moved on before action can be taken. In organizations that are large and complex and in markets that are turbulent, such an approach is just unlikely to work.

An alternative approach is to rely upon customer facing employees to

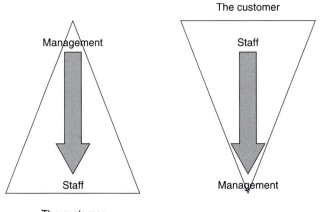

Figure 1.8 Top down vs bottom up?

identify improvements in the way the business runs, improvements that stem from their interaction with the marketplace and with the customer. The role of management changes from proactive to reactive in style, towards one of mentor and coach, to encourage customer facing employees to be equally proactive in the way they approach the customer, to identify as many options for improvement as possible. Managers do not abrogate their responsibilities. Their role is just different. The business unit evolves, driven by what the customer wants and not by what the managers think they want.

Ask any senior manager what percentage of his or her time is spent with customers. Most will give you an estimate that is quite small but one that still exaggerates how much they really spend. Probe more deeply and all too often the focus of the limited time senior operational managers spend with customers is on complaints.

The symbolism within Figure 1.8 is important. In the left-hand diagram the customer is at the bottom, in the right-hand at the top. In a business unit that has a clear product advantage, perhaps a unique product that is ahead of the market, then the left-hand approach is fine, but most organizations will need to consider the approach to its right. The labels that are put to this type of approach vary but include empowerment, customer orientation and the learning organization. Whatever the label we will argue strongly in favour of the bottom up approach making a significant contribution to managing strategy. The role of senior management we believe should focus on defining and refining the values that drive both the internal culture and the external image of the organization. These values are interpreted and reinterpreted at the interface with the customer, by customer facing employees and their immediate management. The process would look more like a circular flow than either of the linear flows implied by Figure 1.8 where more radical ideas that might redefine the company values need to be exposed to senior management for their appraisal. Such thinking is not new but what has been lacking are ways to analyse objectively what the linkages are between internal and external values and how they interact. It is in this arena that we believe we have the most to offer the strategist.

A customer orientation

For a bottom up approach to work an organization has to be focused on its marketplace and on its customers. Businesses can have one of a number of orientations, that is to say the focus of the business. For example a company with a unique and desirable product technology can focus on its products and on keeping ahead of competition in its research and development. Another company, for example marketing life insurance, may decide that the nature of its business lends itself to a sales orientation and an emphasis on persuasively selling the company's products.

A market-oriented company ensures it has regular customer contact at many levels on a regular basis. It undertakes and uses market research regularly to understand what is happening in its market. Surveys of customer satisfaction are used to guide the business. Rewards inside the organization are based upon performance with the customer (Lynch 1997). Market orientation has been associated in some research with more profitable and sustainable results; in other research the picture is less clear (Slater and Narver 1995).

The most extreme form of market orientation is a customer orientation. The customer oriented business is led by someone who is a fanatic about the customer and able to model the appropriate behaviours. Customer facing employees are empowered to respond to customer needs. They feel trusted to run the business. They and customers are regularly asked for their views as to how the business should be run. There are a number of aspects of a market that can promote or even necessitate the adoption of a customer orientation: low growth, concentration, and a lack of fundamental differentiation. But even the most dynamic of companies can benefit from a market/customer orientation rather than a product orientation.

The history of the coffee shop chain, Starbucks, provides an excellent example of the difference between a customer and market orientation and the benefits of both (Schultz 1998). Howard Schultz purchased the business in 1987, when it was still centred on the West Coast of the USA. Schultz's philosophy was to 'delight customers with excellent quality coffee'. Brian Behar joined the business when Starbucks still had only twenty-eight stores. The company history is in many ways a documentation of the struggle between their two different philosophies, Schultz with his emphasis on quality coffee (with what this meant being defined by Starbucks) and Behar, who argued that what the customer saw as an excellent coffee shop should be what Starbucks provided. Behar got his way more than once. Starbucks introduced flavoured coffees, low fat milk options, and iced coffee, not the kind of products that coffee fanatics might regard as the genuine article, but what many customers wanted to see. Customers were able to have their own beans made into their morning coffee.

A customer orientation goes hand in hand with a 'bottom up' philosophy. Top down and bottom up companies can coexist in markets, but they will have very different cultures. One could be labelled as 'authoritarian' or 'paternalistic' the other as 'liberal' or 'fluid'. There is no right or wrong implied here, merely the point that to employees and probably to customers too, the two organizations will appear very different.

If you, the reader, have not already guessed, the approach advocated in this book is customer orientated and bottom up. We do not advocate that every customer's demands should be the drivers of the business. Customers might ask for price reductions that could bankrupt a business and that no sane manager would agree to. What we argue for is that managers should consider any suggestion from customers no matter how stupid it might seem, no matter how far removed it appears to be from the company's vision of itself, and see whether there is profit in introducing the idea.

Mission and vision

Earlier the word 'vision' was used in Figure 1.2 at the top of the pyramid describing how organizations approach strategic management. The point was made that a vision is essentially qualitative, but, together with a mission statement, it can provide a sense of direction. Mission and vision were popular in the 1980s. Annual reports would present them to external stakeholders. Time and effort would have gone into deriving them inside the organization before-hand. Their popularity has declined recently, mainly we believe because many mission and vision statements have been more motherhood and apple pie than the type of document that can direct, let alone inspire, an organization.

A company's mission and vision has long been regarded as a way to express a company's 'corporate character' (Campbell and Tawaday 1990) or 'personality' (Want 1986). In a study of 100 global brands by Opinion Research Corporation International (1999), the biggest internal obstacles to realizing corporate brand potential emerged as a lack of clarity in what the organization/brand stood for. The most successfully positioned companies and brands in terms of growth, financial performance, visibility and market share are those that have linked a powerful brand positioning to an inspiring, overarching vision (Hogan 1998).

Since Peter Drucker (1973) emphasized the importance of mission and vision to business success, a stream of literature has attempted to define both, locate them in the strategic management framework, and suggest an ideal format and content. Academic writers are still unclear about what such statements should include (Klemm *et al.* 1991) but one model summarizes the main elements that are common to much of this research (Figure 1.9) namely: purpose, strategy, values and behaviour standards (Campbell and Tawaday 1990).

A mission statement defines the purpose of the organization, for example when IBM wanted to emphasize that it was more than a manufacturer of hardware it coined the slogan 'IBM sells solutions, not products'. The vision statement is often longer, setting out the company's view of itself into the future. One of the better examples would be Hewlett Packard's, 'the HP Way'. There are similarities between the ideas of vision and identity that will be discussed in the next chapter. For the meantime we would emphasize our support for the idea of companies having strong philosophies, principles, charters, mission and vision statements (whatever they are called) that provide their readers with a clear picture of who they are.

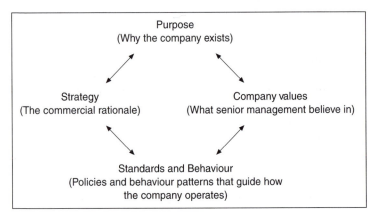

Figure 1.9 Mission and vision.

Source: The Ashridge model from Campbell and Tawaday (1990).

According to Kotter (1996) an effective mission and vision statement has the following attributes:

- *Imaginable*: conveys a picture of what the future will look like.
- *Desirable*: appeals to the long-term interests of employees, customers, stakeholders and others who have a stake in the enterprise.
- *Feasible*: comprises realistic, attainable goals.
- *Focused*: is clear enough to provide guidance in decision making.
- *Flexible*: is general enough to allow individual initiative and alternative responses in light of changing conditions.
- *Communicable*: is easy to communicate, can be successfully explained within five minutes.

Many companies have lists of principles or values that guide them. We will seek to build on this idea to provide the frameworks that we call the reputation chain and the reputation paradigm to make it easier for managers to use mission, vision, and values in their role as strategists.

Implementation

If there is one area where academic thought has failed it is in the arena of implementing strategy. Fine, you have your strategy, you know how to achieve your goal, but how do you convince the employees that your new direction is the way to go? There are a number of ideas that can be useful but none that appears to have the authority that is associated with the likes of a five forces or a PIMS or a SERVQUAL.

A number of options to managing change have been identified. Transforming a business can be a continuous process or involve a step change. The latter can work well only in certain circumstances: in cultures that accept authority (top down) or where the organization faces a crisis and accepts the need for rapid change. This book is not about corporate turnaround, the reinvention of a company, pruning it back to its roots so that it can recover and bloom again. It is more about continuous change and how to promote it and direct it so that it moves the organization forward in a positive way. As has been emphasized there is a fundamental problem with models of strategy that imply that all that is needed is a good analysis. This means that, at best, strategic management is a two-stage process, analysis and implementation.

In a customer-oriented business, the pressure for change comes from the market, sensed by customer facing employees who, perhaps unconsciously, are constantly evolving new ways of serving their customers. They pass these market pressures upwards and on to management, who need to identify what they need to do to make a profitable business from the market feedback. We do not suggest for one moment that every idea that customers have for changing the business has to be taken up; merely that customers and customer facing employees are the best source of ideas to evolve the business. It is the role of more senior management to first explore whether the business can make money from these ideas and then to manage the introduction into the business of those with potential. In such an approach change has to be continuous and strategy evolutionary not revolutionary. It is unlikely that revolutionary change will come from a suggestion emerging from the kind of bottom up process that we advocate. So if you wish to transform your business in the short term look elsewhere. If you want to see it continue to evolve, read on.

Essentially we believe that the stages of strategic analysis and implementation should overlap (Figure 1.10). The whole process will take longer and the implementation phase will appear more tedious and frustrating for those managing change. But the key is that once the organization embraces continuous change then change becomes routine and easier than trying to introduce more radical change once every five years. If you are steering an ocean-going ship you do not keep adjusting the rudder every few minutes, swinging it from side to side, you make small adjustments constantly.

Summary

Strategy is about defining a sense of direction that allows an organization to match itself to its changing environment and, if a commercial organization, achieve above average profitability. Advice on how companies should manage their business strategy has evolved and proliferated. More analytical works, works containing models of how strategy should be managed, gradually super-seded early books from practitioners and consultants recounting their anecdo-tal 'war stories' in the 1980s. One problem with these earlier models was that they gave the impression that they were formulae that can be used by managers to manage the planning process from the top down. New models have been produced in response to the growth in the service sector. As businesses have become more complex, more focused on the service sector and markets have

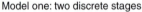

Model one: two discrete stages

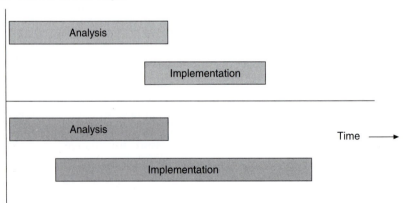

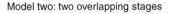

Model two: two overlapping stages

Figure 1.10 Analysis and implementation.

become more turbulent there was a need for approaches to business strategy that go beyond analysis and which are capable of promoting 'bottom up' as well as 'top down' thinking. Continuous change is a good maxim for today's strategic processes rather than seeing strategizing as something that occurs on an annual cycle. A greater customer focus became attractive as a way forward.

Models based around managing vision and mission as the priority for senior management and delegating the detail to 'front line troops' became more interesting but tended to be discarded as the rhetoric they produced appeared too detached from business reality.

From this, albeit brief and selective, history of strategic thought there are a number of ideas that will be referred to in later chapters: that strategy should be about defining a sense of direction; that there are likely to be gaps between how managers see their business and the customers' view of that business, and that an organization's values, mission, and vision somehow define it.

The rest of this book is about a relatively new way of analysing and managing a business unit's strategic situation, the perspective of Reputation Management. It will be of most interest to businesses in the services sector or those with a customer offer that contains a strong element of service but it will still be of value to any organization with multiple stakeholders to satisfy.

We believe that the changes that have taken place in the business and general environments have left a gap for a new approach to thinking about managing an organization's strategy. We aim to fill that gap in the coming chapters by building on the work of others in the relatively new management field of Reputation Management.

We argue that a company can best keep in touch with its market by managing the interface between itself and its customers. The secret to success in our view is for the two most important stakeholder groups for a business, customer facing employees and customers to share the same emotional attachment to the business. We will argue that the external image of many organizations is driven by the way customer facing employees perceive the organization, using what we term the 'reputation paradigm'.

2 The traditional approach to Reputation Management

An interview with a CEO to set the scene, the origins of reputation, the management of public relations, what PR people do, lobbying, how organizations manage reputation, how it is measured, whether there is agreement about links between reputation and performance among managers.

Reputation management is not new. Organizations, individuals, even informal groups have been concerned about the way others see them from time immemorial. What has changed is the way organizations have approached their management of this area and the importance they give to it. The purpose of this chapter is to identify what companies have been doing in managing their reputations so as to identify what Reputation Management means in practice. It draws heavily upon research by Davies and Miles (1998) which drew in turn from an in-depth study of Reputation Management (Miles and Davies 1997). We now draw on an interview with an experienced senior manager to identify how reputation is seen in business.

A practitioner's view

Sir Richard Greenbury was at the helm of Marks and Spencer, in his time one of the world's largest and most profitable of retailers. Marks and Sparks as its customers like to call it, sold mainly clothing but in its British and some of its overseas stores it sold a range of food. Every product was sold under a name belonging to Marks and Spencer, in other words as own brand.

Richard Greenbury left school at the age of 16 and found a job as a junior management trainee with Marks and Spencer. He rose rapidly through the ranks and joined the board aged thirty-three as its youngest director. He became Joint Managing Director in 1985, Chief Executive in 1988 and moved into the chairman's role in 1992. A poll of institutional investors and retailers voted him retailer of the year in 1993. He chaired two government committees, one into corporate governance the other into executive pay. He was knighted in 1993.

In 1997 Marks and Spencer profits reached £1 billion for the first time. A £2 billion global expansion plan was announced to add to a policy of internationalizing the business that had begun in the 1940s. In 1998 the downturn in the Far East and stagnation in the British market saw a dramatic change in the company's fortunes. A boardroom battle to succeed Greenbury, who had announced his retirement earlier in the year, got into the media. Greenbury stayed on for a while as Chairman but soon left. Marks and Spencer continued to decline under two successors. A more detailed case history is given elsewhere in this book. But first what does a manager who has managed a company with one of the best reputations and financial performances, but who has seen its star decline in the corporate heaven, think of reputation and its management?

Reputation

It can take over a hundred years to build a culture and a reputation but it can be destroyed in just a matter of weeks and months.

So why is Marks and Spencer regarded as an icon? Well it was because 12 million people shopped there every week for the simple reason they trusted them. That was the truth, even if they did not always buy. We knew from the figures that only about 8 or 9 million people would make a purchase. But they came every week and back the following week because of a tremendous reputation which had been built up over many, many years.

Product versus image

In the long run one can be certain that you get what you deserve. If you give customers the product they want to buy and it serves them well, and you give them the service they want, I think that will lead to a better reputation. I do not believe that reputation can come before supplying the right product. One of the arguments I had in Marks and Spencer from time to time was with people talking about the brand. The St Michael brand is everything; the brand has to be managed. Of course, but for me the product makes the brand; the brand does not make the product.

If you make mistakes in retailing, particularly with the product, you will pay a heavy price very quickly, because the minute the customer has got a bad product they know about it. But if you then put the problem right, the customer can come back to you. You are as good as last night's performance, so if you give a bad performance you are in trouble, but then you give a good performance and the crowd are back applauding you.

The label on a garment can change people's perceptions of it. It is fashionable at the moment to knock Marks and Spencer even though they still dominate the British clothing market and it can affect the way people feel about the product. Recently one newspaper cut the Marks and Spencer label from a number of garments and sewed in those of some competitors. They asked shoppers to compare these with garments with the Marks and Spencer label still inside. The shoppers preferred those with the false labels.

Every customer has got priorities in their minds. I always think that the first thing that people think about is how much they are prepared to spend. Then what takes over is the design of the product, the performance of the product, the comfort of the product. You might think 'I shall spend a little bit more because if I spend a bit more I get something better'. A younger customer who may buy a product purely for its fashion content might look upon that product as disposable, and therefore would not worry too much about the quality. They would be more concerned that the price was right because they were going to throw it away.

I would say that with everything, that people are trading up. They want better holidays, better cars, better everything. I think that would be true of the food they eat, the clothing they buy, the furniture they furnish the house with. They want better. The question is, how much more they can afford. So I believe that one should be continually trying to trade up and improve the product and give people better, but at prices which they are prepared to pay. You have got to carry customers with you if you are going to trade up.

The CEO

Many great retailers have been heavily influenced by an individual. Walmart was built by Sam Walton. John Sainsbury was also a brilliant retailer. In my own company, Simon Marks was a genius and I think that it is possible in retail businesses for an individual to somehow or other establish a rapport that goes outside the boardroom and down into the business. But I do not think that it is just the man or the woman at the top. In the case of a company, it certainly includes the board. That is why any public argument among board members is so damaging.

I keep a number of quotes from many different people in my wallet. This one is from Winston Churchill, the British Prime Minister during the Second World War, 'In critical and baffling situations, it is always best to return to first principle and simple action'. I feel very strongly that when you, inevitably, have difficult times in business, you must remember what it is you are good at, what are your strengths, what are the things that you do really well.

Another one that I have kept all my life was said by Ray Kroc, the man who founded the McDonald Empire. He built it from nothing to what it is today. Ray Kroc had this wonderful saying, which was on the wall in every outlet in America, 'Nothing in the world can take the place of persistence and determination. Talent will not; nothing is more common than unsuccessful people with talent. Genius will not. Un-rewarded genius is almost a proverb. Education will not. The world is full of educated derelicts. Only persistence and determination are omnipotent.'

Harry Truman was famous for many sayings, 'The buck stops here' and one, that I once quoted at an Annual General Meeting, 'They say that I give them hell, I don't give them hell, I tell them the truth and they think it is hell'. But one of the ones that I always felt was very relevant and which, probably being a blunt Yorkshire man, got me into trouble, was 'Sometimes I was advised to hold my fire, they said, telling the truth would offend people, but whenever I took such advice, I never thought much of myself'. The other one is as follows, 'Once a man starts thinking what it is wise to say and what it isn't wise to say, why, he might just as well cash in his chips and curl up his toes and die', in other words, honesty and integrity. He was famous for speaking his mind.

Keeping a business in touch

It would be interesting to take the top thirty or forty companies in the United Kingdom by market capitalization and look at the chief executive and find out how long he or she has been in that business. Big companies have a problem as people get promoted until they reach the level of their competence. You get an organization that is diamond shaped, because people get into the middle but are not good enough to go further. They stick. They are very important. They have got a lot of experience. They are not idiots but they cannot go any further. In my experience they can make a company become bureaucratic. You cannot dismiss them. You do not really want to because they have not done anything wrong, but they block the way, and do not let the bright young people come driving through.

Listening to staff and customers

I would be in stores two days a week and go to two or three stores in a day. I would nearly always have coffee or afternoon tea and/or lunch with the management of the store and the supervisors. In the privacy of the dining room and without exception I had one straightforward question. 'Right', I would say, 'I know what you are doing well; I know what is successful. I want you to tell me where you are not successful, what you are doing badly'. These people have got a vast amount of information and, if you encourage them, they will tell you, quite openly.

On the sales floor, with the sales assistants, obviously you cannot talk to them about policy, but you can talk to them about the product, because they are selling it to the customer. Again I had two relatively simple questions. 'If it was selling well, why is it selling so well, and if it was selling badly, why isn't it selling as well as we thought? Why have we had to reduce the price or whatever?' The problem with information systems, which have become more and more sophisticated, you know what you are selling. But you do not know why. When you speak to staff, or the customer, that intimacy, especially with good sales assistants, was so rewarding because they could always tell me *why*.

Customers will not speak as easily to someone walking through the store. I could not go to the underwear department and ask, 'Why are you buying that?' Customers want help but they do not want to be interfered with. They will come across and they will tell you if they have a complaint. My Personal Assistant used to type everything up and then every Monday morning, at the operations meeting for all the directors, I would be able to say 'Staff aren't happy about this', and it would cover a wide range of things, not just products but operational matters.

For example after we first introduced fitting rooms we were employing about three to four thousand assistants who did nothing but service the fitting rooms. It was a nightmare, an absolute nightmare. Customers would take eight garments into a fitting room to try on, taking about three quarters of an hour to do so while queues built up. We had to find ways of handling matters and asking the assistants what was the best way.

The media

I think that people can do a much better job of managing the media than I managed to. I am too outspoken, too blunt. And probably, I have too short a fuse to be able to manage the media. Some people do it very, very well. I always feel that Richard Branson seems to be able to manage the media brilliantly. It does not matter if one of his businesses is going badly, he still seems to be popular with them. It is a quality that he clearly has. But the truth is that the media are very, very volatile. If I had my time again as Chairman of Marks and Spencer and as Chairman of the Commission on executive remuneration that I did for the government, I certainly would not today say some of the things I said to the press at the time. Whether you like it or not, they are always going to have the last word. I do not think you can control them. And in fairness, do we want them controlled? After all, we all want a free press. If the price of not having a free press was more control, I am not sure I would want that either. I think it is just something we have to live with.

Staff

I have always believed that one of the principles of business was that the customer and the staff were as important as the shareholder. And in fact, if you could satisfy your customers and keep a happy, efficient, contented staff, the benefits would actually flow through to the shareholders. So I am a stakeholder person, basically. I think the way the customer is treated is very important, but I think so is the way you treat your staff. Because at the end of the day, in a retail business, your staff are your interface with the customer, tens of thousands of them, and if they are not feeling good and right, the way they should be, that they are well looked after, that they are cared for, that you are interested in them, then the customer will know. And it is not about just salary; it is about a non-contributory pension scheme, so it does not cost the staff a penny. And it is not just the perks, free healthcare for example; it is about career opportunities. I think that is a very, very undervalued factor in business today. People should feel 'If

I've really got some get up and go and I've got ability, this business is going to encourage me and allow me to progress'. Progression for ambitious people is a fundamental requirement for happy staff, at every level. I mean that staff can become supervisors, supervisors can become managers and managers can go into all sorts of careers at head office. So progression should be open to everybody which is important.

I am a great believer in one's business life that you must tell people when they have done something well. You must encourage them and praise them, because we all like to be praised. But equally I think it is important that when people do not do their job well, and make a mess of something, that they have to be told that they have not got it right. And to be honest with you, in business if they keep on not getting it right you have to do something about it.

You cannot ask other people to carry passengers; the world is too competitive today. In a football team, if one player is not doing the business, you cannot say to the others, 'Well you've got to carry him, he's not doing very well and he is making mistakes'. You have to change things. Business in my opinion is no different. I am not talking about junior people, because with junior people, the troops, their morale is the most important thing, that they feel good together as a team.

I think people work better in a disciplined environment than they do in a sort of *laissez-faire* environment. We all need discipline in our lives. For the chief executive of the company, the discipline is the discipline imposed by the shareholders. The troops cannot decide what has to be done; they have to be told 'This is what we're going to do', and at every level you have somebody communicating and staff want this as well as suppliers. When I used to go to say, Hong Kong, travelling a long way, I would go out to dinner with them the night before. That was their opportunity to sit with me and talk to me, off the record, casually, about what was worrying them and what they thought we were doing well and badly.

Charity versus dividends

In my time at Marks and Spencer we had a scheme, where the company gave a pound for every pound for any cause the staff raised money for. I was taught and brought up to believe that it was a crucial aspect of Marks and Spencer's reputation. I feel very strongly about commitment to the communities in which you trade. We used to second managers to various businesses including charities. At any one time we used to have about forty people each earning £20,000–£50,000 per annum on the scheme. Sponsorship is just another form of advertising, in my opinion and a different thing altogether. I am talking about genuine giving.

I never regretted it for a second, because of what we got back in terms of reputation and confidence in the business. I used to be asked at every Annual General Meeting, in front of 2000 shareholders about the huge contributions we made. 'Why don't you give this money to us in a bigger dividend?' and I always used to say, 'We think that that's a very, very good investment. We get back reputation, the involvement of our staff, but we also want to do it, we think it's right as a responsible employer'. Obviously, the level of cash flow and the level of profitability impacts upon how much you can afford to give away without upsetting your shareholders. You have got to be sensible about it.

Executive pay

The problem with pay and rations, as I call it, in the United Kingdom, is that it is an unbelievably emotional subject. The British do not look upon pay and rations the way the Americans look upon it. It is still seen as divisive: the senior manager that is earning a million, and the employee on the sales floor who is earning far less. People calculate the ratio of the average staff salary to the CEO's salary, and if it gets to be more than 30 to 1 then it is a disgrace, which is nonsense. You do not see a word of criticism when a sportsplayer negotiates £50,000 a week or an actor earns £20,000 a week on a television soap. Not a word and in my opinion this is rightly so, because they are earning what the market is prepared to pay. So why people get so emotional about what a successful businessperson earns I do not know. Perhaps because there are some terrible abuses by individuals who get bonuses or pay-offs that they should not receive.

Openness

One of the things my committee stopped was the system, by which if someone was dismissed but had a three or four year contract, he or she walked away with three or four years' salary. We created a framework in which it is very difficult now to hide what you are doing as a board of directors. It is all there in the report, an openness, from which the institutional investors in particular can decide if they approve of the way the company is being managed.

Good citizenship

This is very, very important, in my opinion and is fundamental. We are living in a world, reasonably or unreasonably, where your reputation as a business is absolutely crucial. Reputation is achieved in many, many ways. The way you are viewed in the local community is very much the way the staff feel about you as an employer as well as the way the customers feel. The customers and the staff between them, in a very big business, really do make your reputation.

So reputation is important and the media and the relationship between the media and the organization is an issue. The CEO has a central role to play. Reputation without the perception that the quality of product or service is good is not possible, but the image of product affects the company reputation and vice versa. Factors such as executive pay can provoke negative media comment that may not always be seen as rational by the executives who receive high salaries. Reputation involves employees and affects employees. Customer contact and how managers bring information back from the market are issues.

At the time of writing, organizations did not have managers with the job title including the word 'reputation'. So how is it managed? Its origins are in the role of what is variously called public relations or public affairs.

Public affairs/public relations

By the late 1990s most large organizations had departments dealing with what were called corporate or public affairs, corporate communications or public relations. The focus of such departments was on improving the perceptions held by external audiences, where those audiences may have an impact on the organization. Most recently the scope of the activities of these departments appears to have been growing. Post and Griffin (1997) describe the activities organizations undertake in their management of reputation. A similar picture emerges from a study by Edelman (Morley 1998). There is a heavy emphasis on improving the corporate image with local and national government and most activities appear to be externally focused. Figure 2.1 lists those activities identified in the two surveys as being undertaken by more than half of public affairs departments in the USA.

Among the main concerns in the Post and Griffin survey was any gap that might appear between what the various publics might expect from a (large) corporation and the actual or perceived performance of that corporation. Time scales had become more pressing as media issues could explode suddenly and with devastating effect. A similar point emerged from the Edelman survey where Internet usage was a common immediate concern.

- Government organizations
- Community
- Philanthropy
- Issues management
- Media relations
- Public relations
- Employee communications
- Public interest/activist groups
- Crisis issues/management
- Investor relations
- Research and measurement

Figure 2.1 Public affairs activities.

The public relations approach

In 1978 a world assembly of public relations associations agreed upon a definition of public relations: 'PR practice is the art and science of analysing trends, predicting their consequences, counselling organization leaders and implementing planned programmes of action which will serve both the organization's and the public interest'.

Such a broad definition suggests a broad range of activities associated with the PR role, many of which are summarized in Figure 2.2. Organizations typically will undertake part of this work internally and sub-contract part to a PR agency.

Public relations in an organization can be virtually synonymous with media relations. One of the key tasks is the preparation and placing of a press release. Figure 2.3 offers some guidelines as to how to optimize media relations.

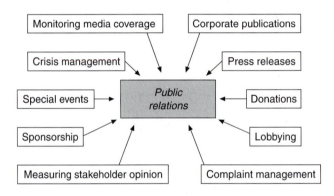

Figure 2.2 The elements of public relations.

> - Learn which media are most influential with your target group
> - Learn what they consider to be newsworthy by forming a relationship with key journalists
> - Do not expect press mentions in exchange for advertising
> - Prepare releases that are succinct, capable of immediate use but which contain adequate contact information for any follow-up and any material such as photos
> - Follow up with the media as to whether they will be using the release

Figure 2.3 Guidelines for media relations.

The image of PR

The traditional image of PR itself could do with some improvement. In Sheridan's play *The Critic* written in 1781, a character named Mr Puff describes himself as a 'Practitioner in panegyric, ... a professor in the art of puffing'. His job involves him in promoting various businesses or individuals in the newspapers by advertisements or by placing articles. As such he represents the forerunner and a parody of both the advertising and public relations agency. He is presented as an unscrupulous rogue, capable of saying anything in his own or in his clients' favour. He catalogues four principles of his profession: the puff direct, the puff collateral, the puff collusive and the puff oblique, all of which involve some form of misrepresentation. If this lampoon of the public relations and advertising industries is somewhat cruel it still reflects a general view that persists to this day that what appears in press releases, in articles in the press, and in advertising should be treated with suspicion. The term 'spin doctor' has crept into the English language to describe someone with the verbal gymnastic skills to make the most negative of incident reflect well on his or her client by turning the sense of the piece.

However the media guarantee the continuation of the press release. Despite the insistence of most journalists to the contrary, the media will sometimes reproduce press releases with little or no original work by the journalist they are supplied to. Second, press mentions are by far a cheaper way to promote a business than direct advertising, ensuring that this method of marketing communications will continue to be important.

An operational problem in using PR is the lack of control the business has over what actually appears in print. The journalist who is creating an original story will act as a gatekeeper between the PR office and the media. But the main issue with PR for us is whether the function is evolving into a Reputation Management role. At present, PR inside an organization is either a subset of marketing or an adjunct to a corporate function or a specialism that is outsourced. The PR manager probably has a background in journalism or the media. PR is a function that is rarely seen as strategic in nature. While there may be an overarching sense of supporting the corporate image, much of PR is short-term and tactical in nature. That said there are many examples where PR can affect an organization or its products in the medium to long term.

Favourable press comment

Product endorsement in the media can be worth more than its weight in gold. A good review by a fashion writer can make or break a designer. A good review in the literary section of a Sunday newspaper can make or break a new novel. The mention of a particular wine on a cookery programme on the television can see sales rocket the following day.

Jeremy Clarkson would be well known to the British public for his engaging reviews of cars on a television programme dedicated to motoring. He is also a journalist and writes for the *Sunday Times*, a middle to upper market paper. In 2000 he reviewed a new version of Ford's Mondeo. The Mondeo is a four-door saloon and is in a competitive sector of the market where most of the large car manufacturers have one or more models. There are two reputations at stake here, that of Ford and that of the Mondeo sub-brand, the associations with the corporate name overlaying those of the product brand of Mondeo.

The car would be regarded in Europe as medium to large sized and was originally targeted at the fleet market to be bought by companies for their sales teams as a value for money workhorse. In Britain the company car had been a tax efficient perk and company cars represented about half of the total market for new vehicles. It was also positioned as a family saloon in the private purchase market. Salespeople often had the option to specify their own vehicle within a price range. Because of changes to taxation the benefit of having a company car had also declined leading some employees to opt for a cash payment that could be used to fund a private purchase. Clarkson's article entitled 'So good that even Gary the salesman will love it' contained the following telling summary of the problems of the Ford name compared with its more glamorous rivals:

> Even if I told you that Ford is donating all its profits to famine relief and that the new car runs on water, you'd still buy a BMW or an Audi or any damn thing so long as it didn't have that plebby, everyman Ford badge on the front...

Describing a Ford as: 'Frill-free engineering for Gary the photocopier sales-man', he pointed out that:

> To attract private buyers, Ford used to load up its cars with all sorts of fruit. BMW would make you pay extra for a steering wheel, whereas a Sierra (*the precursor to the Mondeo*) would come with a whirlpool in the rear armrest.

Clarkson's main point was that Ford's latest product launches had been a surprise with their genuine attention to high quality rather than utilitarianism. After a long list of the improvements Ford had made in the new version of its Mondeo, Clarkson added: 'Gary. You face a simple choice. Buy a BMW and you get the best badge in the business. Buy the Ford and you get the best car'.

Clarkson was seen as an independent journalist and his views would be seen as objective. He would be seen as an opinion leader. The piece was a clear endorsement of the new Ford Mondeo. The article would have repositioned the model's image in the minds of anyone reading it and could, simultaneously, have repositioned the BMW brand as less than value for money.

Negative press comment

Does negative press and media comment have a role in damaging reputation or image in the other direction? The answer is generally yes, but how does it work? Bennett and Gabriel (2001) used the case of the misselling of pensions to examine whether people aggregate successive pieces of unfavourable information received about a business to form a continuously worsening impression of it, or whether they mentally average bad news, so that if successive but still adverse items are less negative the overall image actually improves. Their work indicated that people average bad news. If this is generally the case then it pays to try to counter bad news with good or at least more positive comment in the media. Things will only get worse if successive pieces of bad news are worse than those that came before.

Having a good reputation, as we will point out constantly, is a form of insurance against the inevitable occasions when an organization is commented upon unfavourably in the media. Once a reputation is damaged any news will tend to be interpreted negatively. Much depends upon how the media decide to play a story.

Agenda setting theory

Agenda setting theory holds that the agenda of the media is reflected in the public's agenda but the media's role includes deciding what the public agenda is and so which affects which is unclear. By agenda we mean what people see as important and the way issues are presented. Bob Dole complained about the label of 'old' used to describe him during his presidential campaign rather than words such as 'experienced and mature'. What is considered to be news and how it is reported constitutes the agenda setting role of the media. So who in the media sets the agenda?

Bob Giles, a former editor of the *Detroit News* described the role that Associated Press editors have in setting the news agenda (Giles 2001). Associated Press's editors gathered to talk about the developing stories that are likely to be reported at the top of the evening newscasts and on the front pages of the nation's daily newspapers the next morning.

Before the meeting, the editors will have talked to their bureaux around the world and across the USA to learn of the major news-breaking stories that the Associated Press will cover and pass along to 1700 newspapers and 5000 radio and television stations in the USA and 8500 international subscribers. What Associated Press consider to be news then becomes the news. In selecting certain items and in rejecting others the agenda for the American and international news is set by a limited number of people.

The way that an item is presented is referred to as 'framing'. Framing is the way reporters and editors look at a story. It reflects the premise on which the story assignment might be based. It provides a context for the reporting and the expected story line. Framing draws on journalistic judgement about what is known on the subject and what is important. But the story frame also can be inaccurate if the journalists doing the framing do not fully understand the story or if they are not open to fresh ideas or perspectives. Framing may be influenced by the editorial policy of the paper or station. Thus the same news item will be presented in different ways in different media. The media are also in the business of selling papers or acquiring ratings. They may sensationalize an item and in doing so distort its meaning.

How the media explains a phenomenon is also important. For example is a controversy between two members of the same political party evidence of the necessary debate before any sensible group takes a view on an issue, or is it evidence of a split in a party? Is a plant closure evidence of good management safeguarding the future of the company or of their incompetence in not marketing the right product?

Lobbying, the law and business

One of the more noticeable differences between the job content of European and American public relations/public affairs managers is the heavy emphasis in America on lobbying various government departments and individuals. Not only are local and national governments stakeholders in many types of commercial organization that they have no ownership links with, but government can be a key to an organization's success if it interprets existing or couches new legislation in different ways. The influence that legislation can have on a business sector is rarely given the prominence that it should.

A good example is that of the Japanese retail sector and the pressure placed on the Japanese government in particular by their American counterparts to change the legislative environment so as to open up the market for foreign retailers and suppliers. Much of the battle of will between the two sides was fought out in the media, but both governments would also have been pressured by the representatives of their own constituents, the business people whose futures might depend upon the outcome of such political negotiations. In the case of the Japanese retail sector, American exporters and retailers wanted easier access to the Japanese market.

Local and national planning law is used throughout the world to control the retail sector. Superficially this is to maintain an orderly environment for the average citizen, to restrict opening hours to what is considered reasonable and to ensure that rural and local communities are not bereft of shops. In reality much legislation that has been enacted has also curbed the growth of large scale retailing.

The distribution system in Japan is unique in a developed country. It is multi-layered, with as many as three different layers between a manufacturer and a retailer. With some exceptions, as with milk products, there is little direct negotiation between manufacturer and retailer. Retail concentration is low. There are a great many small, independently owned retail outlets and their owner-managers are an important force politically. Large-scale retailers have been seen traditionally as a major threat to the small-scale, independent retailer in Japan and legislation to protect the smaller business has been a feature of the sector (Davies and Itoh 2001). The Law for the Promotion of Small and Medium Retail Business (the PSMRB law) in 1959, and the subsequent Law for the Promotion of Private Enterprise (the PPE law) in 1959, were specifically designed to promote growth among small and medium sized retailers. The Large Scale Retail Store Law (the LSRS Law) was first introduced in 1973 to restrict competition from larger stores, inter alia, by limiting opening hours. It was amended in 1979 to apply to stores below the earlier limit of 1500 square metres in size (variations in the size threshold also applied in different regions). Thereafter it applied to any stores above 500 square metres in size. There was a rapid expansion of chains of convenience stores of a size below the 500 square metre threshold operated by larger businesses, one of the few ways in which large scale retailing could expand. The number doubled between 1982 and 1994, but even by then they still only represented 3 per cent of all stores, albeit a higher percentage of food sales. The feature dominating Japanese retailing by the end of this period was still the large number of small (independently owned) shops. One measure of the retail structure in Japan is to compare the ratio of citizens to shops in various countries, Table 2.1. The ratio in Japan was very different. In a free market Davies and Whitehead (1995) have argued that the typical shop will become larger as an economy grows due to economies of scope and scale.

Table 2.1 Variations in retail structure from country to country

Country	No. of retail outlets 1994	Population 1994 (000)	Population per outlet 1994
France	326,142	57,900	177.5
UK	306,600	58,395	190.5
USA	977,400	260,660	266.7
Japan	1,499,948	124,960	83.3

Sources: *European Marketing Data and Statistics* 1999, 34th edition, Euromonitor PLC, London, from national sources. *International Marketing Data and Statistics* 1999, 23rd edition, Euromonitor PLC, London, from national sources.

In the late 1980s negotiations between the Japanese and American governments on a wide range of trade issues resulted in the publication in 1990 of a structural impediments initiative. The negotiations were about more than just the retail sector. Change in legislation was argued for to promote the growth of large-scale retailing, so as to promote easier access to the consumer market for American suppliers and also to make it easier for American retailers to enter the Japanese market. Under the new legislation small stores were still to be allowed to retain certain advantages including greater flexibility in their opening hours. Planning permission for large stores had previously needed the consent of local retailers and the planning process could last up to ten years.

The LSRS law was amended in 1992 and was to be abolished to ease the planning process. The PSMRB law was also amended in 1992 but a new law, for the development of specific shopping centres (the DSSC law) was introduced to promote retail business in general and smaller retailers in particular. Nevertheless, a very different legislative environment had been introduced. The new planning application process differed somewhat by size of city but there had been a general loosening of the restrictions on the building of larger stores. Planning applications for larger outlets increased rapidly in the 1980s in anticipation of the introduction of formal legislation. The effect can be judged from Figure 2.4. The ratio of citizens to shops had been moving in the opposite direction to that in other countries but, following the various changes in legislation, the trend changed to be much as in other countries. However the trend was well below that in countries such as the UK as Japanese companies were sometimes unable to take advantage of the more liberal planning environment because of their own poor financial situation or because the new legislation was still a constraint.

It would clearly take a further change in legislation to affect the kind of dramatic change in the retail sector that those who lobbied the American government to facilitate expected. Nevertheless some change had occurred which, without the lobbying, might not otherwise have happened.

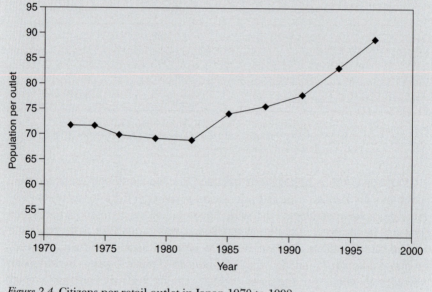

Figure 2.4 Citizens per retail outlet in Japan 1970 to 1998.

Business and its environment

As organizations have become larger, more global and more centralized, their potential impact upon society has become more profound. Society views the modern monolith with increasing suspicion, recognizing that larger organizations in either the private or the public sector have powers that dwarf those of the individual. Large commercial concerns are now bigger economically than many states in which they operate. On a more positive note, larger companies represent a major source of local good, in providing employment, in giving work to suppliers, in creating local wealth that supports other businesses, in providing a social as well as a commercial focus to the geographical area. We talk about companies as being 'part of the community' or 'good citizens' as if they were human entities. And this is how we see them, much as we would see a powerful figure in our own family, someone with the potential to act responsibly and in our interests or to do things of which we disapprove or that might harm our interests. Any society has a set of rules in addition to its formal laws by which it operates. Children are socialized into a behaviour pattern that conforms to a set of norms. If they ignore these norms we seek to show our disapproval and even punish.

The director of a limited liability company must by law act in the best interests of the shareholders. Traditionally this has meant maximizing sales and profit, ensuring the long-term commercial success of the enterprise. Too often such objectives conflict with the formal and informal norms of society. There are mechanisms to rein in any organization that breaks the formal norms, encapsulated as they are in laws. But what of any breach of informal norms? Corporate actions can be legal but unfair or ungenerous. Does this matter commercially? In our view the answer is of course it does! When we deal with an organization as a customer, supplier, official, or as an employee, we do so via a number of transactions. We are more likely to trust an organization of which we have a clear impression and to be suspicious of one we do not know.

If we trust the organization we are dealing with, we are more likely to ignore potential problems, to be more relaxed in our dealings, to be less likely to require formal agreement. In summary we are less likely to increase the cost to the organization of dealing with us. In academic terminology, the transaction costs of dealing with us are lower.

Life has become more complex. We deal with more and more organizations. We categorize them in our minds into three groups: the good, the bad and those we do not yet know. The good we do not worry about. They will not take advantage of us. They will act intuitively in our interests. We treat the unknown with caution. Once we have evidence of their good faith we will be less suspicious. We are definitely suspicious of the bad. They need to redeem themselves in a series of actions that will prove their contrition for whatever wrongs created the bad impression initially. Yes we have short memories, but reputation is cumulative. A bad deed leaves its trace in our memory cells, even if we can no longer remember why.

Public relations and Reputation Management

One of the problems in building upon the PR role to create a broader reputation role is scope. The implications of the changes in the business environment include the need to match better the organization to its environment rather than try to promote a positive picture whatever the reality. So what is different in practice between the reputation manager and the PR manager? First we examine the opinions of a leading specialist in public relations.

Trevor Morris, is chairman of the Good Relations Group, a group of PR companies specializing in finance, healthcare, public affairs and corporate relations. They are among the top ten PR companies in the UK ranked by turnover.

PR agencies

PR agencies should be trying to help their clients to understand their world, to understand that they have multifarious audiences and how best to communicate with them. Ideally that should mean that they help companies to develop distinctive, and real, vision, values and style. By real I mean vision, values and style with substance.

Their role has changed. It used to be much more straightforward, because you dealt with consumers or suppliers or the City or politicians as fairly discrete audiences. The biggest impact on what we must now call corporate Reputation Management has been the emergence of what I call the *new* consumer democracy. The importance of politics has declined. There are lower turnouts at the polls, partly because we think we know what the results are going to be, but also because we do not think it will make a huge amount of difference. Even in America where the result of the 2001 presidential election was far from being a foregone conclusion, the turnout was still very, very low. Why would that be? I believe that power is far more defuse than it used to be and that there are other centres of power. Traditional symbols of power are in decline. In the UK that means the Church and the monarchy.

We are told that of the top 100 economies in the world, fifty-one are now corporations that are enormously powerful globally. Coupled with this is the power of communications, the power of the Internet that undermines any government's ability to control and to influence events. Hand in hand with the increase in corporate power there has been an increase in consumer power, certainly in the developed world as people have become more affluent and better educated. People have shifted up Maslow's hierarchy of needs and now want to express themselves not just as consumers but also as moral, social, political and even spiritual beings. One of the ways consumers do that is through the organizations that they buy from and deal with. For companies it is not now just whether your products or services work, which has become a threshold issue. Companies need to be increasingly transparent with their shareholders and businesses need to publish non-financial information as well. People are also looking to companies to use their power to look after their local communities, to train their staff well, to get involved with education, to look after the environment.

Companies such as Shell or Exxon are inherently exposed to challenges on environmental issues and have to spend time, money and energy dealing with those who oppose or attack them or think that they do not do enough. How you deal with the Third World is another issue that companies have to have a position on that satisfies the new consumer. Nike's alleged use of sweatshop labour generated at least 1500 negative pieces of coverage. There has been a backlash against Nike from the anti-capitalist movement over what could become a mainstream issue. PepsiCo felt it had to withdraw from Burma. Pharmaceutical companies had to agree to open their markets in Africa to generic alternatives.

Another interesting trend is that business has become more part of the mainstream of life. You have lobbyists or pressure groups; you have regulators to make sure they conform, a growing issue for companies. Staff can impact upon your image and having poor relations with your staff can be disastrous if it gets into the media. Ask Bob Ailing of British Airways, what it did to him. The fact that staff and ex-staff are turning to the streets to campaign against Marks and Spencer closing its stores in France is another example.

Some of the antagonism towards Microsoft, for example, is based on their size and dominance, so however well they behave they are going to have problems, and people will want to see them broken up. People do believe that competition is a good thing and they do not see enough competition with Microsoft. It used to be the same for publicly owned companies such as the utilities. They were hated when they were first privatized, because there was no competition. As competition has crept in their loathing rating has gone down because people now feel that they are being tested in the market place and that is fairer.

In summary, there is a much more complicated corporate world than that which existed ten years ago. Previously boards of directors were able to look at their return on shareholders' value, their profitability and that was about it. Now they have to be sociologists, politicians, economists all rolled into one, something that of course most of them are not equipped to do. I can liken trying to understand how a corporation interacts with the world in which it lives as trying to hold a piece of wet jelly in your hands. You can do it but you have to keep constantly moving and the shape of what you are trying to hold on to keeps changing. However much you may research your marketplace, your research only tells you how you were. It cannot tell you how you are going to be. The world moves on so quickly that the need for really expert advice in managing corporate reputation has become far greater.

Good and bad PR management

Bad PR management is first not understanding the way the world has changed, and second trying to remain secretive and not engaging with your audience. It will not wash anymore. One of the reasons is because of the Internet. Almost as soon as something has been typed into a keyboard, then you have to assume that it is more or less in the public domain. There is no point in trying to say one thing internally and one thing externally; internal has become external. There are no secrets anymore. Good PR management is about people who understand an organization's audiences, keep track of them and understand how to communicate with them.

An ability to communicate clearly and effectively is important. There is an element of spin in as much that something well presented and well worded can be made much more acceptable than something badly presented and badly worded. We all know that it is easier to sell a house that has got a nice looking garden and has just had a lick of paint than one that looks run down. It is exactly the same with messages and I do not think that anybody should be at all ashamed of that. Presentation is part of it but not all of it, and a really good PR practitioner and a really effective company make sure that there is substance behind any communication.

The Internet

The big impact of the Internet has been the lowering of the barriers that companies can hide behind. Second allegations that are often completely false and untrue can whip around the world in no time at all. They can be very damaging to a corporation unless it has got a big deposit account of goodwill and a positive reputation for being honest and open, so that people are disinclined to believe any malicious falsehoods. The Internet speeds up the rate of communication. It does not necessarily change the substance of communication. Any message still has to be one that people want to hear, are interested in and believe in and if this is not the case, the Internet makes no difference at all.

Useful models

We use an approach that we call the '180-degree turn'. Most organizations talk about themselves, and yet in fact those organizations and their products are fundamentally dull and of little interest to the audience. What people need to do is a 180-degree turn and talk about what they can do for the audience, how they can help them, what intelligence or insight they can bring to problems and issues of concern to that audience. Instead of talking about home insurance, which is one of the most deadly subjects in the world, an insurer needs to talk about how to manage cowboy builders. The fact that Walmart or Tesco sells food in their shops is not wildly interesting. Tesco's initiative of inviting customers to save vouchers to provide free computers in schools shows that it is engaging with the community and with a modern issue. This is a 180-degree turn from talking about the corporation to talking about the consumer, the community or whichever audience you are trying to address.

PR and advertising

In theory, PR is always better than advertising, because it is effectively third party recommendation. An old saying is that advertising is somebody who goes into a crowded room and says 'Hi, I'm great'. PR is somebody who goes into a crowded room and everyone whispers, 'Hey, he's great'. It is always much more powerful and effective, but few companies pull it off completely. Some pull it off only for a while. Virgin would be a good example and they have been a fairly low-scale advertiser. Advertising is undoubtedly more effective once your products and services are standard and you need awareness and a simple message repeated consistently. PR is not good at that. What PR is extremely good at, and that advertising cannot really do, is to build a more holistic, three dimensional picture of an organization. Your impression of a bank or a retailer is not based on their advertisements so much as what you experience through them and what they stand for, the issues that they have been involved in, even how their management talk. This has become increasingly true of all companies. People look beyond the basic products and services.

Personal reputations

Bill Clinton survived what could have been disastrous media attention about his affair with Monica Lewinsky because those that were against him as a politician were very much against him while the rest of the world, and certainly the rest of America actually did not see his actions as affecting his ability to be President. He caught the zeitgeist of America and indeed there was almost a backlash against the press in the USA for their coverage. More recently, in Britain, when the Deputy Prime Minister, John Prescott punched a protester who threw an egg at him, the press tried to turn it into something big and damaging to the Labour Party, but the public just did not respond. I think people saw it as a natural, spontaneous thing to do, and thought that they might have done the same. And as it was not an issue of life or death it did not really matter. My guess is that Prescott's ratings will go up.

Princess Diana was like something out of a fairytale. She was very beautiful, very pretty in a simplistic way and got engaged in issues that touched some people's lives. People felt that she was vulnerable and a little bit like them. Twelve months after her death some people woke up and were almost embarrassed that they had been taken in. I do not think she was trying to take people in but they had fallen for this modern myth.

Richard Branson, the head of Virgin, is a fairly ruthless, driven businessman, like most very successful capitalists, but he has caught the zeitgeist. People wanted to believe that you could be a hard-nosed businessman, not wear a tie, be a bit of a fun guy and listen to pop music. And that is what he represented; it was a simplified ideal in the same way that Diana represented a different kind of simplified ideal. Such icons will continue to pop up. The fact that we are an advanced society does not mean that people do not want these simple stereotypes. I think that Clinton in many ways was also a simplified ideal, a kind of short cut for people who were trying to understand the world. The problems come when these gods finally get knocked down, when they are shown to have feet of clay that previously they denied, but then of course new gods come along.

Creating an image

PR can present a company at its best, but it cannot make it better than it is. If you try, you risk being caught out and punished. Examples would include environmental over-claims where the media and the consumer bite back. You may not want to actively promote the weak aspects of your business, but nevertheless you should be prepared to answer questions on them if they are raised. You can create an image for an organization, but the organization has to live up to it. If it does not live up to it, then you will get found out, because people are not fools and you cannot make something out of nothing.

Another big change in today's corporations is a focus on internal communications. The employee and customer views on the firm are equally important and they should be very similar. All too often what you have is marketing doing external communication and human resources or personnel doing internal communication. There is, sometimes, an intense dislike and rivalry between the two. Human resources regard marketing as people who do lots of work that is not relevant, the stereotype of long lunches with an advertising agency, while marketing consider human resources to be too soft on people issues or too process driven. The two need to work together and sadly they all too often do not.

Companies often say they put their customers first, but they really mean that they put their staff last. One famous example was the company where the internal communications programme to the staff emphasized being 'right first time', a process driven approach. Meanwhile the external communication to the consumer was all about innovation. If you are going to innovate, then you have to take risks which means that you will not get everything right first time. So, here was this schizophrenic organization with a credibility gap between its external and internal communication. What is needed in modern corporations, is one brand vision that stretches right way across both the internal and the external. Human resources, marketing, and corporate affairs are going to have to work much more closely together.

As we move from a manufacturing society to a service driven society, the old hackneyed expression 'Our staff are everything', will become more and more true. The quality of staff will become critical and your ability to attract and keep the best people and motivate them to perform will be really essential. In some of the more traditional banks you have had very low morale but advertising which claimed that 'we are super friendly; we're a new kind of bank', completely dissonant with people's experience when they enter a branch, or when they call up, only to get somebody who is clearly de-motivated and badly informed. You cannot have a harassed chief executive acting as a conductor trying to maintain one coherent vision. Line functions that have been traditionally separate will have to get their collective act together.

The media

If you give the media good, interesting, hard news then they will tend to go with that rather than necessarily dig as deep as they might. Short term, you can manage the media, to amplify or turn down the likely coverage you get. We see companies timing their announcements to try to manage the media agenda and make sure that they are at the top or the bottom of the news. You cannot manage the media long term. Long-term polluters will be revealed. People who exploit labour will be found out. People who have bad employee relations or poor financial performance will be discovered.

Reputation Management and managers

Miles and Davies (1997) evaluated the management of reputation in fourteen European and American companies (Table 2.2). Access was requested to the 'manager responsible for Reputation Management'. The fourteen companies included organizations of varying size, business type, and country of origin and operation. Some used their corporate name to promote all of their activities (a unitary naming strategy). These tended to be service businesses. Others used separate branding for individual subsidiaries, products, or both.

A number of issues were raised with each company: what overall framework or major objectives they had in their management of reputation; what in their view shaped reputation; how the globalization of markets affected their Reputation Management; what approaches they used in defending reputation and finally what measurement tools they used?

Some general points can be made before the main points to emerge from the study are presented. Ten of the fourteen respondents held the job title of director or the equivalent (vice president) in their organization. Only two respondents were part of or headed large departments whose role was that of managing reputation. For the others, operational matters were either not their concern or they used outside agencies for such work. If the fourteen companies represent the general situation then, companies see the role of managing reputation as requiring fairly senior responsibility (in the smaller organizations contacted respondents tended to be the CEO).

Is there a general framework for Reputation Management?

In the interviews managers tended to emphasize similar factors that they saw as important to their main external audiences. These included to be seen to market quality products or services, to be innovative, to employ excellent staff and to be positively involved in the local or national community. Being seen as performing well in all such areas was a clear priority for those interviewed. This interpretation of the content of the interviews was supported by the responses to questions about what they measured in assessing their reputation, where there was an emphasis on measuring the amount and content of press and other media comment about their organization.

Table 2.2 Companies surveyed

Company name	Main business area	Country of origin	Naming method	Turnover 1996/7 (£m)	Respondent's job title/role
Standa	Retailing	Italy	Unitary	440	Chief Executive
Anheuser Busch	Beer	USA	Product branding	7500	Executive Vice President and Chief Communications Officer
Monsanto	Chemicals/ Food	USA	Product branding	5500	Head of Public Affairs (Brussels)
Co-operative Bank	Banking	UK	Unitary	285	Managing Director
Post Office	Postal and Financial Services	UK	Mainly unitary	6370	Head of Communications Policy
Marks and Spencer	Retailing	UK	Mainly unitary	7800	Corporate Communications Executive
New Look	Retailing	UK	Unitary	242	Joint Managing Director
Prêt à Manger	Food	UK	Unitary	50	Joint owner
Vickers	Engineering conglomerate	UK	Unitary at divisional level	1197	Director, Corporate Communications
Safeway	Retailing	UK	Unitary	6630	Director of Public Affairs
Kimberly Clark	Paper products	USA	Product branding	7740	European Corporate Communications Director
Centrica	Gas supply	UK	Unitary	4200	Director of Corporate Affairs
Virgin	Services conglomerate	UK	Unitary	1800	Group Corporate Affairs Director
London Electricity	Electricity supply	UK	Unitary	1278	Communications Manager

What do managers think shapes reputation?

There is debate about what shapes reputation, the relative importance of culture (Alvesson 1990), design and other tangibles (Olins 1978; Selame and Selame 1988), advertising and public relations (Meyers 1984; Kitchen and Proctor 1991; Wartick 1992), and social responsibility (McGuire *et al.* 1988).

When asked about their views on what shaped reputation, managers often tended not to refer to these issues but rather referred to the need to build and sustain 'core values'. The labels they used varied. Two for example used the term 'principles' but what they talked about or had available in documents that would be used extensively within their organizations tended to be similar. Eleven of the fourteen firms had such lists or they could be identified from the interviews. Honesty, integrity, or trustworthiness were the most prominent 'values', see Table 2.3. Other words, such as 'fun' and 'authentic' may not be immediately recognizable as 'values' but they did give a distinctive picture of what the organization, or rather its senior management, wanted it to be as an entity. A similar picture emerges from research among only American companies, where 58 per cent used value systems as processes to achieve their goals (Morley 1998).

Factors such as advertising, public relations, and design were seen by some but not all as being central to Reputation Management. One interesting issue here was that most respondents had no responsibility for advertising or the design of company premises while most were responsible for public relations. One complained about the lack of coordination between what he was doing

Table 2.3 Respondents' descriptions of core values

Teamwork	Value for money	Authentic
Continuous improvement	Service	Caring
Sharing in success	Reliability	Providing innovative solutions
Listening to each other		Sustainability
Having fun doing all of that		
Customer orientation	Quality and excellence	Trust
Speed and decisiveness	Participation	Being part of the national infrastructure
Team and individual responsibility	Integrity	Offering a personal service
Cultural diversity		Being unique in its ability to reach everyone
Honesty		
Integrity		
Results orientation		
Straightforward	Good management	First class customer service
Pleasantly surprising	Quality products	Value for the customer
Human	Honesty	Partnership with suppliers
Family orientated		Social responsibility
Helpful		
Engaging		
Conduct all relationships in a straightforward trustworthy manner	Quality	
	Value for money	
	Innovation	
We care	Fun	
We value the worth and respect the dignity of every person	A sense of challenge	
We say what we do		
We honour commitments		
Teamwork achieves better results		
We strive to be better		

and what was happening in 'marketing'. The external media were seen as an issue for the communication of reputation rather than its creation. Occasionally design was seen as having a more fundamental role, certainly in service businesses such as retailing where it could be used to create an atmosphere that would influence customers and staff alike. The same could be said by a minority for advertising but three of the fourteen spent little or no money on this and some of the others who did such as the Cooperative Bank (who position themselves as an 'ethical' bank) questioned the validity of advertising 'what you are not'. Managing corporate values and public relations appeared to be the only widely used methods of shaping reputation.

Where the chosen corporate values had come from was one issue that emerged from the interviews. In some instances, and the most widely documented would be that of Marks and Spencer, the values (or in their case principles) had been established far back in the company's history. They had evolved but had remained remarkably constant over time. Other companies had derived their lists more recently, as a response perhaps to an organizational change and often as part of a systematic attempt at culture management.

Do managers accept that reputation and financial performance are linked?

Given the well developed line of research in both the business and academic press about the linkages between reputation and financial performance (Fryxell and Wang 1994), the reactions to this part of the study were surprising. A minority vociferously challenged the line of questioning, arguing that Reputation Management was not to be associated (cynically) with increasing profit. Fostering positive corporate values was seen as a valid goal in its own right, given today's society. Some saw it as positively dangerous to link reputation and profitability.

Others held different views. The Cooperative Bank for example clearly believed that its ethical positioning adopted in the 1980s had benefited it financially as well as providing a cultural platform. Examples of the links between a fall in external reputation and a decline in sales were often given. One interesting concept emerged from the interview with Safeway where changes in reputation were seen as being a leading indicator for the company of a future change in financial fortunes. An improvement in reputation measures heralded a subsequent increase in sales and vice versa.

Given the antipathy towards associating financial performance with reputation it was no surprise that Reputation Management in some companies was an activity without a budget. This finding is not totally different from that in Morley (1998) where a quarter of American companies had a budget of less than $1 million for their global communications. More interesting was that few of the fourteen companies had a defined budget for reputation building, even in those companies where senior managers appeared to be convinced about the existence of direct relationships between improving reputation and improving sales and profit. Budgets where they did exist tended to be defined and cost justified for specific activities. A major sponsorship might be assessed by an increase in certain figures for example. Only one company, the Italian retailer Standa, appeared to budget for its Reputation Management as a whole and to have clear associated measures of cost effectiveness. Here the issue had been one of the turnaround of its department store chain where expenditure on redesign, for example, was appraised against changes in sales figures. Another retailer, New Look, saw the issue of budgets as irrelevant, explaining by emphasizing that virtually everything the company spent money on could be considered to be contributing to reputation. These comments aside, the service businesses in the sample tended to be more convinced of the linkages between investment in reputation and commercial success.

How is a change in reputation managed?

Virtually every interview produced a great deal of material about managing a change in reputation. Three quite different types of change situation became apparent: evolving the existing reputation, a change of name, and globalization. Companies often commented on the need to evolve culture to meet better changing market circumstances. Vickers (a defence systems and engineering company) for example had been moving from a diversified conglomerate to a more divisionalized structure requiring a more cohesive culture across previously separate business units. In a similar way mergers or de-mergers created a need for, this time, a more radical approach to change either due to the fusion of two previously competitive organizations as in the case of Kimberley Clark and Scott or in the creation of new entities as larger businesses divided themselves into smaller more agile units as in the cases of utilities companies Centrica and London Electricity. The third situation arose from a move into a new geographical market (as part of globalization) where the native culture was not in tune with the values that had led to business success in the home market. Two retailers offered the same example of where the 'value for money, money off' approach they had used successfully in the British market had caused suspicion in, respectively, France and Spain, where a discounted price implied that the retailer wanted to get shot of goods of perhaps questionable quality quickly. Each business had to change its orientation to selling quite fundamentally in the new country and in doing so had had to change what it regarded as a major plank in the way it did business. There were some points made about the value or otherwise of being seen as 'British' or 'American' outside of one's home market. Some stereotyping of country images was expected by some managers, but the points made were rarely central to the companies' views on what was critical in managing reputation.

A majority of respondents appeared to believe that they could manage a change in organizational values, identifying first an appropriate set of values and then communicating these to employees and customers. The validity of such an approach has been challenged by academics (Alvesson 1990), but it was advocated by a number of experienced managers.

How do companies defend reputation?

The literature on crisis management is extensive and Davies and Miles expected that this would be a major concern to managers (Siomkos and Malliaris 1992; Wartick 1992; Fink 1986). However little emerged from the interviews.

Companies were well aware of how crisis management formed part of Reputation Management. They appeared to have a planned approach to crisis management but this was a reactive rather than a proactive approach. Only two companies, Anheuser Busch and Marks and Spencer offered examples of where potential crises (a factory closure and the IRA bombing of Manchester city centre) had contributed positively in their view to the reputation of each organization. In both cases the public's view of the organization had enabled each to act in a positive manner, defusing potentially difficult situations. In general it appeared that the companies aimed to manage their reputation positively such that in any crisis they would have a reservoir of goodwill that would help see them through.

How do companies measure reputation?

Respondents were asked what measurement tools they had used, what they measured, and what they did with the results of any systematic measurement. While both frameworks (Kotler and Barich 1991) and techniques (Kruskal and Wish 1978; Allan 1992) are available for image measurement, the companies were reluctant to provide specific examples of what they did to assess and track their reputations. Many argued that it was too ethereal to measure. Most used one or more proprietary measures of media exposure (column inches of newsprint, number of mentions of specific issues related to the business). Few had used any of the market research tools (positioning analysis, multidimensional scaling, etc.) that could be used to assess and track actual consumer opinion. Measurement appeared to be more *ad hoc*, and issue based.

The British Post Office was unique in employing regular monitoring of a list of dimensions of its public persona. Standa had measured the change in customer expenditure for different levels of refurbishment to assess the cost effectiveness of their investment programme. Kimberley Clark had introduced a 'balanced scorecard', a battery of measures with targets for improvement on each, to track its progress in the culture change programme that had been introduced following its merger with competitor Scott Paper. While companies appeared to be less concerned with measuring their external reputations, most did conduct surveys of employee attitudes. However it appeared that these were generally concerned with specific issues rather than with the image of the company to employees.

Asking about measurement did reveal much about the origins and function of the respondents and their roles. In larger companies, which tended to employ director level people with job titles including the phrase 'corporate communications', there was a clear focus on the media. Whatever else they did, media relations and media monitoring were important. As such the origins of their role appeared to be in public relations in most organizations. These observations are compatible with more quantitative research that emphasizes the use of press releases in Reputation Management (Carter and Dukerich 1997).

The fact that few were involved in *market* research as opposed to media or employee research is significant. This was still part of the role of the 'marketing' function. In theory this is a potential area of inter-departmental conflict. In one retailer, Safeway, this was mentioned as a real issue. Interestingly, since our study, corporate communications has become part of the marketing function in that company.

The status quo

Reputation Management is still in its infancy as a business discipline and so looking for any patterns in what managers are doing may be premature. Apart from a focus on the media, which reflected the origins of the function in 'public relations', there was no clear blueprint for the role of reputation manager that (at least in the companies studied) focused on corporate communications. However there are some pointers that emerged from the survey that indicate where the role is evolving.

Point 1: Reputation Management is a senior responsibility

What is interesting was the seniority of the majority of respondents. Four out of the fourteen were CEOs. Only four did not hold the title of director or the American equivalent, vice-president. Over 80 per cent of managers in a parallel survey agreed that reputation was ultimately the responsibility of the CEO (Miles and Davies 1997).

Point 2: Reputation Management is not a budgeted activity

Contrasting with the idea that reputation is important, is the issue that no specific budgets are allocated to manage reputation in the way that marketing departments have budgets for brand management. There were few examples of companies setting an annual budget to maintain or improve reputation linked to a financial or financially related goal. The refusal of one respondent to discuss the issue of a Reputation Management budget, claiming that everything the company did could impact upon its reputation, illustrates the counter view that reputation is so central to business success that it cannot be a budget area. Yet companies do allocate budgets to components of Reputation Management, such as corporate communications and do measure outcomes, such as the extent of press comment.

Point 3: Reputation Management is neither a role nor a function

There are a number of ways in which the lack of formalization of the role, despite its apparent importance, can be interpreted. One is that here is a new role that has yet to become clearly defined. New business functions do not emerge frequently and it is worth recalling that marketing as a function dates only from the 1960s. Purchasing or procurement evolved out of buying as a professional role in the 1970s. Logistics developed from transport via physical distribution management in the 1980s. New functions may have problems establishing themselves with credibility. Strauss (1964) commenting on the rise of purchasing as a business function, saw the setting up of professional organizations and qualifications as a step towards the 'professionalization' of a new business function and its selling of itself to senior management. Reputation management has no need of such devices as it is already regarded as a top level role. What is then surprising are the limited number of professional organizations, journals, and qualifications serving the area to inform those in such a role. Public relations is seen as a profession with its own professional associations and it is possible that these might evolve to fill such an obvious gap. In the survey no respondent held the job title of 'reputation manager' and, although there are examples of such, if reputation is currently an accepted business function or role it would be reasonable to expect to see such titles in more common use.

Point 4: Reputation Management crosses traditional line and corporate functions

If media relationships are one cornerstone of Reputation Management then another is that of a responsibility for organizational culture, two very different aspects of the company. Managers saw themselves as guardians of corporate values, something central to any organization. While what were held to be values can be critiqued, most interviews identified an overt list of things respondents wanted their organizations to stand for. To many, establishing appropriate values was an end in itself. It was not a stepping stone towards higher profits or lower costs. Many challenged the appropriateness of linking the two while others, tending to be in the services sector, saw the two as welded together. However others saw the two as so inter-linked as to be inseparable.

The particular relevance of corporate reputation to a service business has been noted by others (Berry *et al.* 1988; Alvesson 1990; Balmer 1995). Reputation management in service businesses had much more to do with positioning the business simultaneously to employees and to customers than in the manufacturing businesses interviewed. In the latter the existence of individual brands could insulate the company from its customers making any dysfunction between culture and image almost immaterial. In a service business, the customer and employee interact to create the product that the customer pays for. The customer for many service businesses such as hotels, restaurants, airlines, enters temporarily albeit peripherally into the employee's culture. The customer may be able to see and will probably be able to sense the supplier's culture. The interrelationship between culture and image may be crucial to Reputation Management. Respondents in service businesses were more likely to accept the idea of linkages between reputation and financial performance and to be managing culture and external image as a coherent whole.

One explanation here is that in a service business a good reputation acts as an antecedent for both employee and customer attitudes as they enter the service encounter. If both expect a positive exchange then the encounter is more likely to be so. Sales will be higher as would repeat business (following a satisfying encounter). Staff retention will be better than in businesses where encounters are less positive and therefore costs could be lower. If this scenario is valid then Reputation Management could be central to most service businesses.

In service businesses such as leisure services, store retailing, banking, hotels, restaurants and education, the linkages or lack of them between identity and image could be key. When values such as honesty/sincerity are promoted successfully *inside* a service business, then they should become more apparent to customers as elements of corporate image.

If this perspective is correct, then Reputation Management becomes more than a function or role. It becomes a way of thinking about the business, and one of especial value in the services sector that is coming to dominate commercial activity in developed countries. As most public and not for profit organizations are also part of the services sector, then the notion of reputation could provide a focus for the majority of organizations.

Point 5: Reputation Management is different from PR management

Reputation managers embrace part of what used to be called PR, but PR appears to be more about presenting the company as it is in the best possible light. PR is less about developing the reality of the company itself, which is surprising given the attitude of many of the managers interviewed. As three respondents to the survey explained, 'In the past companies were known for their brands. Now they need to be known for themselves'. 'If a company is shown to be a sham, then markets and communities can be very unforgiving'. 'Treating people well is only, after all, enlightened self-interest'.

Reputation Management is then about who or what the organization really are, and improving on this is good for business.

Sign and symbol

However an organization defines the role that is entrusted with managing its reputation the role will be concerned with the management of an image. In Chapter 4 we discuss the idea of the company as a brand and define brands primarily in the context of their ability to create an emotional link between the stakeholder and the brand. Such links are in the mind rather than in reality, but someone's perception is the reality for those responsible for marketing a brand or for managing the reputation of a more complex entity such as an organization.

Throughout the book we refer to tangibles such as a building design or a company logo that can affect our impressions of the organization. In Chapter 10 we talk about visual identity. Many believe that such tangibles communicate to us via the inherent symbolism through the shape, colour, and words that surround them. One area of study that has informed our understanding of the importance of symbolism is that of semiotics.

Semiotics is essentially the study of signs and their meaning. Its origins are probably in the symbolism of language but today it refers to the more general issue of studying something that stands for something else. One theme is to recognize the transformation of meaning in and by different media. In the context of PR this can refer to the use of a press release by a journalist to create a totally different meaning from that intended by the person who wrote the release. The same message will often transmit a different meaning to the public depending upon the medium that carries it. Thus if a piece is carried by television, radio, and the press it is seen through the medium that carries it. Television is more dimensional than radio and the press but the written word can be reread and reflected upon while a broadcast is unlikely to be recorded and replayed.

Live television and radio are more personal. We are there with the presenter. Those who have had training in media awareness will have been asked to remember that television is a very different challenge to talking on radio or giving an interview to the press. A television camera can focus on the speaker's face giving a totally different image of the speaker and his or her words. In a close-up, the situation is more intense. We are more conscious of the licking of the lips, of the blink rate, of the beads of perspiration forming that imply that the speaker is under pressure and perhaps not telling everything. We can over-interpret these physical signs adding meaning that is not really there.

We cannot see the person speaking on the radio and if we have never seen them we can create a mental picture of what they might look like. Why else are we so surprised when we finally see the radio presenter in the flesh? The tone of voice and the choice of words are all signs that we use to create a mental picture of the presenter. In the flesh they are completely different, strong evidence of our need to form a clear picture of someone and how we will extrapolate from limited evidence. We may do the same with brand names and logos but it is also possible that we only do this when we have no choice. Once we have evidence then any inherent symbolism may become drowned. GEC a leading European company changed its name to Marconi, a name with inherent symbolism, when it acquired businesses in the USA and did not wish to be confused with America's GE. All went well until tangible news of a slump in their new markets sent their share price tumbling. The Marconi name offered little protection.

Who needs to consider reputation?

Jorge Coelho has been in political life in Portugal since before the revolution in 1974 when the military dictatorship ended. He was a member of the Macao government before its independence, served as Deputy Prime Minister, Minister for Internal Affairs, Minister for Communications, and Minister of State with responsibilities for public infrastructure. At the time of the interview he was the executive coordinator for the Socialist Party as well as being a Member of Parliament. We were interested in exploring the relevance of reputation away from a commercial context.

The image of political parties

There are many different political objectives. These can be the winning of elections, to hold on to a particular result, to pass a message, to generate a movement of opinion. We do our research, both quantitative and qualitative and evaluate the strengths and weaknesses of both our party and the opposition. We have certain principles, values and our strategy has to reflect those. Our image has to be in tune with our strategy.

Political leaders are protagonists. I would say only about 15 to 20 per cent of voters base their voting decision on ideological principles. The leader embodies the message we are trying to put forward. The majority of voters look for some kind of identification with a project that might solve their problems. It is their interpretation of the various projects put forward to them that might make them choose one party or the other.

The majority of people make their decision without reading a manifesto. There is a message, there is a format and there is a collective 'state of mind'. As a politician you have got to be able to read this. If change is needed, you have to embody change.

Political leaders

I admire Nelson Mandela. He fought for a cause and had an incredible capacity to forgive. He also had the ability to make a distinction which is crucial in politics, and that is separating the fundamental from the peripheral. Helmut Kohl was extremely important for German unity and although recent events have put a cloud over his image, he was an extremely important politician in his time. King Hassan of Morocco had an incredible knowledge of international affairs and he impressed me very much.

There are also some less obvious cases that are worthy of our attention. Take for example the small country of Cape Verde in West Africa. Look at how they adapted to democracy. Much of this is owed to the quality of their leadership.

I know Tony Blair personally. I have closely followed every major run-up to an election in the UK on the ground. He is an intelligent person, who has created a new and more credible ground for the British Labour Party. He took the party from the hands of the unions. Unions belong in companies. They are not in the business of running countries. He has clear principles and a deep knowledge of the history of the United Kingdom.

Politicians should have values, principles, and rules of engagement. Companies sell products and look at issues like quality control. There are points in common between the way companies and politicians try to manage image. Both resort to studies to accomplish their objectives. Companies have responsibilities with their shareholders, but they also have a social, institutional role.

Leaders, whether they are politicians or not, often make an immediate impact on you. For example I first met Richard Branson on the night Labour won the election and the first impression is one of exuberance.

Country image

Portugal does not have much of an image. In the last ten years much incredible effort has been put into changing this, but much has yet to be done. It is important to be selective about target markets. Portugal is now one of the largest foreign investors in Brazil particularly in the areas of telecommunications, distribution, and the financial sector and has to do the same in Spain. Generalized approaches lead nowhere. The ICEP (Institute for Foreign Trade) is reformulating its strategy. It has more than sixty delegations all over the world and the purpose of this is to assess what can be done.

The Portuguese people go very much in cycles of unfounded optimism, which alternates with deep pessimism. It is part of the national character. They do not have an adequate image of their country. The success of Expo 98 helped to improve the national ego and there have been some visible improvements to the capital city, Lisbon. The problem was that, up until 1974, the Portuguese were completely inactive, but the conditions for improving the country are now better.

There is little that is very distinctive about Portugal. The Portuguese have some positive characteristics. They go abroad and typically hold executive positions wherever they go, but there is nothing distinctive about them, unless you consider fado (traditional music).

People who know Portugal find the country attractive at various levels. The reality is far superior to the stereotype. To most people, contact with Portugal enhances their opinion of the country. But Portugal is not yet a brand, while the USA is just like a brand in my opinion. It has a clear and distinct image internationally.

Managing the media

The Portuguese have to adapt and conduct an intelligent policy of collaboration with the media. Politicians have to make concessions and trade with them. This notion of the Portuguese sitting down on their own and formulating policy belongs to the past. They have got to live in the present, find solutions, and discuss them in and with the media.

The Internet has had a huge impact on political communication but still lower than what has been anticipated. Every political party worthy of its name has a website and so do newspapers but the Portuguese are still far from our objectives using that medium.

Crisis management

Politicians, perhaps even more so than businessmen, have to deal with crises. Mine was the collapse of a bridge in the north of Portugal. Many lives were lost and there are various inquiries currently in process. Even knowing then what I do, I would have done the same with the information that I had at the time. I had ordered the building of a new bridge, I had visited the bridge before and I knew of some minor problems with paving, not of any structural issues that might have caused what happened. I am proud of what I did given the circumstances. But being in public service presupposes a certain way of being. People generally advised me not to resign, but I think much of the advice was given out of friendship. This was a solitary decision and I only discussed it with others after having met the press to announce my resignation. There was a need for someone to assume political responsibility and fall on his sword. A company in a crisis may not need to offer up a senior manager even when things go very wrong. Perhaps that will have to change in the future.

Reputation plays a different role, perhaps even a more fundamental role in politics than in commerce, but there are many similarities between the issues in both spheres. While we are concerned mainly with commercial issues in this book, reputation is relevant across many types of organization and even to individuals

In summary

Reputation is still a woolly concept, a mixture of constructs – but so was marketing forty years ago. It appears to have been evolving from what was once called public relations in some countries and public affairs in others. The role of what is now called corporate communications or corporate affairs is already broader than that of PR and one stage in the possible evolution of PR into Reputation Management.

The role of reputation manager has now moved up the corporate ladder to be seen as a role requiring a senior manager or director to be in charge. One key area of concern is that of company and organizational values. The original external focus of PR has been joined by an internal focus because the two are seen by some at least as being linked. But few reputation managers agree that the main purpose of the evolved role is to promote business performance. (We would hope to change their minds.)

There are a number of issues that emerge from studying what companies are already doing. They do not always have or do not always use formal measurement outside the quantity of press mentions. Without established measurement tools for reputation it will be impossible to be convincing about any linkages between reputation and performance. Without any such linkages budgets for Reputation Management will remain indefinable and this may act as a barrier to the functions evolving further from their origins in media management. A number of respondents to the Miles and Davies survey complained of inadequate resources but resources can only be expected to follow evidence of quantitative links between reputation and performance. Those managers who deny links between reputation and financial performance are less likely to obtain significant budgets for their work.

In the coming chapters we will first summarize what are, in our view, the main tenets of Reputation Management, cover some of the constituents of the role in greater depth than we do in this chapter, and develop our own views on how reputation should be managed.

3 The reputation paradigm

The tenets of reputation, multiple stakeholders, interdependency between the main elements of reputation, reputations have value and create value, reputation rankings reflect performance not vice versa, reputation can be measured, reputation can be researched using an interdisciplinary approach, our model of reputation, the reputation chain.

The purpose of this chapter is to identify and describe the reputation paradigm, the shared view of the subject area and to describe how this book adds to the existing body of knowledge. We explain how reputation can be used as a strategic approach in managing a business.

Even though many of the authors writing about the subject area of corporate reputation come from very different academic disciplines and backgrounds, the inclusion of the word 'paradigm' in the title of this chapter was intended to emphasize they have a shared perspective, a single way of looking at business. It is relatively new and different from what has gone before. There are then a number of tenets or central beliefs and approaches within the study of reputation. The most obvious difference from much of what has gone before is the multiple stakeholder perspective.

Tenet 1: multiple stakeholders need to be considered

Businesses can have a number of orientations as we described in Chapter 1, towards their products so that they gain a competitive advantage through superior products, towards sales so that they outsell similar companies, on operations so that they are world class in supplying the market, or on the customer such that they satisfy at least one market segment better than anyone else. Most organizations will have a blend of orientations with one dominating their philosophy, rather than just the one orientation. Most will have some element of market and customer orientation; otherwise they cannot know what the market wants or what threats exist that need to be dealt with.

A customer orientation is fine, but customers are only one of the 'stakeholders' that a business needs to concern itself with. An organization's stakeholders are 'any individuals or groups who may benefit from or be harmed by the actions of the organization'. For example shareholders are as important as customers to senior executives, who have to operate the business on their behalf. Many executives will have their pay linked to the company share price. If a share price falls, then the link becomes more obvious if key shareholders deem that someone else might do a better job. In any company but particularly in a service business recruiting and retaining quality staff can be a central issue. Staff will be internal stakeholders. After all most of us change jobs only every seven years, meaning we may have only six or seven employers during our careers. We stake our futures with an employer and our resale value as employees in the market may depend on the reputation of whomever we have worked for. Suppliers will be concerned about various aspects of the companies they supply to. If they extend credit then they too become financial stakeholders in the business. Whole communities can depend upon a single organization. It may be the dominant employer in the area; it may operate a chemical plant that could damage the local area. It may be a major source of income for local government and a source of the money needed to sustain a local infrastructure. The community has a stake in the business and is as much a stakeholder as an investor. Stakeholders can be usefully categorized into those who will be closely and immediately affected by the organization and those where the effects may be indirect, longer term, or non-existent (see Figure 3.1). Here stakeholders likely to be affected most include customers, staff, and suppliers and they will interact with both the organization and each other. Less directly affected will be the media, competitors, and the population as a whole, whose involvement will be more occasional. Essentially their well-being is less likely to be determined by the actions of the firm.

The problem for a profit oriented organization is where to draw the line between being a valued member of the community and being seen positively by others outside the box in Figure 3.1, a good corporate citizen, and at the same

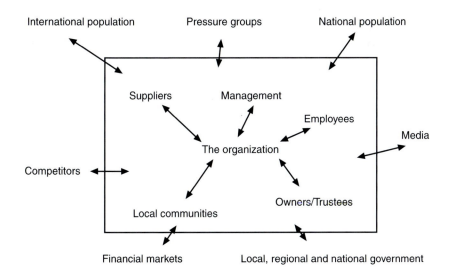

Figure 3.1 A stakeholder model of the organization.

time a source of profit for its owners/or shareholders. Beauchamp and Bowie (1993) suggest two guidelines to help managers recognize their responsibilities: a principle of corporate rights and a principle of corporate effects. The first holds that organizations must not violate the legitimate rights of others to determine their own future. The second holds that the organization is responsible for the effects of their actions upon others.

Referring to Figure 3.1, if a for profit organization ignores the consequences of the effects its products may have on society as a whole, then it may not damage its short-term profitability. In the long term a company in the asbestos business or a company marketing small arms may wish that previous generations of managers had taken a less selfish view of their business, as society reacts against the position that the company saw as inviolate. Suddenly stakeholders appear in the form of their lawyers bringing class actions or legislators introducing new laws because of issues that were never considered at the time when decisions could have been taken to recognize the potential problems.

Each stakeholder may have different expectations, satisfiers, and perspectives. Fombrun's (1998) thinking on the issue of differences in stakeholder orientations is summarized in Figure 3.2. Four stakeholders are represented. Each is looking for something different. Employees might be looking for an employer they can trust, customers for a reliable company, investors for a company that is credible and the community as a whole for a business that is responsible.

A number of writers in the area have pointed to the same thing, that different stakeholders may hold different views of the firm and that what satisfies each may also differ. The challenge of the stakeholder approach is to reconcile the different views and different priorities of each group. Doyle (1998) talks about the tolerance zone that exists, that region of operating where not every

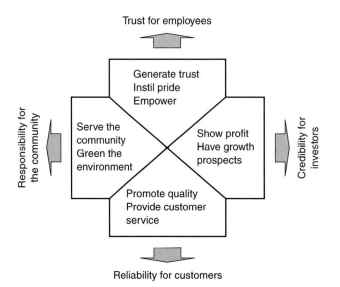

Figure 3.2 The stakeholder perspective.

stakeholder will be satisfied but no one stakeholder will feel that the organization is acting in an unacceptable way. The management of corporate reputation is about more than just how companies should approach the management of any one stakeholder's perception of reputation; it is about how the perspective that has been evolving in this field can be usefully applied to managing the business as a whole.

Tenet 2: the main elements of reputation are linked

Reputation has a number of elements, the two most important being the views held of the organization by the two main stakeholders, employees, and customers. Because the study of corporate reputation is relatively new, some of its terminology has yet to be standardized. In some writings about corporate reputation, the term 'identity' is often used to refer to tangible imagery (logo, building design, colour, etc.). We prefer to refer to these as corporate visual identity. To confuse matters further, the terms 'image' and 'reputation' are often used as if they are interchangeable.

In this book the following definitions are used:

Image is taken to mean the view of the company held by external stakeholders, especially that held by customers (see for example Bernstein 1994).

Identity is taken to mean the internal, that is the employee's, view of the company, following Albert and Whetten's (1985) notion of 'How do we see ourselves'.

Reputation is taken to be a collective term referring to all stakeholders' views of corporate reputation, including identity and image. (See for example Fombrun 1996; Hatch and Schultz 1997; Balmer 1998; Davies and Miles 1998.)

Different stakeholders can have different images of the same organization. In particular, as the SERVQUAL model made clear (Chapter 1) there are likely to be gaps between what the company thinks the customer wants it to be and what the company is perceived to be.

To make matters worse, the company communications may be trying to promote a third perspective, what the company would like its customers or other stakeholders to think it is. See Figure 3.3, adapted from Davies and Miles (1998).

The relationship between identity, image and culture is a central issue in this book. Hatch and Schultz (1997) provide one view of this relationship (Figure 3.4). Identity and image are both embedded in the culture of the organization. All three interact. Image is influenced by the experiences external groups have with the organization. Identity is similarly influenced by the experiences of employees at work. If the vision and leadership of the firm are appropriate, then identity and image will overlap. Each of the first three figures in this chapter tries to paint a picture in their own way of this relationship. The most important point to note however is not the differences between the representations, but that each of the writers on the subject share the idea of a linkage between image and identity.

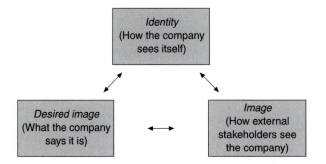

Figure 3.3 Gaps in reputation.

The implications of this thinking are profound and shape much of what we argue in this book. Basically if image and identity are linked in causality, in other words one drives the other, then (external) image can be managed by managing (internal) identity. How identity can be managed and what links there are to culture are discussed later in this book.

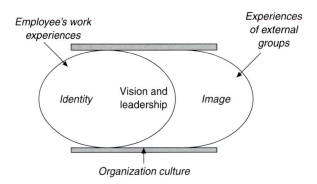

Figure 3.4 Organization culture, identity and image.

Source: Adapted from Hatch and Schultz (1997).

Tenet 3: reputation is created through multiple interaction

First, what exactly is a good reputation? Such an obvious question has no simple answer. Fombrun (1996) talks about the benefits of a favourable reputation as including: 'premium prices for products, lower costs of labour and capital, improved loyalty from employees, greater latitude in decision making and a cushion of goodwill when crises hit'. (Few of these links between reputation and financial performance have ever been proven. They remain intuitive rather than demonstrable links.)

If you accept the potential for reputation to affect commercial performance, it follows that a reputation is something worth acquiring, developing, and defending, so:

How do you get one?

An early description of how we form a view of an organization and how therefore a reputation is created comes from Bevis (1967) and that was (in his definition of image): 'The net result of the interaction of all the experiences, impressions, beliefs, feelings and knowledge that people have about a company'. Corporate reputation is then unlikely to be created through one type of contact alone. Our image of a company will depend upon how we are treated by staff, our preconceptions formed from contact with other similar companies, the national origin of the organization, its product type, its communications. Based on Bernstein (1984) Figure 3.5 provides us with a graphic picture of this complexity.

Bernstein argues that our image of an organization is seen through a number of filters, in particular the industry the company forms part of and its country of origin. For example we may have a stereotype in our mind of all oil companies and all companies that are German. Organizations can do little individually about such fixed preconceptions. They can use only those elements in the outer ring. A major issue in this book is to identify the role and relative importance of factors such as advertising and personal contact in the creation and modification of image.

The contacts we have with an organization are a mixture of tangible and intangible, the rational and the emotional. We can read and study an article about an organization. We can use or consume its products. We can visit its premises and meet its staff. All of these are tangibles, all capable of rational

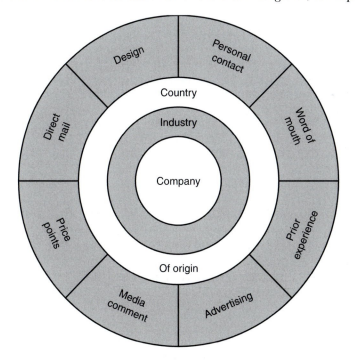

Figure 3.5 How reputation is created.

assessment. At the same time we receive more ethereal communication, the tone of the press article, our subjective judgement of the newspaper as a reliable source. When we meet a company's employees we can judge them objectively by their height, weight, apparent age, product knowledge, the time they spend with us. Or we can judge them subjectively by the look in their eyes, the colour of their hair, or whether they have any. We can stereotype them from our experiences of previous contacts with the myriad of other people we have met. In doing so we risk forming a totally inaccurate impression of them and potentially of the company that employed them. We are taught as managers not to jump to a conclusion about a potential employee at an interview, that first impressions should not count for much, that it should take twenty minutes or so to form any impression of an individual. Unfortunately the typical customer will form an impression within the first twenty seconds of a customer facing employee.

As the employee serves us we will continue to develop our impression of him or her and the employer. But our initial stereotype will be hard to break. We will tend to seek evidence to support our initial picture and select from the cues that we are being given only those that support our first reaction. The role of advertising may be important in preconditioning our image of an organization prior to our experiencing it. At its best it will give us a favourable view that will be confirmed by the actual experience. If the advert over claims and the experience falls below our expectation then the company is wasting its money, the electrical store that claims to have the widest range of fittings for the home, but has nothing to tempt us, the restaurant with the sophisticated title that promises us an evening to remember but delivers one that we would prefer to forget. What matters is the actual experience and the match between it and our expectations. Get both right and a good reputation is guaranteed.

The identity employees have of an organization is formed in the same way. The new employee learns quickly. The induction process or the lack of one informs him or her about the company, its history and culture. History it has been said does not exist; the only reality is myth and legend. This play with words is intended to make the point that history can be manufactured and managed to reflect the needs of the company while myths and legends are more honest portrayals. They are unreal and idealistic, yet somehow give us a clearer picture of reality. Stories of the founder hiring and firing his first staff, nearly going broke, breaking the rules, may not appear in the official history but will be told and retold, complete with embellishments, by employees using such myths and legends to cement their identity. The new employee learns quickly from the peer group about the informal rules and norms that glue every organization together. In doing so they learn 'how we do things around here' about the culture of the organization.

Yet again there will be a mixture of rational and emotional cues to guide us. There may be a vision and mission statement that extols the virtues of a brighter future. At the same time there is Joe the cynic in the canteen who offers to 'put us right' about the reality, or at least the one he has constructed in his mind. We meet people and see how they treat us. We try to be ourselves with one group only to be rebuffed. We try to fit in and get accepted. We begin to accept what we find or we leave. If we stay we probably become more attached to the business we have become a part of. We accept and embrace the identity that is around us.

One of the issues that emerges from any discussion on image and identity is the importance of the intangible and emotional aspects of both. Certain things about an organization we can measure: what are their prices, what do they sell, what do they make, how many are employed, how much profit was made last year. Other aspects such as whether the company is a pleasant place to work, what the atmosphere is like, what kind or organization is it, all these are important but more difficult to assess let alone measure.

We believe that the way employees feel about their organization will affect the way they deal with customers and therefore the way the customer feels about the organization.

Tenet 4: reputations are valuable and have value

What is surprising is that companies do not always appear to recognize that corporate reputation is a significant, albeit intangible, asset. One explanation is that it is difficult to value a reputation. Other assets such as land or buildings can be valued because there is a market for such things allowing a comparison between what is being valued and similar items that have been sold previously. At the end of the day, something is worth only what someone else will pay for it.

Ascribing values to corporate reputations is not then easy, but interest in valuing them and other intangibles is increasing as companies can include valuations in their balance sheets. Up until recently it was only possible to include a valuation for 'goodwill' or other ways of describing intangible assets purchased in an acquisition for example as a value that is written down over time. A strong brand or reputation increases in value but this requires some accepted methodology to provide an acceptable figure.

Various proprietary methods are marketed to provide a valuation for a corporate brand name (Kumar 1999). A more straight forward approach to scope the size of such an asset in financial terms is to compare the value of a company's assets as shown in its balance sheet with its share price. Companies such as Coca-Cola have stock values that are large multiples of their tangible asset worth, due entirely to the company's ability to earn revenue (Fombrun 1996). This in turn can be taken as a measure of its reputation.

One option that is easily used to provide management with a quick but telling idea as to the size of the asset represented by their corporate name is to give them the following scenario:

> Imagine that you had to give up the use of your company's name, but that you had the chance to pay a percentage of your annual revenue, as a licence fee to continue to use the name. What percentage of your turnover do you think it is worth?

In reality companies such as Christian Dior license the use of their names to other organizations in exchange for a percentage of revenue. The percentages charged vary, but are typically between 5 and 15 per cent. Not surprisingly many managers tend to choose a figure of around 10 per cent of turnover.

> Now estimate how long you would make a contract for, to license back the use of your own name.

Managers tend to opt for a period of about ten years or more with an option to continue. A cash flow of 10 per cent of turnover over ten years is worth one year's turnover, ignoring the cost of capital. Even after calculating a net present value for the revenue stream the figure represents a significant percentage of a company's annual turnover. Companies spend millions insuring tangible assets against loss and damage through fire and other disasters. They spend little to ensure that their reputations remain in good order. They spend little on understanding what their reputation is and what the issues might be with it, at least in comparison with what a reputation is worth.

A key tenet of the reputation paradigm is that reputation has value, and that this is substantial for most organizations. Valuation is a more contentious area but companies such as Interbrand specialize in such work and their figures have been included in the annual report and accounts of companies. We would expect such inclusions to become routine in the future.

One issue is how do reputations link to financial value, why indeed should they be valuable? Reputation could influence financial performance in a number of ways. As we mentioned earlier a strong reputation may attract and retain better employees and motivate them to go that extra mile in their work. It may attract more potential customers and make any customer less price sensitive. It will allow customers to give you the benefit of the doubt in any situation that might otherwise reflect badly on the organization. Suppliers will be more willing to supply not only because they might believe that you will deal with them fairly but because they can boast about having you as one of their customers.

This quotation, from J. Paul Getty, makes the point that reputation affects the propensity of others to deal with you, 'If you have a reputation for always making all the money there is in a deal, you won't make many deals'. In other words if you get a reputation for unfair dealing then others will refuse to deal with you and anyone who does will be nervous of doing so again. A business in a monopoly position that exploits its market power too aggressively will come to the attention of regulatory authority. Technically monopoly exists if one competitor has as little as 20 per cent market share. This level of concentration in market power will trigger an interest in whether the company is exploiting its position. Action will follow, as in the case of Microsoft, if regulators perceive that the monopoly is exploiting its position.

Competition too can be influenced by reputation. In the Maltese Falcon, Sam Spade remarks, 'That kind of reputation might be good for business – bringing in high priced jobs and making it easier to deal with the enemy'. If you have a weak reputation among your competitors or an image for incompetence you risk being the focus of competitive action more so than a company whose reputation is to respond quickly and aggressively to any challenge. Gordon Barton, one time CEO of IPEC the Australian transport and courier group once told one of us that he believed that the first people that should see his corporate plans were his competitors, so that they knew if they challenged him in the direction he planned to go down, then they would be in for a fight.

Tenet 5: reputation can be managed

There does not seem to be much point in writing a book about Reputation Management if it cannot be managed, but there is less consensus on this issue than on others. If your image with your customer is driven by the identity that your customer facing employees have of you, and if identity in turn is affected by your culture, then, as culture is difficult to 'manage' can you manage reputation? Clearly there are those who believe that you can.

In Figure 3.6, van Riel and Balmer (1997) suggest how companies can manage their external image (they use the word 'reputation' to refer to external image) through the 'corporate identity mix'. The mix consists of three elements, the behaviours of (in particular customer facing) employees, corporate communication (including advertising, but not only advertising) and symbolism. Corporate symbols will include tangibles, such as buildings, and intangibles, such as design.

Topalian (1984) lists tangibles such as the company size, its products, structure and softer issues such as behaviour to employees and customers, culture, mission, standards and priorities as influencing external image. Barish and Kotler (1991) provide a long list of attributes that might affect image including all the elements of the marketing mix (the four Ps and two Ss) plus corporate social conduct, conduct towards employees, business performance or reputation. Herbig *et al.* (1994) link external image and reputation (defined as the consistency of outcomes with market signals over time) with credibility (the belief that a company will do what it says it will). The idea of consistency is useful in that it emphasizes the need for coherence between the many factors that can influence image. The idea of credibility stemming from image provides a useful explanation as to why reputation is such a strong paradigm.

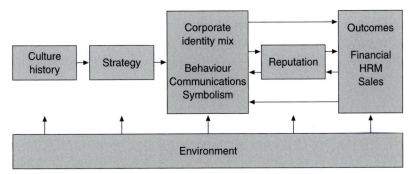

Figure 3.6 Identity, reputation, and outcome.

Source: van Riel and Balmer (1997). Reproduced with the kind permission of Professors Balmer and van Riel and MCB Press.

One issue is exactly what do we mean by managing reputation? Are we aiming to promote positive internal values because these are inherently valuable or are we aiming to enhance measures of outcome especially sales growth and profit? While there is a great deal of claiming that reputation and business performance are linked, such claims often come from analyses of data from the *Fortune, America's Most Admired Companies* survey. As we will explain later the problem here is that the *Fortune* reputation measure includes an appraisal by business people (not customers) of the financial performance of the companies included in the survey. It will be no shock that financial performance correlates with reputation measured in this way.

The jury is then out as to whether there is clear proof that reputation does in fact drive financial performance. There is even less clarity as to how the link operates. It is one of our objectives to explore how reputation links to financial performance and therefore to test whether it is worthwhile spending significant time and money to manage reputation.

Once we have answered these questions then it is essential to answer the question, 'How can reputation be managed?' Our starting point is the assumption that image (the external stakeholders' view) is linked to the internal view (identity). If this is so then the external view can be managed by managing the internal view. Again the issue is how. We will provide examples from our work of Reputation Management in practice. The examples will include those that are implied by Figure 3.6 but also from the involvement of customer facing employees and their managers.

The role of key individuals

Dowling (1993) emphasizes the 'style' of the CEO in determining the mission and vision of an organization and thence its image. If a business is small then it

Laura and Bernard Ashley began in business in London in the 1950s. They designed and sold textiles in local stores. The business grew to become an international company with its own manufacturing and retail stores. It sold ladies' and children's clothes, wallpaper, paint, fabric, furniture, lighting, perfume. What linked this disparate range of products together was a unique sense of design. Laura Ashley's biographer described this in a television programme about the firm as a 'romanticized view of the past'. One of her designers added that, 'Mrs Ashley believed that a design would only sell if it had a sense of nostalgia'. He explained how she would search antique shops looking for old designs that could be recast in a modern idiom. Laura Ashley died as the firm that she gave her name to launched its shares on to the London stock market. The firm never lived up to its potential and saw a series of chief executives come and go. The view of the company and its brand shifted. In its 1995 annual report the then chairman Hugh Blakeway Webb described it as, 'English virtues of the countryside, of the family and traditional values'.

Ann Iverson took charge in 1995. She had a reputation of being a successful turnaround specialist with experience of retailing in both Europe and America where she was born. The next annual report quoted her as saying that, 'Our research supports the brand values our customer identifies with: love of flowers, family, romanticism, freedom and simplicity and tradition'. That same year in a newspaper interview she was quoted as explaining, 'Laura Ashley is a brilliant brand that has shown great resilience and still has great potential. It's English, it's feminine. But it doesn't have to be floral'. The reference to 'floral' reflected the dominance of flowers in many Laura Ashley designs.

The new collection became more mainstream, less evocative of the past. The business in America was changed by the introduction of larger stores with a greater emphasis on furniture. Sales slumped in America. The share price dived. By 1999 the company was all but bankrupt.

is clearer how image and identity can be strongly influenced by the character of the founder. How this is retained as the business grows is unclear but anecdotal evidence suggests that this is important. The example of the Laura Ashley company is relevant here. This brief history of corporate decline also introduces the association of corporate branding with corporate reputation.

The management's perception of the Laura Ashley brand had either changed or, more likely, after the death of the founder, there was no one to articulate the real ethos of the firm. The values of the founders can have a strong influence on the image and identity of the companies they create. Often the personality of the founder will appear to dominate the personality of their organization. The image of Virgin is often associated with the image of its founder Richard Branson. If he were to leave the organization, one issue is whether the image of Virgin would change.

Tenet 6: reputation and financial performance are linked

How, if and why reputation is linked to the financial performance of an organization is a controversial area and forms a major part of this book. Senior managers appear to be convinced that this is true, Miles and Davies (1997). In fact which CEO would admit that having a bad reputation in the market is something that can still mean excellent financial performance? In markets where products are similar, technologies can be copied, real levels of differentiation low, concentration high and real sales growth low, then a market orientation is more likely to be adopted by an organization. Many service businesses operate under such conditions.

Market orientation involves responding to the market and particularly to the customer. In a crowded market customers may not have the time to investigate all possible supply options. In this case they will often short list a consideration set of options from which they will make an informed decision. Every company should ensure that it is part of as many consideration sets as possible for the customer. At least then there is a chance of gaining customers. And why is it, if it is not down to reputation, that customers will short list some but not all potential suppliers?

In this way it is possible to explain how a good reputation can benefit an organization. But reputation is about more than just the customer view. It is about attracting and retaining the best employees, finding it easy to be trusted and being well treated by suppliers, being seen as the kind of company able to influence local and national government.

In the key area of customer relationships, a good reputation is likely to reduce transaction costs (because the customer trusts you to offer a fair price and not to hide things). In the labour market it will reduce labour turnover and attract better quality, more productive employees. The relationship can be modelled as in Figure 3.7. A good reputation will precondition the various stakeholders to expect a positive interaction. There can be little surprise that this leads to a greater likelihood of an actual interaction that is positive which in turn leads to customer satisfaction and employee motivation. This model of how reputation can drive business performance is derived from Davies and Miles (1998).

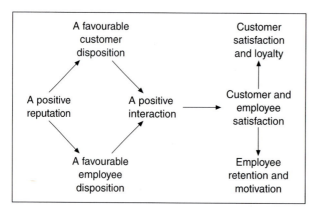

Figure 3.7 Reputation and business performance.

However we all know of companies that appear to survive and to prosper despite a reputation for being aggressive, being a poor employer, exploiting its workforce. Surely examples such as this would be impossible if reputation was as valid an approach as we imply? One answer that surprised us was that companies can have what might be regarded as a negative image but still prosper from it, if the market circumstances allow.

Beyond a limited number of generalizations little is known as to the detail of Reputation Management for better performance. One of the challenges we aim to respond to in this book is that of proving the link between reputation and financial performance.

Tenet 7: relative reputation (ranking) drives financial performance

If the issue of the management of reputation is somewhat controversial then the issue of measurement and links to financial performance is highly controversial. Central to this is the idea of ranking. The best known system of reputation ranking is that from the *Fortune* magazine.

Fortune's list of America's most admired companies (AMAC) are chosen from the largest US companies (ranked by revenues) and a small number of the largest US subsidiaries of foreign-owned companies. They are sorted by industry and the ten largest selected in each industry to constitute fifty-seven separate groups. To create the rankings 10,000 executives, directors, and securities analysts select the five companies they admire most, regardless of industry. The group is told to choose from a list containing the companies that ranked among the top 25 per cent in the previous year's survey; the list also included companies that ranked below the first quartile overall but finished in the top 20 per cent of their industry. To create the industry lists the executives, directors, and analysts are asked to rank companies in their own industry on eight criteria: quality of management, quality of products/services, innovativeness, long-term investment value, financial soundness, employee talent, use of corporate assets and social responsibility. *Fortune* rankings co-relate with financial performance leading to the conclusion that a relatively good reputation ranking creates relatively good financial performance. In reality the reverse is more likely to be true.

The *Fortune* approach has been criticized as being overly dominated by the financial performance of the companies (Fryxell and Wang 1994). These authors question the validity of the reputation measure, claiming that there is only one underlying factor, financial performance, and that the halo effect and the orientation of the respondents ensures that this dominates the rankings. It is not surprising therefore that reputation ranking co-relates with financial performance. The argument is that it is the performance that creates the reputation not the relative strength of reputation creating financial performance. Research using the *Fortune* data also demonstrates the strong inter-linkages between the various items in the measure (Sobol and Farrelly 1988; McGuire *et al.* 1988). The question remains as to whether this is proof that reputation, measured relative to other companies in the same sector on the eight items, is created through being better at those same items.

Whatever the reality, we love rankings, whether they are tests of products by trade magazines and consumer organizations, opinion polls of politicians and political parties or play lists of pop records, but how useful are they to predict the future? One survey using a very similar approach to that of *Fortune*, reported a Marplan survey of 650 marketers, where companies were rated for their marketing expertise (Anon 1986). Top of the list was Sainsbury, at the time the leading British food retailer. Its main rival Tesco, was rated much lower. Since the survey Tesco has out-marketed Sainsbury and taken its place as the leading British food retailer. In the same study, Woolworth Holdings, now Kingfisher, ranked fourth from last. In the following years it outperformed its sector. 'Nothing succeeds like success' as the saying goes, and it appears to be true of reputation rankings which seem to reflect past glories and not to be very useful at predicting future success.

Yet rankings remain the main method of measuring reputation. If they were the perfect guide then only the top ranked provider would succeed. Second, what happens to companies too small to be included in such rankings or not for profit organizations? Rankings also tend to rely upon objective data or on the opinions of experts rather than actual customers. Where actual customers are polled, they tend again to be asked questions about objective and rational factors. Why we prefer one organization rather than another can depend upon rational factors such as price or quality, but it can also depend upon a sense of affinity. We can have an emotional bond to the organization. We do not always give money to a charity for rational reasons, but why do we give to one rather than to another? Quite simply because we have a greater attachment to one type of cause. We will be challenging the status quo that rankings are the best way to assess reputation.

Tenet 8: reputation can be measured

While rankings of reputation appear to be less than useful to the business manager seeking to improve reputation, the reader must not assume that reputation cannot be measured. A tenet of the reputation paradigm is that reputation, however ethereal, can be measured. But there are problems with existing measures. Fombrun (1998b) critiqued a number of commercially available measures of reputation on two grounds: the choice of criteria used in the assessment having no theoretical foundation and the sample of respondents to such surveys being normally that of executives and business analysts. Fombrun *et al.* (2000) propose an alternative to existing indices that could overcome many of these criticisms, particularly those from an academic perspective. Their measurement tool includes six dimensions drawn from an appraisal of the reputation literature. One value of their approach is that the same dimensions are used by different stakeholders to measure reputation of many different types of organization.

Generally speaking companies tend to build their own scales to measure their image or identity. Marwick and Fill (1997) illustrate the ad hoc approach to reputation measurement that is common in the field. Their study in the aerospace sector began with the selection of attributes specific to the industry, for example product reliability. Customers were asked to rate attributes for importance and for image compared to the client company's competitors (worse–better) and for image compared with customer requirements. Their work revealed gaps between the images held by different stakeholder groups (for example on cooperativeness). However are reliability and cooperativeness relevant to all businesses?

We believe that there is a need for a generic scale to measure both internal and external aspects of reputation, image, and identity, a scale that is capable of assessing our attachment to an organization as well as the more tangible things we might be able to rate them for. To demonstrate that image and identity are linked the two should be measured using a similar scale.

Objective matters, such as the size and sales level of an organization can affect reputation but how do you measure the emotional attachment that we have to a company? The issue of measuring reputation is considered in some depth in Chapter 6.

Tenet 9: reputation can be lost more easily than it can be created

Alexander Pope put his finger on it when he wrote, 'At every word a reputation dies'. A reputation takes time to create and to develop but it can be lost in minutes through an unfortunate action, indeed a single word. A structured approach to crisis management is now established within many organizations. The defence of reputation is the subject matter for Chapter 5.

But why are reputations so fragile? The reader will forgive another quotation at this stage, this time from Elbert Hubbard, 'Many a man's reputation would not know his character if they met on the street'. This is a pithy way of explaining that the image (in our terminology) that a person or an organization presents can be very different from the reality that is within. In Chapter 2 Trevor Morris explained that it is not possible to hide the reality of an organization's behaviour from the public any more. If you are a charlatan you will be found out. Someone will cry out that the king has no clothes, that the idol has feet of clay.

A good reputation is like an investment in credibility. No one is without some fault and no organization will deal fairly with every stakeholder all of the time. We cannot hope to satisfy every stakeholder that even the most honest of transactions is perfect. So all of us will have to accept criticism both honest and dishonest as a fact of everyday life. The issue is whether the mud sticks or not. Many a politician has been nicknamed 'Teflon man' after the non-stick surface, because no amount of criticism seems to affect them. One issue is the source of the criticism. If the politician's attackers are other politicians or media known to have a political bias, then the credibility of the source will be lower than say a respected independent journalist. If the attack is based upon hard facts and an emotional issue then it will do more damage than generalized claims of incompetence or misjudgement. The message and the medium are both important.

Tenet 10: reputation can best be studied using an interdisciplinary approach

This last tenet is somewhat technical in nature but it helps to explain why Reputation Management as a perspective has been slow to emerge. Other perspectives on corporate strategy have been based upon a single approach, in research terms upon a single academic discipline. Thus Michael Porter's work is based on an economic perspective of business. The PIMS paradigm emerged from empirical studies of business practice; Henry Mintzberg's approach is based on an organizational behaviour perspective. By comparison those who study Reputation Management come from diverse backgrounds. The profusion of meanings associated with terms such as 'identity' has been mentioned earlier. To those coming at the area from a design perspective (Ind 1992) the word evokes all that is to do with graphic and building design. To those from an organizational behaviour background identity is about how people and organizations see themselves. For those from a marketing/strategy background the word can be a synonym for image.

Overlaid on the perspectives of different backgrounds are different perspectives on the ideal research method. In academia there is a long standing debate (OK let us be honest, a long standing war) between those who believe that you can demonstrate causality between phenomena, for example that a measure of reputation drives business performance (labelled as positivists) and those who believe that social science is not similar to natural science and that hard and fast theories that X causes Y are unlikely to be useful in understanding social phenomena. To business practitioners such debates can be frustrating. They realize that even the most sophisticated statistical analysis is capable of misleading and that even a Marxist sociologist can have an idea that will improve management practice. However for good or bad, books such as this tend to be written from one perspective or another. What is different about the work reported in this chapter and elsewhere in this book is that it is drawn from many perspectives. The value to the reader is that each can illuminate what is a complex area. Sometimes different perspectives are irreconcilable, but often they are complementary.

The main author and his team are predominantly positivistic in their perspective. We believe that you can measure reputation. We believe that reputation drives financial performance in predictable ways. We believe that, despite its complexity, there are some 'rules' for Reputation Management that will bring increased business performance if followed and reduced business performance if ignored. The last section of this chapter attempts to summarize what we have taken from existing thinking on how reputation is managed, why we feel this is a useful paradigm for today's context and, finally, what we have added to the paradigm.

In summary: what is Reputation Management about?

So what is reputation? If we say someone or something has a clear 'reputation' we are saying that we expect that entity to behave consistently and therefore predictably in certain circumstances. We build this expectation through an accumulation of all of our experiences and interactions together with reports of those of others, together with the (filtered) views of others of the entity's reputation. We constantly evolve our expectations as experience accumulates and as we accept some or all of the views of others and the evidence of our own experience. Our first view is likely to be a simple stereotype based upon limited information. We draw upon a library of stereotypes to make an initial judgement (all German companies are efficient; all oil companies damage the environment). This simple starting point can change dramatically but is more likely to evolve. Indeed dramatic change in reputation is the exception rather than the rule. However, highly significant incidents, such as a crisis, can trigger a change in our views.

Our perception of reputation can also be shaped in part by the deliberate actions of the entity we are appraising, motivated to mould our perceptions to create a favourable disposition towards it. An individual or organization can manage our view of their reputation through what it chooses to communicate to us. Formal communication will dominate this process when the entity is something we cannot or do not interact with. Thus a product brand is normally something we cannot interact with while the image we have of a service organization we use every day will be dominated by the informal communication we are involved with, by being with employees or being in a building associated with the entity.

We also form an impression of organizations by working with or for them. If the organization is our employer, the experiences we have during the working day, the ways of working, its rules, its culture, the views of others when they discover where we work all influence what we have called 'identity'.

Somehow reputation and financial performance are interlinked but those links are not obvious. To help understand what drives performance we need better measures of reputation.

Our approach

Central to our view on Reputation Management is the idea that identity influences image, that the views of employees of their organization will influence the views of customers. The level of effect will vary. The views of customer facing employees are more likely to influence customers in organizations where the customer interacts directly and face to face with the employee.

Equally central to our thinking about Reputation Management in organizations is the notion of harmonization. Superior reputations exist when those aspects of reputation that satisfy customer facing employees also satisfy customers. In such cases the emotional aspects of the corporate reputation work together. Not every aspect of the experiences that employees and customers have will satisfy them, but some will dominate satisfaction. Reputation management is about ensuring that the same emotional attachments satisfy and motivate both key staff and customers. But this is not enough. For reputation to work well for a business, customer facing employees have to have a rational reason for being satisfied if their customers are satisfied. This may take the form of an incentive scheme or a share ownership scheme, something that will provide a logical link between staff and customer satisfaction.

Our model: the Corporate Reputation Chain

Figure 3.8 summarizes our thinking as to how the various elements of reputation might tie in together and how they might affect staff retention and business performance. The two 'mights' indicate that from our experience the links in the reputation chain are not always in place.

Reputation management should be concerned with two things, image and identity. Within these, managers should seek to harmonize those aspects, providing both emotional and rational links that can complete what we call the reputation chain. In the following chapters are a number of case examples designed to give life to the model in Figure 3.8.

The model is not intended to represent reality. It is an ideal. The links in the reputation chain are rarely all in place. It is the role and objective of managers to work to ensure that these links are forged such that image and identity do harmonize, that there are links from image to sales or some other objective measure of performance, that there are positive links from identity to staff retention and ultimately that identity can be linked through to performance.

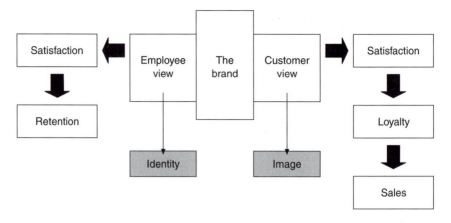

Figure 3.8 The Corporate Reputation Chain.

4   The company as a brand

What is a brand?, metaphors in understanding 'brand', the role of advertising, positioning, country of origin (COO) effects, industry effects.

The purpose of this chapter is to explore what can be learnt about the management of reputation from our understanding of 'the brand'. Many products and services have names but how many are brand names? Do brands have to be names? Can a company name, even one that is composed, as so many are, of initials or a compression of the founders' names be regarded as a brand name? The answer to all of these questions is yes. Anything can be a brand, anything that has associations that are not apparent from an objective assessment of the entity that is purchased can be regarded as a brand. These associations are intangible and emotional in nature. Understanding what is a brand is neither easy nor clear, because of the difficulties inherent in assessing anything non-rational.

In this book we are concerned with organizations and the idea that an organization can be thought of as a brand. Such thinking is useful when it comes to understanding the reputation of an organization.

The branded organization

We associate the word 'brand' with products, particularly those that are heavily advertised. But company names can be brand names too and this is very much the case in the services sector. Hotels such as Hilton, restaurants such as McDonald's, airlines such as Lufthansa, business schools such as MBS, tend to have a number of things in common. The first is that the name of the organization, the corporate name, is the same for the service that the customer buys, for the company employees work for and for the company the supplier sells to.

But product marketers are often changing the way they approach markets and emphasizing their corporate names as well as their product names. Companies who in the past relied on having names for themselves that were not used for products are changing their approach. Take the Ford Motor Company. Their first car might have been known by the Ford name but in modern times the Ford name has been a family name for a number of separately branded models. At the model level each has a further level of branding with labels such as: Executive, Popular, L, GL, GLX and many more. Special editions are given individual names. What is interesting in the context of this book is the approach Ford have adopted following their purchase of a number of other manufacturers. They now control a range of corporate names such as Volvo, Mazda, Lincoln, Mercury, Jaguar and Land Rover. Do you, as some car companies have done before, rationalize the names selecting only the one umbrella name and sell them all from one location? Clearly not. The Jaguar customer is looking for a different product than that sought by the Ford customer. The Jaguar customer is also expecting a different experience when buying and maintaining a car compared to the Ford customer. This will mean that different service criteria will be important in selling one brand than in another. Ford have sometimes located their different marques on the same or adjacent sites but they have kept the experience separate.

There is a certain snobbery about the use of the term 'brand' suggesting that the label should only be applied to high image items such as fashion names or to heavily advertised products such as detergents. A retailer or a bank name cannot become a brand name. But any name can also be a brand name if it represents to the observer more than just the word itself.

Our first problem is then to identify just what a brand is. There are different definitions and brands have many more roles for both seller and buyer, Davies (1992). Figure 4.1 summarizes many of these by suggesting that there are probably six different ways of looking at a brand or, put another way, a brand has six different assets.

Differentiation

Definitions of brand frequently emphasize a brand name's power to allow us to differentiate between otherwise similar products and services. Gardner and Levy (1955) in their seminal article argued that a brand name is more than just a label employed to differentiate, but in doing so they imply that differentiation

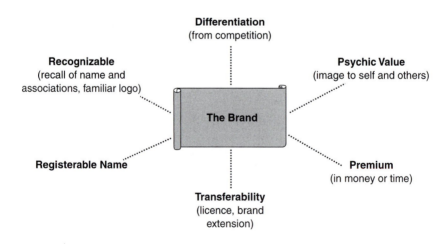

Figure 4.1 The six assets of a brand.

is a key role for a brand name and that this was indeed its original role. In its original sense a brand was a device to indicate who owned a particular cow. Products have been marked with a distinctive sign for other reasons, such as which brick maker in ancient Egypt made a particular brick (in case the building fell down and someone had to shoulder the blame). In more modern times the customer's image of a product can be changed dramatically if a different brand name is placed on it.

In Britain there are three major manufacturers of chocolate, Cadbury, Mars, and Nestlé. The first two, with their brands Cadbury's Dairy Milk and Galaxy, dominate the market for bars of milk chocolate. In market research customers are equally divided in their preferences if they are given the products 'blind' in other words with no way of knowing which product is which. When buying they purchase far more Cadbury's Dairy Milk. The explanation has nothing to do with different levels of distribution or differences in price. In non-blind taste tests where respondents to the market research are told that one product is Galaxy and the other Cadbury's, there is a significant preference for Cadbury's. And it makes little difference which product respondents are told is which. The only possible explanation is that the label is more powerful than the product.

In taste tests Pepsi claim that their product researches better than its arch rival Coca-Cola, yet in most markets Coca-Cola outsells Pepsi. While brand names do help us to distinguish one product from another, differentiation is not the only function of a brand name. Somehow the name evokes other associations. While brand names are associated with specific products, a brand is not the same as a product. The same name can be used for example to label totally unrelated products or businesses.

Transferability

A genuine brand name is then somehow separate from the product or service that it is used to label. It has a life of its own that is independent of the product it identifies. As such it can be beneficially transferred from one product to another. Transferability is what distinguishes between a name and a brand name. Whether the name has been transferred to another product or service is not an absolute test for the name being a brand. For example Coca-Cola was until relatively recently used to label only the original product it has been associated with for decades. But if the name has been transferred beneficially then you certainly do have a brand name and not just a label.

When transferred the brand name will take some or all of its positive associations with it. These associations are often about quality. Indeed a brand is often preferred to an unbranded item due to its implied warranty of *consistent* quality. Strong brands transfer across different types of product, such as the Virgin brand which began as something associated with records and has since been applied to companies selling insurance, operating planes and trains, selling cars and financial services. The list appears endless and this is one of the concerns that the name loses something of its distinctiveness if 'stretched' too far.

Psychic value

Many associations that we make with brand names are less than totally objective and are more psychological in nature. As people we have symbolic needs that can be provided by a car brand that suggest that we are successful or by a fashion brand that suggests that we are up to date. We might wish to impress others or merely to support our view of ourselves. Such psychic dimensions are difficult to measure because we are reluctant to admit to some of the motivations behind our choice of one brand over another. Yet advertising, particularly that on the television and in the cinema, is clearly trying to suggest that we will be more attractive to others if we drink a certain beer, or more successful if we drive a certain car. Surely we drink beer to quench our thirst and get merry? Do we drive a car merely to get from A to B? Of course we do not. Brands have a symbolic and emotional role in our lives that is central to their value. Which product would a young male wish to have in his hand in a bar on a Saturday night, a glass of lemonade or a bottle of a heavily promoted beer? Why do we spend so much on designer clothes compared with the equally good functional quality and design available in a retailer's own brand merchandise? One answer is that when we put on an item marked Calvin Klein or Gucci, we put on more than the article itself. At least for that first moment we put on the imagery that the brand owner has carefully crafted to provide us with an additional reason for buying the product, one that we would be reluctant to admit to and to discuss, but one that is real enough.

Recall

Traditionally we assess the power of a brand by measuring the aided and unaided recall of a brand name. For example we may ask a sample of the world's population, 'Can you name a leading brand of soft drink?' If Coca-Cola is not mentioned then we can ask whether the person has heard of Coca-Cola. The first is a measure of recall, the second a measure of aided recall or recognition. International rankings of brands often use recall as their only measure of brand strength. But just because people can recall a brand name does not mean they will buy it. The name Coca-Cola is heavily associated with one product. While you can argue that the name has been transferred to other products such as Diet Coke and some fashion items, such initiatives are few and far between. Brands such as Virgin which would probably score fairly modestly on recall in the context of soft drinks (the name is used to brand cola) may be stronger brands because they have been transferred beneficially to many other product types.

More important than the recall of the name itself is whether actual or potential stakeholders recall the desired associations. Measuring this is a more complex task than measuring the recall of the name itself.

Recall and transferability are attributes of a brand that are not necessarily in harmony. Recall within a product type may be low if the brand has been transferred widely as the two examples of Coca-Cola and Virgin that have been used here can attest.

Premium

Leading brands tend to sustain a financial premium in the market, especially over unbranded items. All too often a premium is essential to reflect the investment the brand owner needs to fund the advertising needed to promote recognition and recall of the brand name and to build the essential associations. Critics of consumer brands, and these include many consumer groups, ask whether it makes sense for customers to spend sometimes double the price on branded items compared with unbranded or retailer branded items.

A retailer is better placed than a manufacturer to brand its products in a cost effective way. The manufacturer has to speak over the head of the retailer to the consumer. Having a well-known brand is often the only power a manufacturer has over its distribution channel, but one consequence for the consumer of the battle for market power between supplier and retailer is higher prices for the person at the end of the supply chain.

Figure 4.2 illustrates how the comparative selling prices of competing products compared in one study. Davies and Brito (1996) analysed the cost structures of competing supply chains, the example in the figure is for one of their studies, that of margarine. The selling price to consumers for the leading brand is used as a benchmark and set at 100. The supply chain cost structures of the two leading manufacturer brands are compared with that of a retailer's own brand. The number two brand in the market at the time sold at a slight premium to the price of the leading brand while the retailer's own brand was considerably cheaper. The cost of raw materials for each product was remarkably similar. The retailer's gross margin, shown here as its added value, is highest for the number two brand, possibly because the supplier needed to give a bigger incentive to the retailer to stock and display their product than from the leading brand. The retailer's gross margin, as a percentage of selling price was higher for their own brand.

The explanation for the differences in selling price lay mainly in the internal costs of the respective manufacturers. A different manufacturer made each product but the technologies used were almost identical and quite

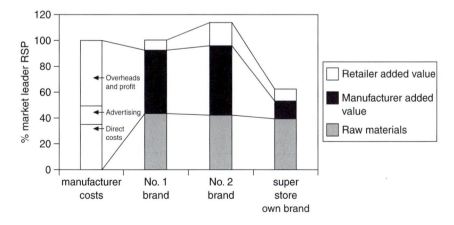

Figure 4.2 Supply chain cost structures for competing own brands and brands.

straightforward. Vegetable oils that had been processed to make them into fats were delivered to each company as hot liquids. Normally the oils were a predetermined blend of different types (sunflower, groundnut oil, etc.). All the manufacturer had to do was to mix in any supplements, flavours, and colouring and to cool the hot raw materials as they were put into the final packaging.

The costs of the leading brand manufacturer were higher due to advertising but also due to large profit contributions.

Davies and Brito used a technique called trade off analysis in getting consumers to compare the three competing brands. Consumers were asked to spread the margarine from each sample on to bread so as to compare the taste of each. Respondents were asked to express a preference if each product was sold at the same price. The relative price of their choice was then raised and they were asked to choose again. The process was repeated until the full range of prices charged in the marketplace had been covered.

Many respondents preferred the own branded product even when the prices they were told were the same for the three products. These results reflected other research where the actual quality of own brands in blind taste tests was judged to be the same or superior to that of the leading brand in the sector. At market prices few respondents would still choose the leading brand in the research experiment. Interestingly, although the identity of the products was revealed to the respondents at the end of each interview, when they were interviewed again some months later, few of those who had purchased the leading brand prior to the research had even tried the retailer's own brand and fewer still had switched.

One issue that emerges from an analysis of supply chain cost structures is that retailers do not spend as much money on branding themselves and their own label products as do manufacturers. Typically a food retailer will spend less than 1 per cent of turnover on advertising, a manufacturer about 5 per cent. A company such as Procter and Gamble spend up to 40 per cent of turnover on all aspects of marketing. To manage their supply chains they need to spend heavily on consumer advertising, trade marketing, and marketing research. Their logistics costs are far higher than for a retailer dealing with an own brand supplier. Many own brand suppliers sell only own brands. They probably have a limited product range. Their emphasis on research and development is low as they tend to copy existing lines. Their marketing costs are low because they spend little on advertising and their trade marketing costs are also low as they do not have to distribute their products widely and certainly not as widely as a branded manufacturer. What is interesting about the comparative supply chains is that the main differences in cost structures between them are found in the internal cost structures of the main players who constitute the supply chain. Discount retailers have lower internal costs than full service supermarkets and own brand manufacturers generally far lower cost structures than brand manufacturers.

Retailers brand themselves and their own brand products using corporate branding while manufacturers with a plethora of brand names can only use consumer advertising. We are not anti-advertising but clearly believe that advertising is not the most cost effective way to create a corporate brand. Corporate branding is not without cost but is more concerned with the recruitment and retention of quality customer facing staff, their training, and the presentation of the environment they work within to the customer.

Manufacturers of brands have much higher internal costs compared with those of own brand companies. The explanation appears to be that the former employ many more 'managers' than the leaner own brand companies. The premium in price that leading brands have to charge to pay for the higher costs of their supply chains can only be justified if customers perceive that they are getting something extra for that premium. If a retailer can brand itself more cheaply than it costs a supplier to brand its products, then the traditional competitive advantage to the supplier of branding is lost in negotiating with the retailer. In some markets retailers have become strong brands. Supplier products have to be genuinely innovative if they are to succeed or the supplier has to vertically integrate to protect its access to the end customer. Any distinction between retailer and product brands has become increasingly blurred.

Money is not the only resource that we are willing and able to exchange for a brand. We will often travel further to visit a more attractive restaurant or leisure centre. We will spend longer somewhere that the 'branded experience' is more satisfying. Compare the queues somewhere such as Disneyland with the amount of time we would be prepared to visit, say, a bank, and you have a good example of what is meant by a branded experience. We are taught that when visiting France a good measure of the quality of a restaurant is the length of the queue or the difficulty in booking a table. In all such cases we exchange time to acquire the brand and time is as valuable if not more valuable than money.

In Chapter 3 we discussed the idea of brand valuation in the context of corporate reputation. The value of a strong brand name is worth up to a year's turnover. A brand can be licensed to produce revenue streams equivalent to around 10 per cent of sales turnover, again indicating that the value of the brand name to the product it is associated with is equivalent to a capital sum of about a year's turnover. However you calculate the value of a brand a strong brand has a capital value of something in the order of a year's sales. Brands can be bought and sold, licensed and valued. The size and nature of the asset a brand represents is indicative of its strength. Their value can now be included in a company's balance sheet in some countries as part of their assets, yet the focus is often on a valuation from the perspective of a single stakeholder, that of the customer. As we argue throughout this book, the company name or brand has value in dealing with many stakeholders.

Brands are assets that can be invested in to enhance the price the customer is prepared to pay. Brands can be created in a number of ways and creating and managing a superior experience can be more cost effective than using advertising.

Registration

Finally and more pedantically a brand's strength depends upon the owner's ability to register the brand name. The rules differ from country to country but basically you can register the same name in different domains or areas of use, but you cannot register a name if someone else has already claimed it or if the name you choose is a word in common use. For example it would not be possible to register 'Classics' as a clothes brand because many retailers refer to a range of products using the word. You could however register a design or logo with a distinctive presentation of the word but you could not protect the use of the word itself. In the current context the registration of names on the Internet has been an issue, with entrepreneurs registering existing trading names in the hope of selling them on to the company using them in traditional markets.

Some brand names do not transfer from one society to the next often due to the literal meaning of the word. In Spain a leading brand of soft drink is branded Revoltosa, the connotations of which in Spanish are positive but in English, negative.

Metaphor and brand

Brands are complex entities and we can understand more about what we mean by 'brand' by using different perspectives. We use metaphorical expression when talking about complex entities to help our understanding. As this is the approach we use in this book to understand corporate reputation it is useful to spend some time examining the benefits and issues associated with the use of metaphor.

Metaphors pervade our every day speech and thought. They have a number of roles and forms (Black 1962). They can be used rhetorically to entertain and divert. This is a major role of metaphor in a literary context. For example the statement 'Roger is a lion' is not meant to be taken literally but to provide us with an instant, figurative picture of Roger's character (Black 1962). The metaphor also serves to inform us about Roger and in particular about his character. In this example the metaphor works through the associations we can make with something that is better understood or just easier to understand. More fundamentally the use of metaphor forces the reader to connect two ideas. The target of the metaphor, in this case the character of Roger is seen through the metaphor, the lion, which filters and transforms our view of the target. It helps us to make sense of something that is too complex to describe or define easily.

Davies and Chun (2002) have argued that there are three main or root metaphors and a much larger number of sub-metaphors in common usage when talking about brands. These three root metaphors are: brand as differentiating mark, brand as person, and brand as asset (see Figure 4.3).

Brand as differentiating mark

The word 'brand' is itself a metaphor. As a metaphor it signifies a mark that identifies something. The metaphor is so commonly associated with the concept of a brand that the idea of a brand as distinguishing or differentiating appears in many definitions of the term brand itself (Kotler 1988; de Chernatony and McWilliam 1989; Murphy 1990; Doyle 1990). Once a metaphor becomes a term then, by definition, it loses its creative power. A term has a specific meaning, while a metaphor does not. The whole essence of metaphor is to expand our thinking about a complex entity, not to narrow our thinking to the confines of a specific term.

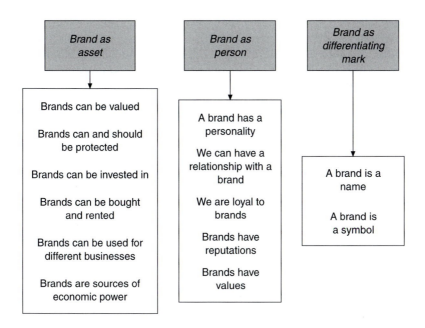

Figure 4.3 Metaphors for a brand.

The idea of a mark that is unique to a particular brand is the root metaphor for a number of sub-metaphors that have become important practical issues for many brands. First, there is the brand's name itself and the logo that is used to present the name. Some claim that there is an inherent advantage in a 'well chosen name' (Berry *et al.* 1988), that initials or locations should be avoided in favour of names that give 'character' to the brand as names can have inherent meanings or associations (Collins 1977). Companies spend large sums with consultants to identify brand and company names that have an intrinsic meaning and to research existing names to ensure that any inherent associations do not impede their using any names they already have. However the value of specific names can be exaggerated. Companies such as Mars, the confectionery and food group, sell the same consumer products in different geographical markets under different names. It is not uncommon for the same name to be used to label different products. If names have intrinsic meaning, then this should not be possible. When Mars were faced with the need to harmonize their use of names across various markets they decided to rename a strong brand in the UK, Marathon, with the name Snickers, the name used to label the same product in other countries. The word Snickers has no meaning in English but has all kinds of possible connotations in an English context. The change was not without its critics, but it was done all the same and as far as is known the same brand values transferred successfully across to the new name. A leading brand of German domestic equipment is Bosch. In France the word is a pejorative term for a German and this association is well known in other countries. If the word's intrinsic meaning was vitally important, the brand would not sell well in Europe.

The symbolic significance of logos has received considerable attention in practitioner-oriented books (Olins 1978; Selame and Selame 1988). Brand logos are probably more important as a topic than brand names to discuss in the context of their having an inherent meaning. We used the example of the Mars company above in the context of confectionery. The same name is used to label a division specializing in vending machine electronics. It is used by a totally different company, Mars Crucible, who make foundry products and by many other companies, including a taxi firm and a transport company. In the case of Mars the food business it is the family name of the founder. In any research into the fundamental associations with the word 'Mars' doubtless there would be many derived from the planet or the god of war. Another meaning would be from the verb to 'mar' or to damage something. The name might not be at the top of any list of ideal names for a food company and yet Mars Inc have one of the strongest reputations as an organization. What matters is not then so much the name as the associations that can be made with it. A name with a natural meaning may provide a short-term advantage, but that is all. By contrast a logo, through the use of design, can have inherent associations depending upon the style of that logo and the use of symbols.

When used in practice the brand name generally forms the central part of a logo. In terms of metaphor, the name or logo can take on the role of icon or more precisely symbol, and a new sub-metaphor is evoked. The sub-metaphor of brand as symbol, an emblem, something that is generally accepted to represent something else, adds to the blander notion of a means of labelling or identifying. The idea of a brand being an emblem allows us to see a brand name or logo as something that is OK to put on the outside of clothing rather than hide away inside. A T-shirt with a well-known brand name on it can sell for ten times the price of a plain T-shirt. A brand name can be used to adorn consumer durables such as a car or a hi-fi. As consumers we pay to advertise the product for the supplier because it also adds to our own prestige to be associated with a leading brand name.

A logo is not only a way of presenting the company name attractively. It is probably a far more powerful way of adding associations than by spending time worrying about any intrinsic associations with the brand name itself. The typeface, colour, and associated design will carry more powerful symbolic messages to the stakeholder than the name itself. In a later chapter we examine the use of logos as part of a section on corporate identity.

The idea that a brand name represents something else leads to the question, 'What something else?' One answer is provided via the root metaphor of brand as person.

Brand as person

The personification of the brand, or more precisely the use of the personification metaphor, can be seen in a number of works on branding dating from the 1970s. King (1973) was one of the earliest of authors to develop the idea when he insisted that the main difference between two competing brands, where the products were similar, lay in the different personalities projected by each brand.

Thus Keeble (1991) could claim that while competing soap powders Ariel and Persil both had different market positions, only Persil 'had a personality'.

One of the earliest uses of the person metaphor was not in the area of product branding at all but in retailing with the expression, 'the personality of the retail store' (Martineau 1958). Martineau was using the idea of branding to include the company name above a retail outlet. This was also one of the earliest acknowledgements that company names can usefully be seen as brand names. One extension of the 'brand is person' metaphor is to recognize that if we can test the 'personality' of a human then the metaphor implies we can test the personality of a brand. Generally brand personality is still seen as being accessible for researchers more through qualitative than through quantitative means (Durgee 1988; Hanby 1999). The researcher asks the respondent to imagine that the brand has 'come to life' as a person and to provide examples of what that person might do or what its personality would be like. For example, 'What newspaper would the brand read? Where would it go on holiday? What car would it drive?' There is no scientific validity in the answers that are produced. Brands are not people. They cannot come alive; they do not drive cars or go on holiday. But we are quite comfortable to pretend that they do. In fact it makes it easier to talk about a brand using such a 'projective' technique. Brand as person is one of the best examples of the use of metaphor in understanding what a brand really is and in analysing it and we use it when measuring corporate reputation.

The idea that we can have a relationship with a brand is an extension of the brand is person metaphor. Fournier (1998) takes this sub-metaphor into the brand arena by examining various types and styles of relationship that individuals may have with specific brands. Thus concepts such as trust and friendship are introduced to describe the interaction between human and brand in much the same way as it would be natural to discuss the relationship between two people. Similarly if the brand is another person we can become 'involved with the brand' (Laurent and Kapferer 1985). People we are involved with mean more to us. We are more interested in them, notice things about them more, and react differently towards them compared with those we feel we have little to do with. We are highly involved with only a few people and more involved with certain types of person (such as friends and family) than with others (such as strangers).

Individuals have values and so must the brand as person. Corporate reputation research has adopted the sub-metaphor of brand as a person with values in such definitions of the corporate brand as 'a set of values perceived as typical for a specific company in the eyes of a variety of stakeholders' (van Riel 1997).

Brand as asset

The statement that a brand is an asset opens the door to a number of ideas in addition to those listed earlier when talking about brand valuation. An asset is an item of property and one specifically of worth. Thus the metaphor suggests two things: first that a brand must belong to someone and second that it has a value that can be determined. Ownership implies something that can be tested in law, which implies in turn that such ownership should be protected under

Table 4.1 The image of brands and own brands

Image cluster	Timotei	Sainsbury's frequent use	Wash and Go	Tesco's 2 in 1
Natural	15	9	–	2
Gentle	25	18	2	4
Relaxed	9	3	–	–
Quiet	12	17	–	2
Conservative	9	–	–	0
Active	–	–	45	30
Sociable	–	–	6	3
Young	–	–	6	6
Cheap	–	–	–	3
Happy	2	–	21	12
Curious	–	–	2	–

law. This is only partly true in reality. While trademarks, company (in this case brand) names and logos can be registered in most countries, it is more difficult to protect the imagery that is associated with the brand name due to advertising and packaging. This is an issue with retailer's own brands and other competing brands that ape the 'get up' of more established brands in the expectation of advantage (Davies 1998) (see Table 4.1).

Many retailers, but also some manufacturers copy the presentation of leading brands in the same market sector. This copying can be too close and become passing off, the wrong committed by someone who represents their products as being those of another. Most commonly, similar sounding names are used together with similar designs and colours of packaging. In one experiment shoppers were asked to compare the brand imagery of two leading manufacturers' brands of hair shampoo with the brands sold by two retailers which happened to look very similar (Table 4.1) (Davies 1998).

The personification approach was used to get shoppers to provide their image of each brand. Respondents were asked to imagine that each product had 'come to life' as a person and to offer words that described the character of that person. Similes were grouped together to provide a profile of the image they presented. The Sainsbury Frequent Use product was packaged in a similar way to that of Unilever's Timotei and Tesco's 2 in 1 packaged in a similar way to Procter and Gamble's Wash and Go. Both of the last two products were combined shampoo and conditioners. The data in the table reports the number of respondents (of the fifty who were asked to rate each product) who used a word or its simile to describe the personality of the brand.

The imagery of the own brands is very similar to the manufacturer's brand that they appeared to mimic. This is unlikely to be an accident. The imagery of the two manufacturers' brands reflected the advertising campaigns that were being used. Timotei's television advertisements showed a blonde woman washing her hair in a pool in the forest. The word 'timotei' is Finnish for 'grass'. The Wash and Go advertisement showed a short haired brunette in the changing rooms of a sports club explaining that she did not have the time to take a bottle of shampoo and another bottle of conditioner into the shower with her and that she got around this problem by using Wash and Go. Television advertising to create such imagery is not cheap and it appears that the two retailers were taking a free ride.

The 'theft of identity' that is represented in these examples of own branding was not against any law at the time of the research except potentially in some countries where passing off is regarded, not as part of consumer protection legislation, but as part of unfair competition law. Where the relevant law is within consumer protection the view is often taken that passing off is concerned with ensuring that the consumer is not disadvantaged by any copying. In Britain this has been interpreted as meaning that if the customer benefits from lower prices then copying is not against their interests. In other countries where the issue is part of unfair competition legislation, the owner of the original brand can sue if there is evidence that a new brand has copied its get up and that in doing so has damaged the franchise the first comer had created. If the copying is too close, so that the consumer would be confused as to which product is which, passing off can be evoked directly in most countries. The law is now being strengthened to provide more protection for a company when it launches a new brand. It is now possible for example in Britain to register the shape of packaging as part of any moves to protect a brand franchise.

The valuation of brands has received some attention historically (Smiddy 1983) but the level of interest in the ways in which such value should be calculated has increased recently following the decision to allow the inclusion of valuations for intangible assets within the balance sheet (Arnold *et al.* 1992; Ward and Perrier 1998; Ambler and Barwise 1998; Kerin and Sethuraman 1998). We have added our own, simple approach to brand valuation in suggesting that as a rule of thumb a strong brand is worth about a year's turnover.

Assets are something that should be seen as investments for the future. Until the recent changes in accounting convention, the acquisition of intangible assets required that the value should be written down over time. In other words the 'asset' was seen as something that declined in value to the organization, just like plant and machinery that needs eventual replacement. Strong brands should increase, not decrease, in value over time, and somewhat faster than assets such as land and buildings that are revalued from time to time. The metaphor of asset and the sub-metaphor of brand as investment allows us the idea of a need to revalue brands periodically. What are needed are easily understood and non-controversial methods for brand valuation that can be used in support of the metaphor.

Assets often need to be invested in, to be refurbished so as to ensure their future worth and usefulness. Accounting conventions allow for provisions to be made for the refurbishment of fixed assets and for any improvement to be added to the value of the asset. Advertising can be argued to be to the product brand asset what maintenance is to the building asset. If the metaphor is taken to its full extent, advertising expenditure should be capitalized at least in part. In corporate branding staff training appears to be an important way of improving reputation. What about the idea of capitalizing that? Realistically, neither suggestion will be adopted but the idea that brands are as much an asset as any land or building has now been accepted.

An asset can be bought and sold. In the case of a brand, its use can also be licensed, the equivalent of renting or hiring out the use of an asset to a third party. As the asset is intangible, it can be rented to more than one party simultaneously.

Finally, assets can be applied in a number of ways. Plant and buildings can be used for a number of businesses. So can the brand asset. The phrase 'umbrella brand' sounds like a very different metaphor but the underlying root is really that of asset. An asset is more valuable if it can be used as an umbrella over a number of brands. It reduces the cost of launching new brands. It reduces the cost of promoting existing products if the brand name is the same. We do not mean that the umbrella will keep something dry or shaded. The phrase 'brand stretch' has the same inferences. How far the brand can stretch may have as its origin the simile of making money go further but the issue is the value to the company of being able to apply the brand name to as wide a range of products as possible.

Brand building and advertising

The traditional way of thinking about brand building is to think about consumer products and the traditional way to build a strong brand is to advertise. Relationships are claimed between market share for consumer brands and share of advertising voice (Jones 1990). Advertising 'voice' means little more than advertising expenditure and so the main tenet of brand building has become that to build a successful brand you need to emphasize media expenditure. But advertising is only one way to build an emotional attachment to a brand.

The marketing mix identifies those elements that a marketer has to juggle with to create a marketing platform. Traditionally it consisted of four elements, product, place, price and promotion, to which have been added sales, service and most recently, people (see Figure 4.4). The marketer adjusts the elements to create differentiation and to manage a brand over its lifecycle. For example pricing strategy can differ at the beginning and end of the lifecycle. Nowhere in

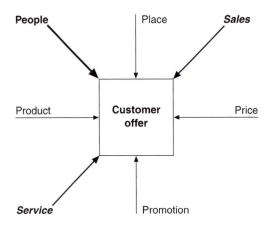

Figure 4.4 The marketing mix.

research on the marketing mix is there a statement to the effect that one element is more important than another. Indeed that is the whole point of the marketing mix to emphasize that there is no ideal mix and that similar products can and should be marketed using very different mixes so as to create differential advantage. That said, the gradual addition of new elements, especially that of 'people' indicates that somehow thinking has changed as to what a marketer needs to consider. The main issue for us here is the role of advertising.

The role of advertising

Consider the example of Starbucks, a coffee shop originating on the West Coast of the USA that became an international brand within five years without the 'benefit' of advertising. That is not to say that the company did not use any communication to create interest in itself. For example many openings saw a jazz musician playing outside the store. The sound could be heard for a block or two, just about the catchment area for a Starbucks.

Starbucks tends to employ outgoing staff, for example actors or musicians resting between jobs. There is a great emphasis on the experience that customers can expect. The company is unashamedly not the lowest in price, explaining that their focus is on giving the customer a bit of affordable luxury. All these elements will contribute to our image of Starbucks, an image unaffected by advertising.

Thomas Lipton, who was a retailer as well as a tea merchant, wrote a book in the 1920s in which he extolled the virtues of what he called 'advertising'. By this he did not mean media advertising (because there was neither the media nor the ability to read that would make this possible or effective at the time). He wrote about getting local farmers to paint on the side of their pigs 'I'm on my way to Liptons' and to employ a sculptor to fashion statues in butter in his store windows.

In the 1980s in the UK the leading banks spent between them about £1 billion a year on media advertising, with slogans such as 'the listening bank' or 'the bank that likes to say yes'. One television advertisement showed a customer explaining to another that his bank opened another counter if there was a queue. The media took great delight in publicizing any example of a loan being turned down by banks claiming to listen or to say yes, or banks that claimed to open more counters when they were crowded but did not.

Another bank promoted itself on an ethical platform. A journalist decided to test them out by pretending to be a businessman seeking funding for a new business venture. He presented his phoney plans to a number of banks. It should have been obvious in his view that the new business was a brothel. All but the one bank (the one who positioned itself on an ethical platform) apparently agreed to loan money to help launch the new business. For the ethical bank, the press coverage that this created was positive, the word of mouth for such a racy example was positive. The press coverage and the word of mouth for the other banks, who were pretending to be what they were not, could only have been negative.

There was no evidence that the media advertising from the main banks did anything positive for their income. There was little or no research identifying that customers had changed branches because of it. Commentators explained that no bank had the courage to stop advertising. Perhaps they were taking the maxim ascribed to a number of businesspeople earlier in the century, 'I know that half of the money I spend on advertising is wasted. My problem is I do not know which half'. In the case of the banks the answer was that both halves were wasted.

Shostack (1977) a bank executive and an academic writer, had tried to tell the banking fraternity years earlier that images for service companies, which are intangible, are created through tangibles (such as building design) while images for tangible products are created through the intangible imagery of media advertising. It is counterproductive to advertise an experience that is not delivered when the customer turns up. In contrast an image for being more beautiful, more exciting if you use this or that brand works because the user recreates the intangible imagery in his/her mind when using the product. Other people will also ascribe some of the imagery of the brand to the user, for example we form a picture of the driver of the car in front of us from the brand name on the boot.

The role of advertising is different in creating a brand image for a service company or a corporate reputation for any company. Advertising cannot generally be used to *create* an image in such circumstances. However if the company has created a different experience for the customer then this can be *communicated* using advertising. As with all such statements there will be exceptions. The most obvious are when the corporate brand and the product brand are the same. This is the case with Coca-Cola and with retailers such as Gap, Limited, Marks and Spencer and Tesco who sell much of their products under their own names. A brand image for Gap can be created around their products and some of this imagery will transfer to the branded experience expected in their shops.

Figure 4.5 shows the results of two studies of retailer advertising. One sector, electrical goods retailing, relied on price, manufacturers' branded merchandise

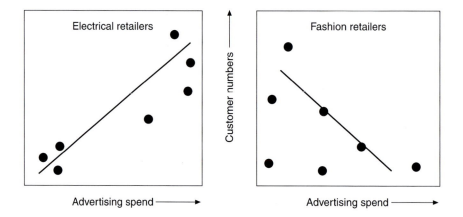

Figure 4.5 Advertising in the services sector.

Source: Davies (1991).

being promoted with promises of discounts. In this example if you spent more on advertising you generated more customer flow. The other sector was department stores. Here the higher spenders attracted fewer customers. This graph does not prove that such companies discouraged customers the more they advertised, merely that there was no positive relationship between advertising weight and patronage.

When advertising is used to communicate factual information about service companies such as the discount prices and product availability in an electrical retailer, then it can be effective. In Figure 4.5 the main content of the electrical retailers' advertising was to inform about product and price. It worked. The retailers shouting the loudest and with the most attractive products and prices, created the most customer flow. If the offers for product and price were matched by what was in the store, then customers will buy. In the fashion retailer example, a number of retailers were trying to create an image for being exciting and fashionable. Unfortunately what was promised in the advertising was not credible and was not delivered inside the store. The advertising did not work.

Advertising in the context of corporate branding has one main role, to provide factual information. If the stores had been exciting then it would have been worthwhile boasting about it in advertising. No advertisement will create an exciting store when the reality is fundamentally boring.

Positioning

Positioning is defined in the marketing text books in the following way (Kotler and Armstrong 2000). 'Positioning is the place the product occupies in consumers' minds relative to competing products'. And also: 'Positioning is the way the product is defined by consumers on important attributes'.

Positioning requires a frame of reference and this is normally other products in the market that are competing. Thus the market for bread may have two important characteristics, health and price. Products can be 'positioned' on these two dimensions as in Figure 4.6. The figure uses the basic technique of gap analysis where only two attributes are used to identify the positioning of all product types. There is an apparent 'gap' for breads which are low in price but which have an image for being healthy. It may not be possible to fill such a gap, but if it is, it may be better for one of the manufacturers of white sliced bread to reposition its brands into this gap. Alternatively a new concept might be developed to fill the gap such as white bread with added vitamins that would cost little more to produce but which may have a healthier image.

More sophisticated methods of producing positioning maps are available, such as multidimensional scaling (Davies and Brooks 1989). Maps showing competing products can be produced from data scoring each product against any number of attributes. Two dimensional maps can be produced to visualize such information. It is also possible to position company reputations or images using the same techniques. For example Figure 4.7 maps the UK ladies wear market.

The figure was derived from actual purchase data. Retailers that were used by the same customers are positioned close together and retailers that do not share the same customer base are positioned far apart. There are four main segments.

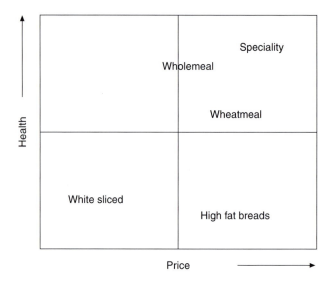

Figure 4.6 Product positioning.

In the bottom right-hand corner are retailers catering for the younger, more fashion conscious but more price conscious buyer. Above this is a more affluent segment of about the same age grouping that are looking for a more formal and tailored look. In the top left-hand corner are the department stores occupying the segment with the single largest share of the market. They cater for an older more affluent clientele. In the bottom left are the more price-led chain stores.

The study examined the positioning of competing retailers over two years to check on the positioning of one brand, Etam. Its position had been more in the

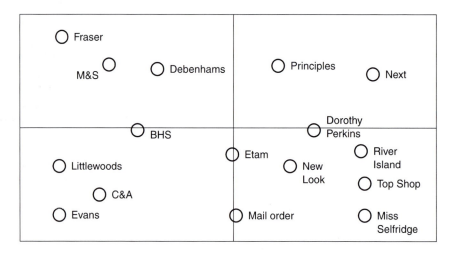

Figure 4.7 Image positioning.

bottom left-hand sector, but its management had decided to reposition the company in the more dynamic, bottom right quadrant. They had succeeded in doing so by changing the store design and the merchandise, but sales had suffered. One view was that they should have changed the name as well as the look of the store.

One of the principles of branding is that the brand name is the shorthand for all the associations that its management seeks to make with the brand. The brand becomes an icon, an encapsulation of the brand image, an image that is evoked every time the brand name is seen or heard. If the imagery is changed but the brand name remains the same, then customers may become confused. Existing customers will see the familiar brand name, but realize once they are in the shop that the product is aimed at a different group. The target group is confused because they like the product but do not associate themselves with the imagery they associate with the brand name. A radical repositioning takes time in the services sector or may entail a change of name.

Rational or emotional?

Customers can value brands on rational or emotional attributes. The speed and service frequency of a car are rational attributes. So are the data provided by consumer organizations on the number of faults and breakdowns experienced by owners. Design is more emotional in nature. It is also very subjective and difficult to assess objectively. Factors such as the sex appeal that a particular car may bestow on its owner might be an important factor in purchase but be virtually impossible to measure or to get potential owners to admit to as a factor. Some believe that it is the emotional dimension to a brand that is its most valuable asset, as can be seen in this definition of a brand: 'A company with a price advantage can be undercut. A company with a performance advantage can be outflanked. But a company with an emotional difference can potentially demand a premium forever'.

The Country of Origin effect

In Chapter 2 we discussed the model of Bernstein that sees corporate image as being viewed by the stakeholder through a number of lenses, the two main lenses being the country of origin of the business and the industry that it is in. The Country of Origin effect can best be illustrated in the context of Germany and German goods.

Before 1918 nobody knew where a product came from. In that year Germany lost the First World War. To punish German industry and to warn the European consumer of that time, German manufacturers were obliged to put on each product they exported 'Made in Germany' labels (in English). Very soon it became a sign of quality (Morello 1984: 5).

The implications of Morello's comments are profound. If a company can be identified with a particular country then part of its image is predetermined. German cars are generally referred to as more reliable, irrespective of knowledge of relevant attributes in car buying (Johansson *et al.* 1985). Bannister and Saunders (1978: 562) define Ccountry of Origin (COO) effects as:

> Generalized images created by variables such as representative products, economic and political maturity, historical events and relationships, traditions, industrialization and the degree of technological virtuosity which will have effects upon consumer attitudes additional to those emanating from the significant elements of the products.

There is a general tendency to mentally associate reliability and overall perceptions of quality with the level of industrialization of the country of origin of the product in question (Schooler *et al.* 1987: 53). Some studies have suggested that such effects are more likely to influence purchasing decisions than just an evaluation of actual product attributes (Johansson and Nebenzahl 1987).

Stereotypes result from preconceived perceptions of national characteristics, history, traditions and political or social factors. They can be product dimension-specific (Han and Terpstra 1988). For example German products tend to be seen as high on prestige value but low on economy. Latin countries suffer from an impression of being 'laid back', places to holiday in rather than to do business with (Morello 1984). Halfhill (1980: 26) found differences among attitudes expressed about product classes (mechanical, food, and fashion merchandise) and the national image.

Some consumers appear to be unaware of, or indifferent to, the country of origin effect, while others search for such information (Reierson 1966; Hampton 1977). Stereotypes such as the COO effect will be used when other product information is missing, less so when more information is available (Erickson *et al.* 1984). There are also other studies suggesting country of origin effects are more important for some products than for others (Gaedeke 1973; Lillis and Narayana 1974).

In general, perceived risk either increases or decreases when the consumer was made aware of the country of origin as perceptions of quality are particularly susceptible to the COO effect (Lumpkin *et al.* 1985: 168). If the image is positive then fine and distributors will be quick to exploit them (Kaynak and Cavusgil 1983: 153).

The COO effect will vary depending upon the country it is measured within. In one study of Japanese consumers' perceptions of European Countries and products (Dentsu 1994), the Japanese public associated Europe with history, tradition, and well-designed products, but that they assumed that non-Japanese products would be lower in technological sophistication and not always suited to their needs. Thus *any* European company exporting to Japan could have this imagery as its starting point.

While most research into the COO effect has been done with consumers as the focus, commercial buyers can be influenced similarly (White 1979). If a retail buyer believes that their store's customers believe that products from a certain country are superior then this will influence buying decisions. But buyers can have their own preconceptions, prejudices, and stereotypical images. In one study of the perceptions British retail buyers held of Portuguese suppliers (da Silva *et al.* 2001), buyers tended to stereotype the entire Portuguese textile industry as likely to be slow to respond, to have acceptable but not high quality but to have low prices. The reality at the time was that Portuguese manufacturers had benefited from substantial capital investment in their textile industry, investment aided by the European Community after Portugal became a member. At the same time labour costs had risen as the standard of living and wage rates in Portugal began to approach levels in other European countries. The study showed that Portuguese exporters were sensitive to the image they had among overseas buyers but underestimated it.

The main drivers of the COO effect appear to be: the level of industrialization of the country, with developing countries being saddled with the image of making poorer quality products; ethnic origin where Latin countries lose out due to a perception of being laid back, but benefit from the same image in markets such as tourism (Zajonc and Markus 1982). Other than that perceptions vary and can be highly product specific. In some instances these images are valid. Porter (1998) identifies a number of product types that individual countries appear to be better placed to produce. A country may have an economic advantage in supplying one type of product or service and have industries that have achieved competitive cost structures through their accumulated experience in such activities. In other cases there is no real foundation for our stereotypes, which are probably a function of our extrapolating from limited knowledge of a country gained from the media, holidaying there and experience of other products in the same category (Morello 1984).

Industry image

There is less research on the effect on all companies within the same industry, but the issues are similar to the COO effect. For example this quotation from G. K. Chesterton illustrates the way in which food retailers were once viewed:

God made the wicked grocer for a mystery and sign,
That men might shun the awful shops and go to inns to dine

Today food retailers are trusted more than many other institutions. In one survey leading British food retailer Tesco were trusted only slightly less than the BBC (Mintel 1998).

In the same survey the major oil companies came at the bottom of the list of companies the British public would trust. Oil companies appear to share a similar problem. They are seen generally as very large and powerful. The products they produce are essential in the daily lives of most of us, yet at the same time they are associated with many modern day ills, particularly global warming. Other industries that are at risk include those involved with armaments, tobacco and testing products on animals. At least with a minority in society such companies will start a metre or two behind the rest of the field in the race for a positive reputation.

There are no easy or obvious answers. At the time of writing the tobacco industry is under fire. Their traditional arguments, that they create employment and that people should be free to choose their products or not in a free society, have been undermined by the counter arguments, that cigarettes are deliberately made to be more addictive and that the tobacco companies have always realized that smoking can damage health. If the latter arguments hold sway, then it is conceivable that tobacco companies could be bankrupted by litigation on behalf of individuals or health authorities claiming the costs associated with smoking related diseases.

The stereotyping of an industry can be avoided. The Body Shop is a part of the cosmetics industry. It is a multinational. It trades with the Third World. Founder Anita Roddick emphasized that her products were not tested on animals, a feature of most cosmetics; that they were not over packaged (originally you could refill her, basic, containers) and; that she aimed personally to support Third World initiatives particularly those associated with women. In doing so she positioned her own company, repositioned her competition and created a strong corporate reputation and all within a market, cosmetics, that would not have been everyone's first choice of a sector in which to launch an ethical positioning.

In summary

Ideas from branding are useful in understanding corporate reputation as company names can be brand names in the eyes of customers, one of the more important of stakeholder groups. The heavy emphasis on media advertising in the branding literature may create the impression that corporate reputations can be promoted using advertising. That is not what we suggest. Indeed we argue the opposite. Advertise an image that you do not deliver and you will dissatisfy your customers.

Brands have many useful attributes, promoting recall, as assets, in delivering premium in the market, and in creating perceived differentiation. Brands are complex phenomena but we can simplify such complexity using metaphors such as brand as person.

The image of an organization will be affected by the stereotype that we have of the country and the industry that the organization comes from. There will be little that can be done about such stereotypes other than to be aware of them and to realize that in the absence of any information provided by the organization, the customer will fill the void with the nearest stereotype he or she has to hand.

5 Defending a reputation

Crisis management, pre-emption of crises (case histories of BSE, Coca-Cola, Perrier and Ratner), transaction analysis, the crisis management team, choosing reputation partners carefully (Ford and Firestone, IBM and Intel), dealing with pressure groups (McDonald's and McLibel, Shell and Greenpeace), losing reputation slowly (Marks and Spencer).

A key issue in Reputation Management is defence. Corporate reputations are constantly in danger of being eroded, damaged, dented or even destroyed. Exxon once took a pride in naming each of its oil tankers with the company name. The strategy changed after the *Exxon Valdez* collided with an iceberg in Alaskan waters. The cost of the clean-up and lawsuits was estimated at $2.5 billion. The effect on Exxon's share price was a fall of about 5 per cent of value, valued at $3 billion. All together the incident cost Exxon shareholders close to 10 per cent of their investment value, only a quarter of which was due to the direct cost of cleaning up the spillage. If the possibility of such an incident had been foreseen, the ship would probably not have been named the *Exxon Valdez*. Similarly the calculations made as to the likely cost to the company of procrastinating over settlement did not appear good enough to predict the true cost to the company both directly and in the longer term. Their delaying tactics painted a negative view of Exxon as an organization. The issue is once again whether seeing the role of an organization strictly as maximizing shareholder returns, while consigning the role of corporate citizen to second place, makes financial sense any more.

Crisis management

Defending a reputation starts with thinking the unthinkable and then planning for that eventuality.

A crisis is an event or series of events that can damage a company's reputation. Typically crises interfere with normal operations, attract external, particularly media, attention, damage profitability, and escalate if not well handled. A crisis occurs when the reputation of an organization is threatened or harmed by bad media comment leading to short-term loss of sales and profit and long-term damage to reputation.

There are many things that can threaten reputation: sabotage, fraud, product boycott, the restatement of a financial position and disasters caused by employees or by bad planning by management. Many are avoidable if management recognizes that crises *can* occur even in the best run of organizations. Acknowledging the potential for a crisis is part of avoiding a crisis, especially the type of large-scale industrial crisis caused by human error.

The number of large-scale industrial accidents has been increasing exponentially during the last century. Of the twenty-eight major incidents that occurred up until the 1980s, half occurred in that decade alone (Shrivastava and Mitroff 1987). The disaster in Bhopal, India in 1984, when poisonous isocyanate gas leaked from a plant located next to an urban area, killed 3000 and affected half a million people. In 1986 30,000 died when a nuclear reactor melted down in Chernobyl, within the then Soviet Union. Millions were affected across fifteen countries. Such incidents can be foreseen by thinking the unthinkable. Safety systems can be put in place to minimize the chances of such disasters. Technological failure *can* be prevented by better technology or by a better understanding of the risks of modern industry.

But technical or human failure is not the only cause of a crisis. Shrivastava and Mitroff (1987) define two dimensions to categorize crises, an internal/external dimension and a technical/social dimension. Thus Bhopal and Chernobyl are typified by failures in internal systems and in the core technology of each organization. External issues such as natural disaster and civil disorder can also create crisis situations. The explosion of an IRA bomb in the centre of Manchester in 1998 caused widespread destruction including that of a large Marks and Spencer store. One shopper thrust a small baby into the arms of a shop assistant as she went to check on the safety of another child. The shopper recognized the member of staff because of her uniform. That level of trust in an organization is symptomatic of a strong and positive corporate reputation. No one was killed in the incident but the emotional effects on the retailer's staff were profound. The store took three years to rebuild during which time the retailer relocated to occupy parts of two nearby buildings. Staff needed to be reassured about their jobs and the commitment of the company to retain a substantial presence in the city. However, they, like the shopper with the baby had sufficient trust in the company that few staff decided to leave. In a time of crisis a company appears to draw on a reservoir filled from its actions in the past. If you are trusted then people are more likely to rely on your response to a crisis. In later years as we will explain in this chapter, Marks and Spencer appeared to lose the confidence of the British people.

In the 1980s there was a spate of attempts to extort money from companies or similar acts of terrorism with no apparent motive, that involved tampering with products. Johnson and Johnson experienced two such events, one in 1982 and again in 1986 when tablets of Tylenol were poisoned. Such incidents are external to the company and beyond its control. The failure, if there is one, is also of a social nature. Some incidents are caused by internal social problems, for example when someone makes a mistake or a disgruntled employee commits an act of sabotage.

The actions that management can take ahead of such crises will differ with the type of incident. In each case it will help if the company has a clearly defined plan to deal with any type of crisis.

According to Murray and Shohen (1992), Johnson and Johnson survived their Tylenol crises for a number of reasons:

- a strong and positive reputation before the crises;
- being open with the media at the time of each crisis and after;
- chairman James Burke took clear and public command;
- the media perception that J and J were not to blame.

By the time of the second Tylenol incident Johnson and Johnson had a formal process in place to handle any similar event, a crisis plan, as part of a systematic approach. Johnson and Johnson are now closely associated with having a positive approach to managing crises. The Tylenol example is so widely quoted that any reader of a book on reputation would be expecting to see it mentioned. Johnson and Johnson's positive handling of a difficult situation must have added significantly to their reputation.

The crisis management team

A key step for any company is the creation and training of a crisis management team. There is a consensus as to what this involves.

Problems occur in any crisis if it is unclear who is in charge. The nature of a crisis means that time is short. Something is happening that has already got out of hand. The media are demanding a statement. Suppliers and customers are making threats. Production is being lost while everyone waits for a decision. The problem is who makes the key decisions and who decides what to say to the various stakeholders who expect a clear lead. The first advantage of having a team in place with defined roles for each member, is that it is clear who will take responsibility. No one talks to the media for example unless it is a member of the team.

The team needs to be trained. Simulated crises can be used to test their mettle and to give them opportunities to experience the real thing before it happens. The team knows where to meet and all communication about the crisis both internal and external are channelled through the one location. The worst situation in a crisis is that no one from the firm at its centre is available for comment. The media will always seek to fill any such vacuum and find their own authority figure. To quote C. Northcote Parkinson: 'The vacuum caused by a failure to respond is soon filled with rumour, misrepresentation, drivel and poison'.

Five crisis management elements

There are a number of phases or stages to a crisis, Mitroff (1988). Figures 5.1 and 5.2 identify the typical patterns that can exist inside and outside the organization. Initially there will be some isolated events, issues raised by 'overly concerned' members of staff or mentions of potential issues in the specialist media. These may be ignored but, ideally, management move to respond to such early

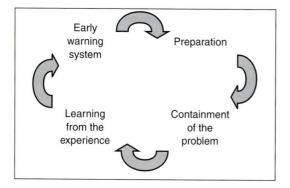

Figure 5.1 Phases in a crisis.

Source: Adapted from Mitroff (1988).

warnings so that the potential dangers are averted. Sometimes this is not possible, for example when Monsanto developed its genetic modification approach to develop news strains of crop seeds. Some reaction was quite predictable and inevitable. Having an early warning system at least allows the company to prepare and then to contain as many problems as it can. Once the crisis is over the organization should endeavour to learn from its experience so as to be better prepared for the next crisis.

Auditing the risks that a situation might pose can prevent some types of crises, for example of having a chemical plant next to a residential area. An analysis of the risks could lead to the redesign of the process, the introduction of new safety procedures.

The phases of a crisis are reflected in the escalation of media comment (see Figure 5.2). In the early phases when the issue is still being scoped or understood

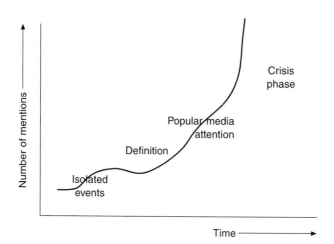

Figure 5.2 The escalation of media comment.

there will be limited public visibility. Comment, if it exists at all will be in the specialist media. Once the issue broadens into a crisis, because something has happened, then the level of media comment rises exponentially. It can become unmanageable with the firm on the back foot defending attacks from all directions and unable to take any initiative. It is essential therefore for an organization to have an early warning system in place to pick up the first signs of a storm that is brewing, to solve the problem or to gain control over the communication process.

The structure of this chapter is to rely heavily on actual case studies of crisis management or mismanagement to illustrate the main principles of preemption and to emphasize the need to recognize that crises are not always about handling rational issues in rational ways. Ignore emotion and you will probably fail to manage a crisis.

Pre-empting a crisis: mad cow disease

Rarely can a crisis have been so predictable or so devastating to an industry as the BSE crisis in Britain in the 1990s and which extended into the rest of Europe after 2000. The links between BSE (bovine spongiform encephalopathy) in cattle, more commonly known as mad cow disease, and CJD (Creutzfeldt-Jakob disease) in humans, and the uncertainty of the extent to which humans might be infected, will ensure that the crisis will also be one of the longest in history.

BSE is a disease of the central nervous system of cattle. The infection attacks the lower part of the brain filling it with holes, hence the name Spongiform. The most likely cause is an infectious protein (prion) converting normal protein molecules into dangerous ones that attack the brain. However the pathology is still unclear. Prions are not destroyed in the processes normally used to manufacture animal feed nor in domestic cooking. Similar forms of the disease have been detected in different species. BSE was thought to have originated in sheep (this form of the disease being known as scrapie). It appears that the disease can cross from one species to another. CJD, the human form, has similarities to BSE. CJD is a degenerative disease of the human brain resulting in the loss of coordination and faculties. It occurs throughout the world, killing about one person in a million. If there is a link between BSE and CJD then British people who ate beef before firm controls were introduced in 1989 may be at some (probably small) risk of infection. However, one eminent microbiologist has estimated that between 5000 and 500,000 people may become infected.

In March 1996 Secretary of State for Health, Stephen Dorrell, told the House of Commons that the most likely explanation for the ten new cases of CJD in people under forty-two was exposure to BSE before a ban was introduced on bovine offal in 1989. The implication of his words was that the problem had been solved. Yet the implications of the BSE crisis for the beef industry first in Britain and increasingly elsewhere in Europe are still huge.

The history of BSE is a long one. According to the website documenting the crisis (www.bse.org.uk) BSE was first recorded in sheep in 1732 and in cows in 1883. It was widely known from the nineteenth century that animal feed could contain offal from other species. Indeed the practice was often commended and larger-scale plants were commissioned in many countries to convert parts of animals not used for human consumption into animal feed. This would often include the brain and spinal cord of domesticated animals or even whole carcasses of animals deemed unfit for human consumption.

Concern over the use of certain animal remains in animal food surfaced in America in the 1970s leading to a decision by the US Department of Agriculture that carcasses of sheep with scrapie should not be used in animal feed. In Britain examples of BSE were said to have been detected in cows in 1985. In America similar findings occurred in 1986 and 1988. In 1986 and 1987 BSE was identified in antelope in a UK wildlife park. The disease was first formally identified in cattle in 1986. In 1987 a research paper describing BSE was given limited circulation. Other publications followed in that year. These were the early warnings that were ignored.

In 1988 the British government began legislation to limit the BSE problem. A working party set up under Sir Richard Southwood to investigate concerns that BSE was entering the human food chain, made their first recommendations in June 1988. By September 1988 most animal feed compounders could report that their feedstuffs now excluded suspect material. In November the use of milk from suspect cows was banned for other than feeding to their own calves.

In January 1989 a BBC television programme on BSE brought the matter more to the attention of the public. It was re-screened in July. This marked the start of the exponential rise in media comment predicted by Figure 5.2. The government announced that the sale of cattle offal (liver, etc., thought to represent the most risk of transmitting BSE to humans) would be banned. That month the European Commission banned the export of any UK cattle born before July 1988 (the date that the law on animal feed had changed) and the offspring from any suspect herds from the UK into other European countries.

In 1990 further evidence that BSE could move between species came with the discovery of similar disease in other species. The EC imposed further restrictions on the export of British beef. Calls for the slaughter of all British cattle and for re-stocking were made in the press but discounted by officials. The British press also claimed that the EU decision was not motivated solely by a desire to avoid the spread of CJD but by attempts to benefit the farmers of mainland Europe. After all the British were still being told it was safe to eat British beef. Agriculture minister John Selwyn Gummer had publicly fed his young daughter Cordelia a beefburger in an attempt to allay public concern.

In 1991 there was the first case of a calf being born with BSE after the ban on animal sources being used in animal feed. That year bone meal from suspect sources was banned for use as a fertilizer. In 1992 press comment included the view from one expert that existing actions had failed to halt the spread of BSE. The official committee disagreed but further restrictions on the preparation of meat were still introduced. The official view was that the number of cases of BSE had now peaked (at 0.3 per cent of the national herd). In July the total number of confirmed BSE cases recorded reached 100,000. From 1993 onwards the number of cows identified as having BSE did decline rapidly, but public concern was not so easily assuaged. Sales of beef and particularly minced beef and other similar products such as beefburgers and sausages declined (see Figure 5.3).

According to research company Mintel the value index of beef and veal

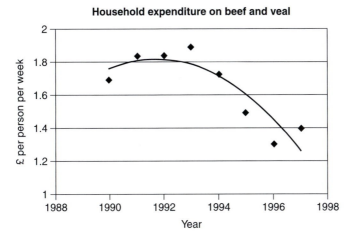

Figure 5.3 The effect on expenditure on beef from the BSE crisis.

Source: *Family Expenditure Survey*, CSO, HMSO.

dropped 18 per cent in real terms from 1993 to 1998. Only 38 per cent strongly agreed to a survey question asking whether people felt that beef products such as mince were safe. Confidence was higher for joints of beef and steaks where consumers could feel surer about what they were buying.

In May 1995 the first case of so-called new variant CJD was discovered in a man aged only nineteen. Thus far the theory had been that mainly those exposed to BSE infected meat over a long time period would be at risk. The incidence of CJD among farmers with infected herds was also reported to be high. The UK government banned all vertebral tissue from entering the food chain. In 1996 the European Union banned all export of British beef. The following press statement was released just prior to the ban:

Sir Kenneth Calman, Chief Medical Officer said today: (20 March 1996)
'The statement by Spongiform Encephalopathy Advisory Committee (SEAC) of the description of a new variant of CJD which has a distinct clinical and pathological appearance, is a cause for serious concern. While there is no direct evidence of a link between BSE and this new variant, pending further research, I agree with SEAC that the most likely explanation is that these cases may be linked to exposure to BSE before the SBO ban in 1989.

'I have always sought and followed the advice from the experts in this field, notably SEAC, and ministers have always followed this advice.

'While the theoretical risk has always been acknowledged, and the measures which have been introduced to control the spread in cattle, have had as their basis the reduction of any possible risk, these new findings are important.

'They have a number of implications:

- these new findings suggest that there may have been an association between eating bovine products, which may have been contaminated by infected brain and spinal cord, and a risk of developing CJD before the introduction of measures in 1989.
- there remains, however, no scientific evidence that BSE can be transmitted to man by beef. However, risk analysis suggests that even the likelihood of the extremely small risk of transmission increases when non-muscle parts from older cattle are eaten. It is essential therefore that the source and quality of beef is clear and that the public can be assured of these measures.
- current measures must be rigorously enforced. This is at the heart of the issue. SEAC will recommend that effective training measures should be introduced and consider this further.
- further research is urgently required and this will be funded.

'For this reason it is considered that an additional measure, the de-boning of beef in specified plants with full supervision by the Meat Hygiene Service in cattle over thirty months of age should be introduced. This will significantly reduce the likelihood of extremely small risk of transmission from non-muscle parts of the carcass. These will be prevented from entering the food chain. This will be discussed further by SEAC.

'Meat or meat products on the shelf or in carcass form do not need to be removed or destroyed.

'There is nothing to lead the committee to change its advice on the safety of milk. It is considered to be safe.

'The implications for the public who may be worried about contracting the disease have also been considered. At present the overall numbers are very small, but there is as yet no indication as to the likely numbers of patients who may contract the disease in the future. There is currently no clinical test for the disease and today all doctors will be contacted and given further background on the new information.

'The question that will be asked is whether or not I will continue to eat beef. I will do as part of a varied and balanced diet. The new measures and effective enforcement of existing measures will continue to ensure that the likely risk of developing CJD is extremely small.

'There is at present no evidence for age sensitivity and the scientific evidence for the risks of developing CJD in those eating meat in childhood has not changed as a result of these new findings. However, parents will be concerned about implications for their children. SEAC has been asked to provide specific advice on this issue.

'Further discussion will take place over the next few days and additional measures may be considered in the future. As has been said before, should any new scientific evidence become available it will be communicated to the public as soon as possible.'

In December 1996 a selective cull was announced of cattle most at risk of contracting BSE. Slaughtering began in May 1997 of 100,000 head of cattle. In December 1997 the UK government announced a ban on the sale of beef joints containing bone, due to the risk that bone might harbour BSE and be transmitted to humans if cooked with the meat. The BSE enquiry was set up at the end of 1997 to 'reveal the events and decisions which led to the spread of CJD and BSE'. A former chief medical officer, Sir Kenneth Calman openly criticized the chief veterinary officer, Keith Meldrum. Calman's point was that assurances that beef was 'safe to eat' did not mean that there was no risk.

In November 1998, the EU agreed to lift its ban on the export of British beef. However both France and Germany refused to accept the decision. In May 2000 another cow, born twenty-five days after the removal of all stocks of cattle feed containing meat and bone meal from farms, was shown to have BSE. The number of cases of CJD reported in the last quarter of 1998 was the highest on record, but at five deaths was still an insignificant figure by comparison with deaths from alcohol and smoking for example. The ban on the sale of beef on the bone was lifted on 30 November 1999.

The epidemic had now killed more than 178,000 cattle in Britain and been linked to the deaths of more than fifty people from CJD. An estimated 700,000 BSE-infected cattle had entered the human food chain.

The monetary cost had been enormous. Foreign markets worth nearly £650 million a year to British agriculture had disappeared. The cost of compensating everyone in the meat production chain, propping up markets and implementing slaughter schemes was estimated to run to £3.5 billion. The National Audit Office calculated public expenditure on BSE-related schemes had amounted to £2.5 billion since March 1996, when the worldwide ban began, with a further £1 billion expected between 1998 and 2000. By the time other costs are counted, some newspapers were forecasting the final bill to be at least £5 billion.

In January 1998 a £2 million marketing campaign was launched to attempt to restore confidence in British beef. The EU made a financial contribution. Meanwhile, the BSE inquiry itself was estimated to be costing £16 million. The figure included paying for hearing rooms, keeping evidence, and staff salaries. The Ministry of Agriculture was planning to spend a further £12.8 million on research into BSE and related diseases.

Many thousands of jobs in the meat trade and rendering industry had been lost, with a cost to the nation of additional unemployment. Farmers were hit hardest. They were already suffering reduced incomes but those who relied on the meat business had to contend with cattle prices falling from about 120p per kilogram before the crisis, to 95p. Collectively, farmers' incomes plummeted from £4.1 billion in 1996 to about £1 billion in 1998. Some were forced to give up farming altogether. One bank reckoned 25,000 farmers had been driven out of the industry.

Lessons from the BSE crisis

The BSE enquiry made its final report in October 2000. The first of eight volumes contained twenty-four pages of 'lessons to be learnt'. None of the lessons appears to reflect the insights from the crisis management literature. In fact the general lessons from previous crises in other industries appeared to have been ignored. There was a heavy emphasis on the rational handling of a crisis. In a section entitled, 'Dealing with uncertainty and the communication of risk', the following points were made:

> To establish credibility it is necessary to generate trust.
> Trust can only be generated by openness.
> Openness requires recognition of uncertainty, where it exists.
> The public should be trusted to respond rationally to openness.
> The advice and the reasoning of advisory committees should be made public.

There is nothing wrong with such statements but they miss the point. The whole essence of a crisis is that logic is put to one side. (To expect the media for example to deal other than selectively with the facts in a food crisis is somewhat naïve.) In any such crisis the emphasis must be on handling the emotional aspects of the crisis, not just the more rational and information giving tasks. There are some obvious points that could have and should have been made that are germane to the management of any crisis.

Signals that a major problem was looming were in evidence in 1986, but it took two years to even begin to examine the problem formally. It took until 1996 to decide that a cull of animals was the only solution that would meet public concern, let alone stamp out BSE. The problem could have been scoped in 1986. Instead those with responsibility procrastinated while seeking the 'right' answer and by this read 'the right technical' answer. Once the crisis was upon the British government, the relevant ministry and the food industry, the responses were too often driven by events, one bit of bad publicity leading to another action that was not sufficient to stop another event and so on. As the BSE report does acknowledge, the frequent claims that beef was 'perfectly' safe to eat ensured that once scientific evidence emerged that it was not, then official sources lost credibility.

The BSE saga contrasts with a British government ban in October 2000 of a polio vaccine that had been prepared using cattle products that might have been in contact with BSE. The Department of Health were reported as saying that the risks to humans of catching CJD was 'incalculably small'. In a letter to GPs, Chief Medical Officer, Professor Liam Donaldson, said: 'I am advised that the risk of a person contracting CJD from this oral polio vaccine is incalculably small. However, public confidence in medicines' safety is paramount. We have to approach this from a precautionary principle'. So it was acceptable for a manufacturer to have to bear the cost of a product recall when the risks were incalculably small. Why then was it also acceptable for the public to be told it was safe to eat beef with a more calculable risk. Did this have anything to do with the much higher price tag if the entire British herd had to be slaughtered?

The rational argument that beef was 'safe to eat' was not believed. It contrasted with a series of actions to reduce the risk that merely emphasized that some risk was indeed associated with eating beef. Evidence of a human link

(BSE to CJD) was first rebutted and then accepted by officials. The British were asked to accept that while other Europeans thought the risk too high, they could carry on eating domestic beef. While there was not enough hard and rational evidence for government to justify a more radical approach and cull the entire herd, officials ignored the emotional aspects of the crisis. The emotive label 'mad cow disease', a recent history of other food scandals where the Ministry of Agriculture was perceived as siding too much with the producer and too little with the consumer, further damaged confidence in the credibility of official sources.

In hindsight, the cost of culling the entire herd and restocking was probably considerably lower than the final cost of the crisis itself. The possibility of a crisis was entirely predictable, but in the absence of any contingency plan, officials were always reacting to the latest event, trying to catch up rather than lead. It does not matter one iota what leading scientific opinion is on a matter as sensitive as what we eat. What the consumer fears to be the truth is more important. Once the crisis becomes one of confidence then significant, symbolic action is essential. Objectively, eating beef was not the most dangerous thing that individuals could do in the 1980s and 1990s. The death rate from CJD in the UK was about the same as that from malaria (and there are never any queues wanting preventative medicine for this). Road deaths totalled nearly 3000 in 1998, but people continued to use their cars, often exceeding the speed limit, sometimes the alcohol limit and risking their lives and those of others. Objectively, the risks of driving on the road were far, far higher than from eating beef, but the crisis, as are so many, was not only about rational decision making.

Compare the actions of the British government to those of consumer companies Coca-Cola and Perrier facing not dissimilar circumstances.

Handling emotions better: funny tasting Coca-Cola

Atlanta based Coca-Cola is often cited as the world's leading brand. Coca-Cola sells its products in over 200 countries. Three quarters of its profits came from overseas sales. In 1999 people became ill in Belgium and Northern France. They complained of nausea and dizziness after drinking the product. Over 100 were hospitalized including many children. Coca-Cola's first response was to deny that its products could have been the cause of the reported illnesses. Governments in five countries then banned their product. Seven days after the first event, Coca-Cola withdrew all Belgian made products from sale.

They issued a statement explaining that, while there was no health issue in their view, there had been a problem due to poor quality carbon dioxide used by one of their bottlers and that a fungicide used to treat pallets could also have tainted the product. The manufacturer of the carbon dioxide disagreed that there was a problem with the gas. It was also unclear how fungicide on pallets could have tainted the product in bottles and cans.

On the eighth day of the crisis, the problem escalated in France, where eighty people near the Belgian border had fallen ill. The French government ordered the entire stock of Coca-Cola products, whether or not they had been made in Belgium, to be removed from the distribution chain. It was made clear that Coca-Cola's explanation of the odd taste was not believed. Matters appeared to be getting out of hand elsewhere in Europe. A headline in a Swedish newspaper claimed, '200 poisoned by Coca-Cola'. No obvious explanation could be found for the problem. One source suggested mass hysteria following a dioxin contamination scare earlier that same year in Belgium.

By the tenth day Coca-Cola's problem had spread to Switzerland, Germany, and Spain, where its product was being banned. Scientific tests had still failed to account for the problem. Coca-Cola's own explanations could not be substantiated. Despite the absence of any evidence that the company had done wrong, Coca-Cola Belgium offered to pay the medical bills of those affected. On the fourteenth day, full-page advertisements appeared in Belgian newspapers apologizing for what had happened. On the fifteenth day Belgium lifted its product ban, and similar actions followed shortly after elsewhere in Europe.

Lessons

Coca-Cola have received some criticism for their handling of the Belgium affair. Chairman Douglas Ivester had been slow to meet the Belgian Minister of Health. The company had been slow to apologize. Yet there is still no evidence that their product was at fault let alone caused the illness. The only explanation remains that of mass hysteria. Coca-Cola had apologized, made full restitution, and distributed coupons to each of four million Belgian households.

The context is important here. Consumers had been sensitized to problems with the food industry due to recent dioxin contamination of animal feed. Coca-Cola does not generally own its bottlers. Nevertheless they are often a major shareholder and the bottler uses the Coca-Cola brand. Coca-Cola's claim that no real problem existed gave the impression that they did not care enough about customer health. The episode cost Coca-Cola about $60 million in recall costs, but the evidence is that long-term sales have not suffered. In hindsight Coca-Cola's attempt to provide an explanation for the taste problem was the only mistake they made. Another drink company had faced a similar crisis.

Handling the media: funny tasting Perrier

Perrier Vittel is the world's leading mineral water company and part of the vast Nestlé global portfolio. Although its best-known brands are the two mineral waters which make up its name, the company also has a large portfolio of other brands including San Pellegrino, Buxton, Calistoga, Pure Life and Aquarel.

In 1990 the Perrier company was based in France, from where all its water originated. Traces of benzene (a known carcinogen) were detected in their leading brand, Perrier, in America. This happened by accident, as, ironically, due to its purity, Perrier was being used as a standard in an analytical laboratory in North Carolina. The benzene presence, six parts per billion, was unlikely to harm anyone, but for a product positioned on purity, this was six parts too many. The product was withdrawn from the American market.

Perrier UK management called an immediate meeting of its crisis management team. It was a Saturday. Contact was made with analytical laboratories and the Ministry of Agriculture asking for immediate (independent) testing of Perrier products. The tests took forty-eight hours but by Wednesday the team knew that benzene was present in the product on sale in the UK.

In Paris a spokesperson was quoted as suggesting the problem could have originated from a 'greasy rag'. Other explanations were given and then retracted. The UK wanted to withdraw all Perrier product from sale but were overruled by Paris who argued that a single press conference to be held in Paris should be the main source of information and action. But the French had underestimated international interest and the press conference became more akin to a riot. Back in the UK briefings were given to individual journalists. On the Thursday, press advertising announced a product withdrawal, promising refunds. Forty million bottles were returned. The problem did not end here. The environmental action group, Friends of the Earth voiced concern about the low level of recycling of the returned bottles. The water could not be put down the drain until local health authorities had been convinced it was safe to do so.

By now the true source of the contamination had been identified as a blocked filter. This should have been the end of the matter, but it was not. The impression given by the use of the words 'naturally carbonated' in describing Perrier was that when Perrier water came from the ground it already contained carbon dioxide. In reality the water and gas were mixed in the plant. British retailers demanded a change in the product's labelling.

Perrier suffered a drop in its British market share (its share was already declining) from 32 per cent before the crisis to 17 per cent in the first full month after the crisis. In the US the share of all Perrier brands had been 24 per cent. Perrier itself was the number three brand with a share of 5.7 per cent. The company lost share but held most of its ground by promoting its other brands. Altogether the crisis involved recalling 160 million bottles, 72 million were in the UK alone. Advertising expenditure doubled in the relaunch of the brand that followed.

Lessons

The Perrier crisis contains a number of lessons. Crises for a multinational company are inevitably international. Coordination of crisis management globally is essential. The media are, after all also international, and able to report globally. Perrier's credibility fell between the cracks separating the response of their headquarters (that was inadequate) and the more planned and proactive approaches being taken in America and Britain. The general lesson is much the same as with the previous example of Coca-Cola in Belgium. If the public *thinks* there is a problem with a product, particularly a food product, then there *is* a problem, one that can only be solved by disposing of the suspect product, apologizing, explaining with authority what happened, compensating and then recovering.

Respond, recompense and recover

There are 3 Rs in a crisis: 'respond, recompense, and recover'. At the time of writing those responsible for handling the BSE crisis have barely addressed the first R adequately. There has been no recompense for consumers. Farmers, who arguably are in the same role as Coca-Cola, have suffered but have at least received government compensation. There has been as far as the authors can tell, absolutely no public apology from the animal feed industry, farmers, or the Ministry of Agriculture Fisheries and Food. Coca-Cola were criticized for taking fourteen days to address their problem in Belgium. It is now fourteen years since BSE was known to be an issue in the UK. How confidence in beef is expected to recover in such circumstances is a mystery.

A 'foot' note

In 2000 another disease was identified in British farm animals to add to the joys of being a farmer or a butcher: foot-and-mouth.

Foot-and-mouth disease is one of the most contagious of animal diseases and causes death mainly to young animals through inflammation of the heart muscle. It infects two groups of animals: cattle, sheep, goats and antelope, and pigs and warthogs. Symptoms include the formation of blisters in the mouth and between the claws, hence the name. People can be infected through skin wounds or the mucous membranes in the mouth by handling diseased stock, handling the virus in the laboratory, or by drinking infected milk, but not by eating meat from infected animals. Any infection of humans is temporary and mild and foot-and-mouth disease is not considered a public health problem.

Infection can spread easily through direct or indirect contact, through the movement of humans, animals, vehicles and implements, and through the air. Cattle are mainly infected by inhalation, often from pigs, which excrete large amounts of virus through their breathing. The virus is a member of the same family as the common cold virus. Newly infected animals start spreading the virus before symptoms appear so it is often difficult to control the disease before it has already spread. Cattle may be carriers for eighteen to twenty-four months and sheep for one to two months after recovery.

Foot-and-mouth disease is endemic in parts of Asia, Africa, the Middle East and South America with sporadic outbreaks in free areas. Foot-and-mouth disease was last reported in 1929 in the USA, 1952 in Canada, and 1954 in Mexico. The outbreak in the UK began on a farm in the north-east of England. The animals there probably became infected in early February 2001 and late detection meant that full restrictions on the movement of animals were only imposed on 23 February by which time infected sheep had been moved over 400 km to an abattoir in Essex in the south-east of England.

The British government's approach to limiting the spread of the disease was to cull all animals within 3 km of badly infected premises, leading to about 600,000 animals being killed. A less extreme way of curbing the virus is to vaccinate animals but this not a favoured option because many countries prohibit importation of meat from vaccinated areas.

The approach of using culling in one context (foot-and-mouth) and not in another (BSE) is interesting. The long-term damage from having another disease associated with the same food can only be guessed at. Meanwhile BSE had spread to other countries in Europe. In Germany, learning perhaps from the British experience, an immediate cull of suspect animals was announced.

Managing the emotional and the rational: transaction analysis

Transaction analysis theory tells us that there are three states that we can be in when interacting with another person, adult, parent, and child (see Figure 5.4). Our state will interact with that of the other person and different configurations are either positive or negative. Some transactions are complementary, others are not.

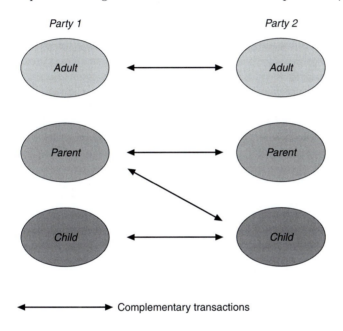

Figure 5.4 Transaction analysis theory.

Two people can talk rationally to each other on the same level, much as two adults would do. In this example the adult mode of the person speaking is trying to speak to the other person's adult mode to create a complementary transaction:

BSE presents a small risk to those who eat beef but if you eat only joints of beef or minced products with this label on it then the risks you run are tiny, far less for example than from over-eating.

If the reply is along the lines of:

You can't trust anything a government spokesperson such as you says. The more you tell me it's safe the more I think you are lying.

then the mode the first speaker has actually contacted is the person's child, the often irrational, playful, overly emotional side of ourselves. The transaction is not complementary. It does not produce the desired result.

Parent mode can be a more complementary posture if the other party is in the mode of child:

> Government scientists have assured us that beef is perfectly safe. Comments in the press are no more than hysteria, designed to sell newspapers, not tell you the facts as we always do.

An anxious child might be reassured by such an approach. But today's consumers are often quite confident in using their own judgement about what is safe to eat, particularly if there is an alternative to the suspect product. The adult mode might respond:

> Please don't tell me what to think. The facts are these. EU scientists disagree with those in the UK. They have banned our beef from leaving our shores. If it's not safe for other Europeans to eat our beef why should we? Why should I feed my children beef when they are happy to eat other meats?

In mass communication it is not always possible to talk directly to the target audience. Messages are filtered or re-interpreted by the media. Tabloid newspapers may deliberately emphasize the sensational; excusing their exaggeration by arguing that no one takes their headlines too seriously. While the adult in us may be able to tell the difference between an objective report and a tabloid shock horror story, the child in all of us will be influenced by the more emotive headlines of the latter.

Many organizations appear to ignore the emotional aspects of a crisis, which is by definition an emotional issue. When people consider any issue they do so along two dimensions, the rational, cognitive dimension that weighs up the facts and provides the objective perspective (the adult mode) and the emotional, affective dimensions where feelings are important (the child mode). When Coca-Cola decided to recall its product in Belgium they were not acting rationally in the sense that they knew that their product represented a risk to human health. In fact they probably believed the opposite – that they were disposing of a perfectly good product. The apology given could have been with clenched teeth. What mattered was these were the most appropriate actions to take. People's emotional attitude to the company had been damaged more than their rational attitude. An appeal to the emotions was appropriate, not one that was necessarily logical at first sight. The symbolism of withdrawing the product and publicly apologizing was important.

'On ev'ry word a reputation dies'

This quote, cited earlier and from Alexander Pope (1688–1744), could be the epitaph for one of Britain's most successful retailers. Gerald Ratner built the largest jewellery retail business in the world. At its peak in 1991 the Ratner group had a global business with a turnover of £1.1 billion and profits of £112 million. It had over 2000 stores, mainly in the UK and USA.

Gerald's father, Leslie, had started the business in 1947. In 1983 it made a loss of £350,000 on a turnover of nearly £26 million. Gerald took over from his father and took Ratners and the jewellery trade in a very different direction. At the time jewellery was a luxury, purchased on special occasions. Through aggressive pricing, and focusing on lower price points, Ratners aimed to attract younger buyers, purchasing jewellery more as a fashion item. Gerald Ratner described his approach as the 'McDonald's' of the jewellery trade. The formula worked and soon Ratners was acquiring the much larger chain of H. Samuel. There followed a series of takeovers first in the UK and then in the USA. In most cases the original retail name was retained to allow different chains of shops to target different customer types.

Ratner had courted the press in his acquisition of H. Samuel. They liked him for his open style, ready quotes and self-deprecating jokes. In April 1991 he was invited to give a keynote speech to the Institute of Directors at London's Royal Albert Hall. Copies of his speech were given out to the press in advance. He had worked on his speech and circulated it to his fellow directors, one of whom had told him it needed a joke. The joke he chose to use had played well for him before. It had even been quoted in the *Financial Times*. Referring to a decanter that retailed for £4.99 he told the audience in the Albert Hall that people often asked him how he could sell such a product for such a low price. 'I say because it's total crap', was the punch line. He went on to explain that, 'We even sell a pair of gold earrings for under a pound. People say cheaper than a prawn sandwich from Marks and Spencer. I have to say that the prawn sandwich would probably last longer than the earrings'.

The speech went well with the businesspeople in the audience and with a journalist from the tabloid newspaper, the *Sun*, who was delighted that Ratner had stuck to his script. The speech made the front page the following morning, under the headline 'Rotners'. Competitor tabloid the *Daily Mirror* headlined, 'You 22 carat mugs'.

Ratners' share price rose during the day. A city analyst explained on the following morning's radio news that investors liked a CEO who had no illusions about what he sold. Ratners' customers had different views and returned recent purchases. Sales volumes dived. Who after all would give a loved one a gift 'from Ratners'? Staff were horrified to see the press coverage.

Shops in the Ratner empire with his name on the fascia represented only 15 per cent of all the company's stores globally and less than 20 per cent in the UK. However 1991 saw the beginning of a recession, a time when jewellery sales could have been expected to decline anyway. The company had used bank loans to finance its acquisitions. Losses, of £120 million, were the inevitable result for 1991/2 and 1992 saw the equally inevitable resignation of Gerald Ratner himself.

The view of some was that the media had built Gerald Ratner up only to knock him down. Dealing well with the media is central to both reputation building and defence, but the main lesson from this example is that detail matters. One further lesson might be that the real philosophy of the company was revealed in the jokes of its leader. Jewellery is a high involvement purchase. Ratners appealed to the less well off, to whom a few pounds spent on a pair of gold earrings was still a substantial sum. Poking fun at the product demeaned the purchase and the purchaser. One interpretation of Gerald Ratner's humour was that he was all too cynical in his approach to business, to his customers and to his staff.

Choosing reputation partners carefully

The reputation of one company can affect another it is associated with. As alliances and partnerships become more common, the danger of a partner causing damage to your own reputation grows. There have been a number of examples where problems with a component have given difficulties to the company whose products contain an item clearly branded by a partner.

Ford and Firestone

Ford are one of the largest motor vehicle companies in the world. By 2000 the Ford stable included other car names such as Mazda, Volvo, Land Rover and Jaguar. Bridgestone-Firestone was also huge in its own right as a tyre manufacturer. Serious problems were experienced with owners of certain styles of Ford vehicle fitted with certain Firestone tyres. The tyres could shred in use causing the vehicle to topple. Deaths were reported from Saudi Arabia, and North and South America. Fourteen million tyres were recalled. Ford accounted for 5 per cent of Firestone's business. The recall would cost $450 million and take some considerable time to implement. The real issue between the two companies was that of blame for the deaths and injuries associated with the tyres. The Firestone brand had suffered from a large recall in the 1970s. While the two multinationals scrapped in the media over the safety records of tyres and vehicles, both brand names risked damage. Finally in 2001 Ford and Firestone announced they were to end a business relationship that had begun when Harvey Firestone had agreed to supply tyres for Henry Ford's model T.

The reputation issues that this example highlights include that Ford, whose dealers would be primarily responsible in law to customers for product quality, presumably felt that they benefited by having a Firestone brand on the tyres it put on to its vehicles, rather than say a Ford branded tyre. Firestone would in turn presumably prefer to supply Ford with a branded tyre. The issue of who might be ultimately responsible for any personal injury claims is beyond the scope of our book. Needless to say, Ford blamed the tyres and Firestone the design of the vehicle. Both reputations are likely to have suffered. Two corporate giants fight it out while those who have bought the suspect vehicle had to wait and worry before their tyres are replaced.

IBM and Intel: the Intel chip that made mistakes

Intel's marketing strategy is to appeal over the heads of the computer manufacturer and directly to the consumer. The 'Intel inside' sticker became as
important to have on your computer as any maker's brand name. Two million
pentium chips sold before July 1994 contained a problem in their floating-point
circuitry. A professor of mathematics at an American college first discovered the
problem. He contacted the chip manufacture who took their time to get back
to him. Frustrated, he went on to the Internet to see if others had experienced
the same problem or whether their chips made the same error. They had and
they did.

Intel first offered to replace the suspect chips but only if the user could prove
that the type of calculations they did encompassed the type of error situation
being complained of. They argued that very few users would ever experience
the problem.

It was only when IBM stopped shipping machines with the faulty chips that
Intel changed their minds. As one user pointed out, IBM were a blue chip
company who could not afford to have their own reputation damaged by the
idea that one of their machines might make a mistake.

Intel then offered to replace all chips at a total estimated cost of $306
million. CEO Andy Grove admitted, 'I don't think we understood the psychology of the marketplace as well as we should have ... millions of consumers who
think they are entitled to judge it better than we are, and we were insensitive to
that ... The perfect chip takes an infinite time to develop'.

IBM's role in the Intel affair is an interesting one. At limited cost to themselves but at great cost to Intel they could pressure a business partner. Indeed
IBM felt they needed to pressure their business partner into a reputation
defence action to protect the IBM name. By having to admit being in the
wrong, Intel risked its own reputation. (Sources: Anon (1995) 'Additional problems for Intel's Pentium' *PCPlus* 23: The BBC's Money Programme, 1995.)

Dealing with pressure groups

In Chapter 1 Michael Porter's five forces model was introduced as an example
of a strategic model. One of the insights from the model is the importance of
the relative bargaining power of suppliers and customers. This is usually
assessed by the relative concentrations in both groups. Thus if there are a
limited number of large customers and a large number of small suppliers the
balance of power in the typical relationship will tend to favour the customer. In
most businesses where the customer is a member of the public the balance of
power will favour the supplier. This balance can be affected by the threat of the
customer to publicize any wrong doing of the supplier. Governments tend to
legislate to protect consumers from rogue suppliers. Another way for consumers to exercise more influence over a large business is through pressure
groups of one kind or another.

The advent of the Internet has added to the potential power of pressure
groups. Members do not have to meet to communicate quickly and comprehen-
sively.

Pressure groups tend to be believed more than the companies they are set up to pressure. Consumer programmes in the broadcast media are particularly powerful in this respect. They present themselves as champions of the consumer and unfavourable coverage of a product can have dramatic effects on sales. So how do companies manage an attack on their reputation from a pressure group and what are the lessons?

McDonald's and McLibel

Views differ on the results and consequences of the longest running libel case in British history. What happened provides a lesson for all companies who use the law to defend themselves against the allegations of pressure groups.

McDonald's are one of the world's largest companies. They are often cited as an exemplar of successful globalization. They have their critics as purveyors of 'junk' food, but they are a feature of almost any town anywhere in the developed world. By 2000 the company had over 28,000 restaurants in 120 countries, worldwide. Some were operated by themselves and some by franchisees. In the UK for example, in 1997, 216 restaurants were operated as franchises out of a total of 836. The cost of a McDonald's franchise ranged at the time from £250,000 upwards. Applicants were required to have at least 25 per cent of this sum in personally owned funds.

A small group calling themselves London Greenpeace (but with no links to the larger Greenpeace organization) had been distributing leaflets in the UK in 1986. These contained allegations about McDonald's in six areas: clearing rainforest to rear beef, recycling and waste, the nutritional value of their food, their marketing to children, cruelty to animals and, their human relations policies.

Under British law anyone sued for libel carries the burden of proof that what they claim is true or at least fair comment. The accused, in this case McDonald's, does not have to prove that any statements about them are false. The only acceptable evidence would be primary sources, original material, not newspaper reports of others' views for example.

The London Greenpeace leaflet was called 'What's wrong with McDonald's?' In 1989 McDonald's produced their 'McFact cards' countering some of the allegations. They hired two firms of private investigators. In 1990 writs were served on five individuals, three of whom took the option of retracting their views and apologized. Two chose to fight, Dave Morris, and Helen Steel, described as unemployed ecologists and anarchists. With no legal training and with no money to hire lawyers, the two had to rely upon their own efforts and any voluntary support they could attract. In contrast McDonald's retained a team of lawyers.

The trial proper began in March 1994. McDonald's issued a press release and leaflet claiming their actions were not about freedom of speech, but 'the right to stop people telling lies'. The early parts of the hearing went in the direction of the defendants on issues such as nutrition and health. The trial dragged on until the end of 1996, breaking all previous records for the time taken to hear such a case. Not surprisingly the media attention it attracted was enormous. In 1996 the McSpotlight Internet site was launched. A book and a documentary film were produced. A three-and-a-half-hour reconstruction of the case was screened by one television channel.

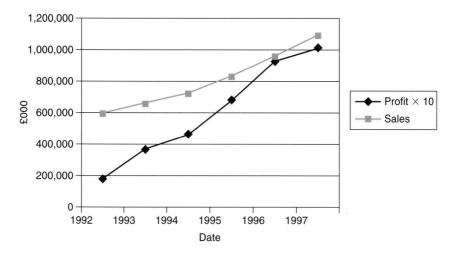

Figure 5.5 McDonald's sales and profits following the McLibel case.

Morris and Steel lost their case, even though the judge ruled that they had justified some of the claims in the leaflet, but they won the publicity war. The total cost to McDonald's has been estimated at around £10 million. If their actions had been against, say, the BBC, then they might have expected to recover their costs. In the event they could well have suffered a great deal more from publicizing their protagonist's case more widely than any leafleting campaign could have hoped to achieve. It is impossible to estimate what, if any, commercial damage was suffered by McDonald's. It is unlikely that they gained reputation as a consequence.

Profits in 1992 for example appear low by comparison with later years (see Figure 5.5), but this is as likely to have been caused by the BSE crisis than anything else. Total UK sales appeared to have been largely unaffected by the McLibel incident. By 1999 and 2000 the total number of restaurants was growing again to 842 and 920 respectively.

The McSpotlight website is mandatory reading for anyone interested in Reputation Management. It looks highly professional and contains material that is far from the emotive rantings that one might expect from a pressure group of 'unemployed ecologists/anarchists'. As the title of the video about the trial has it, this is a meeting of two worlds, two perspectives on business, the capitalist system and life in general that cannot be reconciled. The advent of the Internet and growing awareness among activists that they can take on the corporate giants will ensure that companies have to find ways other than litigation to defend their reputations.

Lessons

‹ The evidence suggests that McDonald's did not lose out by challenging London Greenpeace. The court action was expensive and difficult to justify purely on the grounds of the financial impact of London Greenpeace's challenge. However the case would have given other potential challengers cause for thought. For this reason alone McDonald's would probably argue that £10 million was well spent. (Sources: www.mcspo-light.org/case/trial/story.html Brockes, E. (2000) 'Life after McLibel', *Guardian*, 6 July www.prwatch.org/prw_ issues/1997-Q2/mclibel.html).

A similar situation occurred at around the same time, involving Greenpeace itself and the mighty Shell corporation.

Shell and Greenpeace

Shell were the largest company in Europe. Greenpeace were the best-known environmental pressure group. Shell's plan to dispose of one of its North Sea oil facilities defined a virtual battlefield between the two in the 1990s. Shell co-owned a massive storage buoy that operated in the North Sea, the relatively shallow piece of water separating Britain from the mainland of northern Europe and the German coastline. The use of an intermediate vessel as an adjunct to an oil rig became redundant with the development of new pipeline technology in the 1980s. Shell evaluated a number of options to dispose of one such vessel, named Brent Spar, located off the north-east coast of Scotland and close to the Shetland Islands. Technical studies had led Shell to believe that the best means of scrapping Brent Spar was to sink it in deep water to the west of Scotland and in the deep waters of the Atlantic Ocean. Options such as disposal on land represented a risk due to the sludge at the bottom of the tanks in the massive rig. The tanks contained heavy metals and radioactive materials that had collected there during the rig's working life, all of which were present in the oil extracted from deposits beneath the North Sea.

By 1995, it had taken Shell four years to identify the best means of disposal and to convince the authorities, the British government, that their solution was the best option. The environmental pressure group Greenpeace had different views. They saw Brent Spar as a symbol of industrial pollution, a precedent for the disposal of other rigs and a danger to the ecology of the sea. Armed with £350,000 worth of broadcasting equipment, Greenpeace activists, mainly from Germany, boarded Brent Spar and occupied it, beaming their views to the European media and inviting journalists to the scene of a dramatic confrontation in the North Sea.

Shell sent a mobile oil platform to recapture the Brent Spar. In an operation more reminiscent of a James Bond film, Shell employees were swung from a crane across to the Brent Spar. Images of oil company Shell employees capturing Greenpeace protesters and images of Greenpeace's attempts to frustrate the moving of the platform made excellent television in the coming weeks. Shell were later to admit that Greenpeace were adept at catching the public eye and that they had not taken into account 'hearts and minds' when deciding on their disposal solution.

According to one journalist, Shell fielded 'grey looking men' to argue a logical case, ignoring the emotional one being argued by Greenpeace. Greenpeace also challenged Shell's logical position in adopting deep-sea disposal, but their main success was at an emotional level. Shell could point to the views of independent experts supporting their contention that their option was the 'greenest'. The media gave the impression that the whole 14,500 tonne rig was an environmental risk, not just the few hundred grams of heavy metal and radio active material in Brent Spar's tanks. German Greenpeace saw no problems in being a 'bit naughty' with the truth as to how much contaminant was involved and where the rig was to be dumped. The Shell plan was always to dispose of Brent Spar in deep waters in the Atlantic, not as was being implied, in the relatively shallow waters of the North Sea.

The problem escalated. Demonstrations against Shell in Germany reduced Shell's petrol and oil sales. German ministers complained to their British counterparts. Shell petrol stations were attacked. Chancellor Helmut Kohl complained directly to Prime Minister John Major. Greenpeace reboarded Brent Spar, even though the rig was set with explosives, prior to its disposal. Shell UK came under pressure from its continental colleagues to abandon their plans. While the UK government were still publicly supporting Shell's original solution, Shell themselves had changed their minds.

Greenpeace claimed a victory for consumers. A UK government minister described it as 'blackmail'. Shell briefed a PR company to pave the way for future disposals. Greenpeace acknowledged their exaggeration of the amount of contaminant in Brent Spar. But whose reputation was damaged the most, Greenpeace for exaggerating and being a 'bit naughty' with the truth, or Shell for choosing a solution that ignored the emotional dimension of public opinion?

Views differ as to whether Shell's about turn on the disposal of Brent Spar would affect their image positively or not. In one article, PR specialist Quentin Bell was quoted as believing it would not do Shell any long-term harm. Greenpeace were quoted as holding an opposite view. One other source pointed to the problems any oil company has due to public cynicism about the oil business.

Since this and other public relations disasters Shell has re-examined its approach to reputation and undertaken a fundamental review of its values and behaviours.

Lessons

Pressure groups are powerful. They specialize in emphasizing the emotional aspects of an issue, leaving company management floundering with their more factual platform. Firms have learnt that it is sometimes better to listen to activist groups and to keep them informed on controversial issues. At least managers will know what the arguments are that will be used against them. It is even possible that a compromise solution can be worked out to ensure that media coverage is less than controversial.

Crises in summary

Are there any general lessons to be learnt from the largely anecdotal content in this chapter? These are the more obvious ones:

- All organizations should plan for possible reputation crises.
- Conducting a risk analysis, focusing particularly on risks from fire, explosion, and theft, can identify some potential crises.
- Some issues can be predicted by picking up early warnings, for example from what is being commented upon in the technical media.
- All organizations of any size should have a crisis plan which should include the nomination of a crisis management team.
- In a crisis, all communication must be via the crisis team.
- Don't allow media vacua to occur. If the cause of the crisis and its solution are still unclear then release a holding statement.
- Crises are times of emotion. A purely rational response may not be enough to protect a reputation. Going what appears to be one step too far may be the only way to respond to emotive aspects of a crisis.
- The bigger the crisis the more it is essential for the CEO to be seen to take responsibility.
- Large corporations are vulnerable to attack from pressure groups many of which do not share the capitalist view of business. One answer could be to consult with leading pressure groups on sensitive decisions.
- Crises are often expensive in the short term but rarely appear to damage companies in the long run if they handle them well.

Reputation isn't built in a day . . . but it can be also fade away

Some reputations are destroyed in minutes by a tragic action or a mishandled crisis. Others, like the old soldier, merely fade away. In Chapter 2 we quoted from an interview with Sir Richard Greenbury, one time head of Marks and Spencer. In his era Marks and Sparks, as the British refer to the company, had prospered. Few companies could claim a better reputation. But in the last year of his leadership sales and profit suddenly declined. Other things happened and Marks and Spencer suddenly found itself on the receiving end of a welter of negative publicity. In Greenbury's opinion a reputation takes a long time to build but less to destroy. The company he once managed offers some insights into why and how this is true.

Marks and Spencer was once the most admired of British retailers. The profitability of the British retail sector in the 1980s and 1990s was the envy of the world. There were many explanations (some of which are none too flattering such as collusion over prices and artificial barriers to new store development by competitors), but in general the view was that the British had managed the phenomenon of own branding better than their international rivals. Retailers selling products under their own names tend to position them on price and as bargains. When first introduced into European markets own brands were seen as 'generics', plainly wrapped (such as Carrefour's Produits Libres) and were very low priced. Quality was not always high.

Some British retailers observed that the less well off in society (to whom such products might be expected to appeal) shunned them in favour of smaller amounts of well-known brands. They believed that the poor could not afford to take the risk of buying a store brand. To them it mattered if their children refused to eat own brand cornflakes or wear a T-shirt with an unknown name on the label.

The main buyer of own brand was the more affluent consumer who could afford to be a risk taker. Retailers realized that positioning their own brands more upmarket, at perhaps 10 per cent below the price of the leading manufacturer's brand would work. They could attract the more affluent shopper and the margins they would make would be much higher than from selling most manufacturers' brands. To be credible own-brands needed to be seen as 'brands' in their own right. Leading this trend was Marks and Spencer.

Their origins were humble as a single market stall, started in the open market in the northern industrial city of Leeds by an immigrant from Eastern Europe, Michael Marks, in the year 1884. By 1890 he ran a number of stalls all trading under the sign 'Don't ask the price – it's a penny'. This approach of asking a fixed price was unusual in an era when negotiation or 'haggling' over price was still commonplace. The story goes that Marks did not have enough confidence in his command of English to haggle and therefore refused to by hanging up his notice. Such is the way of business because this initiative, an innovation in its day, worked well for him as customers often shared his views on haggling.

In 1894 Marks took a partner, Thomas Spencer. The business prospered and grew to become a private limited company in 1903. Marks's eldest son Simon became a director in 1911, four years after his father's death. His brother-in-law Israel Sieff joined him on the board in 1917 and by 1926 the two had become chairman and vice-chairman respectively of the company. By 1914 Marks and Spencer were operating a chain of 'penny bazaars' across the country, outlets (mainly in market halls) that were half way between a market stall and a shop. The one-penny price point had disappeared in 1914 but the idea of buying and selling to a fixed price remained after the First World War when the company moved away from bazaars and into high street stores.

The company became a public corporation in 1926 with 125 stores. Money from the flotation was used to expand and refurbish the outlets. At the same time Simon Marks introduced a more professional style of management, borrowed from American retail practice. Perhaps the most significant innovations were however the emphasis placed on quality control and staff welfare. Marks and Spencer began buying directly from manufacturers (thus cutting out the wholesaler) in 1924. This was again contrary to established methods and did not endear them to the wholesalers who guarded their role in the distribution system jealously.

In 1935 a textile laboratory was established to test both garments and cloth and to prepare technical specifications. This was inevitable if Marks and Spencer were to establish and maintain an image for quality. At about this time Marks and Spencer bought an interest in a textile manufacturer but this was a brief flirtation with owning the means of production. With few exceptions Marks and Spencer concentrated on controlling rather than owning their sources of supply, leading to the label of a 'manufacturer in disguise'. To this day virtually all Marks and Spencer products are sold under the St Michael name, a name exclusive to the retailer, or, most recently under the Marks and Spencer name itself.

A merchandise development department was created in 1936 and then a design department charged with improving quality and design. In 1947 a production engineering department was formed to assist suppliers in modernizing their plant.

In the 1920s and 1930s Marks and Spencer was predominantly a textile and home wear retailer. Food was sold but the offer was somewhat different from that today, including for example substantial sales of broken Kit Kat biscuits, a leading brand of chocolate wafer from confectionery manufacturer Rowntree (now part of Nestlé). Simon Marks in particular seemed unconvinced that food held much of a future for Marks and Spencer nevertheless a food development department had been created as far back as 1948.

What has become known as a 'human relations' policy at Marks and Spencer dates to the 1930s. A personnel department began in 1933 and a welfare department in 1934 whose role extended to the well-being of previous employees. Employees today enjoy subsidized meals, services such as hairdressing and chiropody, discount schemes, and a profit sharing scheme. Membership of trade unions among Marks and Spencer employees was and is very low.

Concern over the scope for future growth in Britain and over moves by the Labour government in power in 1945 towards nationalization, prompted Marks and Spencer to look abroad for future growth. A share exchange with a South African retailer was scrapped in 1971 and interest switched to Canada with a 50 per cent holding in Peoples Department Stores. The Canadian business developed into three chains, Peoples, D'Allairds, and Marks and Spencer. However Marks and Spencer found achieving consistent profitability in Canada to be difficult. In 1975 the first Marks and Spencer stores were opened in Continental Europe, in France and Belgium. In 1988 the company acquired Brooks Brothers with outlets in America but also across the world including Japan. Also in that year Marks and Spencer acquired the small American food chain Kings Supermarkets and opened two stores in Hong Kong. The Brooks acquisition brought with it the right to sell food into 258 US department stores belonging to the Campeau Corporation.

By 1990 Marks and Spencer had become one of the world's largest retail businesses. Its core business was still in the British high street where its 281 stores and 8.8 million square foot of selling area gave it annual sales of £4.5 billion. Its UK market share in clothing was 16 per cent, in food 5 per cent. nine hundred suppliers produced goods under the St Michael brand name. Fourteen million customers made purchases each week in their stores. Some 2.5 million possessed a Marks and Spencer store card (the company did not accept other credit or charge cards until later in that decade). According to market researchers Gordon Simmons, in 1987 67 per cent of all British adults made a purchase in Marks and Spencer.

The company was a household name, a British institution, yet Marks and Spencer had rarely advertised in its century and more of trading, although it was highly involved in the community, committing £4 million to good works in

1989 alone. The company name was synonymous with middle of the road reliability, the epitome of Britishness perhaps, the only retailer in the world with a triple A credit rating. It had grown from a single market stall through a phase as a variety chain and on to dominate the British high street with its department-store like outlets. The customer pulling power of a 'Marks and Sparks' meant favourable terms for the company in any new retail developments. Its human relations policies and career prospects attracted and retained good quality staff. Marks and Spencer's positive attitude to staff was reflected in their staff's positive attitude to customers.

The company launched a financial services business that grew rapidly. People bought savings products, unit trusts, and even pensions from what had once been mainly a clothes shop. Yet the company itself found its success in its home country almost frustrating. Each new venture in Britain seemed almost doomed to succeed while, try as it might, its success overseas had been patchy.

Operating losses were recorded in 1989 for two of the three Canadian chains. Profits had fallen by 26.5 per cent in mainland Europe. The purchase price for Brooks Brothers had been high and the bankruptcy of the original owners, Campeau, had cast doubt over the value of an agreement to sell food in all their department stores. One American critic wondered whether Marks and Spencer could mass market the Brooks concept and whether the British food offer would sell at all in the USA or whether Marks and Spencer could introduce the necessary logistics infrastructure in the less densely populated American market. 'Maybe', the article concluded, 'they should have stayed at home'. In Continental Europe the food offer was selling well, better in fact than clothing that was often seen as too traditionally British and lacking fashion appeal. Nevertheless, Marks and Spencer had set their sights on being a truly international business, seeking new locations in Europe.

Greenbury's explicit strategy when he succeeded to the top job at Marks and Spencer was globalization. The primary role of a CEO is probably to continue to satisfy the shareholders with the same rate of growth in their shareholding values in the decade to come as they had become used to in the last decade. Where then other than outside the UK was such growth to come from? Globalizing a retail business had been an objective of many before including Woolworths and Safeway, but few made as much money away from their home markets as they did from the original business. Worse, the original business was almost bound to suffer as it was milked for the funds to support global expansion.

In 1997 profits rose above the £1 billion mark for the first time. The next year they increased but only marginally on an increased turnover. Turnover held at £8.2 billion in 1999 but profits almost halved. UK sales were badly hit but international retail sales went from a £67 million contribution to profits to a loss of £15 million (see Figures 5.6 and 5.7).

There were many explanations for this sudden reversal of fortune: the economic situation in the Far East, increased competition at home, that the company had been too loyal to its mainly British supply base that was now too expensive, that the ladies wear products had been poorly chosen. Whatever the reasons, the reactions both inside the company and in the media were astounding. The first phase was described by Gwyther (1999) in the business magazine *The Economist*. Other press comment below is taken mainly from the British

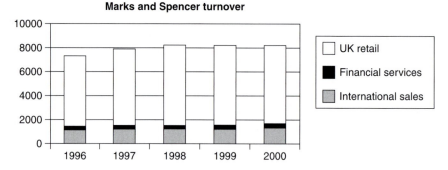

Figure 5.6 Turnover at Marks and Spencer flattens.

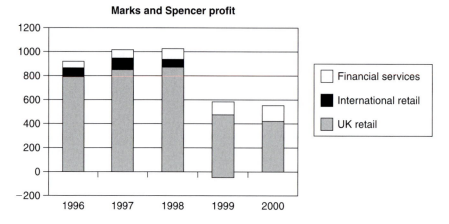

Figure 5.7 Profits at Marks and Spencer nosedive.

newspaper the *Daily Telegraph*, aimed at the British middle class, the core market for Marks and Spencer.

On 3 November 1998 when Marks and Spencer announced a substantial decline in its profits and their share price lost 10 per cent in a single session. The share price had already been declining from a peak of £6.40 but was now below £5. A press report had suggested that Greenbury would soon stand down in favour of one of his two joint managing directors, Peter Salsbury. The other joint MD, Keith Oates was taken aback by the press leak, as he had his own aspirations for the top post. He wrote to the non-executive directors suggesting that he would like to be considered for the post. Unlike Salsbury he had not worked for Marks and Spencer all of his life, but he had headed the very successful financial services business.

The letter somehow leaked to the press. Banner headlines in the Sunday papers talked about a 'War of Succession'. Greenbury was on a business trip in India. He flew back to chair a directors' meeting on Monday 9 November, by all reports less than pleased. It was decided to bring forward the process of deciding on Greenbury's successor. By 20 November every director had been interviewed and a key meeting planned for the 25th. Greenbury was still reported to favour Salsbury and after the meeting it was announced that he would become chief executive with Greenbury remaining in a non-executive role. Oates left the business stating his disappointment at 'retiring early'. He was 56.

The reaction in the media to Salsbury's appointment was not totally favourable. In the *Guardian* he was referred to as 'meek, shy and anonymous'. Perhaps to prove his critics wrong and after a few weeks in his new role, Salsbury removed three directors and nearly a quarter of the other long-standing senior managers. Gwyther described Marks and Spencer as 'a tribe'. The new chief had culled his senior colleagues in a way no tribal leader has been reported as doing in any field studies by anthropologists. The press began to have a field day. A new genre arrived, the management consultant. At its peak there were so many consultants employed that one consultancy was retained to report on the work of the rest.

A new range of 'designer' clothes was introduced in 1999 under the Autograph label (exclusive to Marks and Spencer). Some welcomed the initiative; others worried that the more glamorous look was not what the core customer wanted and, worse, that it made the rest of the more middle of the road products on the sales floor look dull.

Under the headline 'Poor Marks' the American edition of *The Economist* ascribed the financial problems to 'the company's inward-looking culture'. But this had been the company's strength, an evolutionary not revolutionary style with a senior team who had spent their lives in the business. The share price held its ground for the first half of 1999. Then more bad news about clothing sales in particular sent it into another downturn to below £2.50. The share price had halved in two years. Greenbury had finally retired in June 1999 a year before his planned date and the company was looking for a new chairman. He arrived in January 2000 in the form of Belgian Luc Vandevelde the former president of the French hypermarket chain, Promodes. He promised to turn the company's fortunes around within two years.

Following further poor sales results Peter Salsbury left the business in September 2000, together with two other directors. Their total severance pay was given in the press as £1.2 million. There was now hardly anyone left in the senior echelons of Marks and Spencer that had been there two years before. Vandevelde took sole charge. In November he was quoted in a newspaper article as saying that the sudden downturn had come as a surprise to him and to the rest of the struggling retailer's board.

Everything the company did seemed to be met with sarcasm in the media. For example the launch of a new type of gift voucher, a 'gift experience voucher' received the following comment from the *Daily Telegraph*,

Marks and Spencer vouchers can be exchanged for white-water rafting and aerobatic flying classes. I suppose it will allow customers to sympathize with investors, queasy from watching the Marks and Spencer share price dive.

Marks and Spencer had rarely used media advertising to promote itself or its products. Their new campaign featuring a size 16 model was intended to make the point that Marks and Spencer appealed to women of all sizes. It appeared that realism was not what the public wanted as one article commented,

> So what has gone wrong? One analyst blames what he delicately described as the 'fat bird' running around naked on our TV screens.

An interview with the new retail director hired from Kingfisher included the following question,

> 'What are the measurements for a size 16 woman', I ask. Marks and Spencer currently has one – the model Amy Davis – running naked through a field in its TV ad. 'I have no idea', he admits. The answer is 38–31½–41, and it's one of Marks and Spencer's most popular sizes.

The journalist commented,

> He knows virtually nothing about selling clothes. Everyone says that he's brilliant at writing strategy papers, but can he run the country's biggest clothing retailer?

Marks and Spencer had used the fact that their products were manufactured within the UK as part of its marketing. The amount of work that was actually done in the UK had declined with some garments reputedly being part made overseas to be imported for finishing so as to claim they were 'made in Britain'. Realizing the claim was no longer credible and the cost advantages of sourcing in lower labour cost areas, Marks and Spencer had rationalized their UK suppliers in 1999 concentrating on three – Courtaulds, Coates Viyella, and Dewhirst. The move prompted a lawsuit from William Baird, that Marks and Spencer had sacked as a supplier after a thirty-year relationship. The case went in favour of Marks and Spencer but attracted poor publicity. In September 2000 Coates Viyella announced it was to sever its relationships with Marks and Spencer after seventy years. Thousands of jobs were to go from an already beleaguered textile sector. Coates Viyella made a number of key items for Marks and Spencer including the recently launched saucy Satin Rose underwear and Julien Mac-Donald's jerseys for Marks and Spencer's Autograph designer range.

In October 2000 the closure of twenty stores was announced, including twelve of nineteen stores that had only been bought three years earlier from a rival retailer Littlewoods, themselves in difficulties at the time of the sale. The headlines focused on the 1500 staff 'to be affected' ignoring the reality that those who wished would be found jobs within the company and that the typical level of staff turnover in retailing is as much as 50 per cent per annum.

Press articles about quite mundane issues were given headlines suggesting dramatic problems,

> Marks and Spencer goods worthless

for example over an appraisal in *The Times* of attempts to calculate the break up value of the company.

In January 2001 Marks and Spencer had to acknowledge another poor result for the key Christmas trading period. Sales of clothing were down again.

'Just how greedy is Luc Vandevelde?' asked the *Daily Telegraph* in April 2001 under a headline,

> The £5 million man at Baker Street proved to be no bargain

commenting on how much the new chief executive would have cost the company during his initial two year contract. In the body copy the paper added:

> Of course, the bonus shouldn't be paid. It can't be justified on any sensible measure of performance – Marks and Spencer has gone backwards during Mr Vandevelde's reign. Maybe, just, maybe, the non-execs will finally decide to take a stand, and explain to Mr Vandevelde that it isn't deserved at all. After all, they've flunked the difficult decisions in the past.

The item ended with the suggestion that

> It's time to give up the lucre, Luc.

In March 2001 the *Daily Telegraph* included a number of customer comments in an article headed 'Good food hall, shame about the clothes'.

> In the old days, I'd probably have gone to Marks and Spencer to replace (my underwear), but I've grown out of buying them at Marks and Spencer. It's what your mum would approve of. Gap offers better quality and better colours.

And

> The bras are crap. They don't fit normal women. You buy your knickers there and that's it. The other clothes are better than they were, but you know the fine line between fashionable and unfashionable. Marks and Spencer always get it slightly wrong.

There was the occasional positive comment

> What makes me angry is that everyone knocks Marks and Spencer. I think there's a section of the press that really wants to do them down. It's a great British institution and one of the world leaders. Look at the way they look after their staff.

A letter to the *Daily Telegraph* in February from a loyal customer complained

> I was not alone in my almost vain search, but found myself circling the stands with other ladies in the same situation. Bring back the quality, bring back the cut.

Another explained,

> The many letters from shoppers and shareholders agree that the reason for the poor showing of Marks and Spencer clothing is that they do not sell clothes that people want to buy. Why do they still not realize this?

Another complained,

> Recently, I wanted to purchase a size eight sweater. When I tried it on, the image in the mirror resembled a scarecrow. The sleeves reached my knuckles, and the body part reached almost to my knees.

Yet another

> I, too, wrote to Marks and Spencer, mainly to say that it didn't sell enough big sizes (letter, 13 November). I received a similar 'fobbing off' letter, enclosing a magazine advertising, on the cover an article on 'Slimming for Summer'.

And again,

> How can we convince Marks and Spencer, before it is too late, that its clothes never did appeal to the young and trendy, and never will; that the slick advertising and marketing strategies are futile; that all we want is a return to the traditional values of quality and reliability?

And again,

> I carried out a survey of thirty stores, interviewing every manager. Each one agreed with me that the needs of 'ordinary' people were no longer being met, and each had received 'thousands' of comments in this vein. I wrote to every board member with the results of my survey. After three weeks, I received an acknowledgement from Peter Salsbury enclosing a picture of grey-haired ladies in twinsets.

Luc Vandevelde's regime was described in a *Daily Telegraph* article on 19 December 2000 entitled

> A cold, lonely Christmas under the Michael House tree

as

> one where fantastically clever strategic thinkers are increasingly replacing anyone who knows how to sell knickers, lamb's-wool jerseys or bootleg trousers.

Marks and Spencer had seen its own market share of the key UK ladies wear market fall sharply from 16.9 per cent in 1996 to 12.9 per cent in 2000. Arcadia, which owned a number of fashion chains Dorothy Perkins, Top Shop and Evans, was the second biggest ladies wear retailer, with a 12.3 per cent market share. Marks and Spencer were still the leading clothing retailer, despite all the press comment, but it was becoming more and more difficult for the shopper to take them seriously as a main place to shop with comment by fashion writers such as this again in the *Daily Telegraph*:

Last year, they were accused of being frumpy, ageist, 'sizeist' and not sexy enough. Then, last season, they were labelled 'too fashionable' and accused of ignoring their core customers. So this time, perhaps unsurprisingly, they have decided to be all things to all people. The result is a collection of schizophrenic separates and accessories. Some are super trendy, others hybrids of recent catwalk trends. But most would only satisfy the comfy-elas-ticated-waist-and-drip-dry brigade. What is remarkable perhaps is that there were any shoppers other than ever more desperate shareholders in the stores'.

In 2001, following figures for the previous year that sales and profits outside the UK had been poor, the company announced it was selling all its overseas busi-nesses and stores. Thousands of jobs were to go. The move would yield a capital sum to be returned to shareholders. Even so the company were taken to court in France for not consulting with their French labour force (as the law there required). More unfavourable press comment followed but the share price showed its first sustained increase to £2.70 in May 2001.

Lessons from Marks and Spencer

Marks and Spencer is not an example of a poorly handled crisis, unless one regards the key to its decline as the sharp fall in profits in 1999 as a crisis. It is better regarded as offering a series of lessons in Reputation Management that, cumulatively, resulted in a reputation being severely damaged. Richard Green-bury's opinion is that the public quarrel over who was to be his successor was a crucial beginning. It gave the impression of an organization not able to manage itself. Further dramatic changes in personnel did not help. Store closures and the great loss of jobs contrasted with the large payoffs and bonuses announced for executives. The company's press machine still poured out positive messages to the media, but many journalists chose to put a negative spin on such mater-ial. Why? Journalists are stakeholders in such businesses as well. Business and fashion journalists rely upon their contacts for that occasional exclusive, so why bite the hand that feeds you? Obviously because their allegiances are primarily to their own employers, to their readers and viewers and not to any corporation. The perceived needs of their own stakeholders meant that they should use the information they had to further darken the Marks and Spencer image.

The effect on the core customer is the most important issue. Marks and Spencer sold a wide range of products but its core offer was in clothing, which is a very individual purchase. People do not buy clothes solely or even mainly for their functional attributes, such as the wear rating of the cloth or the colour fastness of the dye. These are assumed to be integral at the price points of a Marks and Spencer. We also wear clothes because we like to feel good in them. For some of us this might mean that tired old pullover that an aged aunt had lovingly knitted for us twenty years ago, more of a friend than a garment. For most it is that new item that we have worked hard to buy or spent ages searching for. A plethora of negative comment would impact upon our emotional attachments to the products the company sold.

What appeared to happen in the case of Marks and Spencer is that the customer stopped believing in the brand. It was still trusted, but trust requires evidence. If we have faith in a brand we accept everything the brand offers. We do not question. If the brand name is on a pension product, no matter if it started on a frock, we still accept it as a quality product. One we lose our faith, we descend to mere trust. If the evidence is poor we no longer reject the evidence or rationalize it; we act on it and reject the product not the message.

Marks and Spencer is still a strong brand. It is still the market leader for clothes in the UK and the most profitable food retailer, probably in the world, if measured on the basis of net margin. It has suffered and not only with customers. Its relationships with suppliers were always tough but companies such as Coates Viyella who had supplied them for years suddenly walked away. So did senior staff, some pushed, some jumping ship before they were pushed, but others because the rosy future that global expansion had once promised was now gone with the sale of the overseas operations.

The same content but a different plot?

One of the lessons from the Marks and Spencer example is that the media can use the same factual information to support very different pictures of the organization. A useful way of analysing what is happening here is a framework from Downing (1997). Drawing from themes in drama he suggests that there are four 'plots' that can describe most themes in the way a journalist will play a story about an organization: the quest, the downfall, the contest and the scam. These reflect the four traditional themes in drama: romance, tragedy, melodrama and irony.

In the 'quest' the firm as hero challenges the status quo, experiences setbacks but ultimately triumphs. In the 'contest' the story line becomes a struggle between good and evil, where ultimately one side emerges triumphant. In the 'downfall' the firm as hero is seen to be first successful and then to fall to humiliation. In the 'scam' the hero is shown to be no hero at all. The hero's actions are shown to have been an attempt to fleece others.

Marks and Spencer had once been the hero who could do no wrong. They developed own brands to offer the audience quality products at a price they could afford. The play is rewritten and Marks and Spencer has its rivals (other retailers) who try to overcome its market dominance. Despite all, the hero triumphs, though perhaps the audience is left with a less than secure view of the hero's infallibility. In the next version the hero is seen to fail, but mainly because of fate or external events. This would equate to the company's failure in its attempt to become global. In the final version the hero is seen to be the cause of his own downfall. The audience is exposed to his duplicity. This certainly describes the way the media tended to play stories about the large payoffs for senior mangers and the bonus for the new chief executive.

A summary of reputation defence

Reputation can disappear quickly or it can fade away. Crises can sometimes be foreseen and can always be prepared for. The media can turn on an organization and this should be no surprise, as the media are not paid to be a free communication channel. The same story can be made to play quite differently in the media and it is worth positioning any communication clearly as one type of plot or another.

Part 2

Managing reputation by managing corporate personality

In this part of our book we present what is largely our own work on reputation. Our approach is analytical; we like to show mathematical co-relations, for example, to argue that one thing is related to another. One of our main contributions to research into reputation has been the development of a scale to measure how different stakeholders see an organization, what we call the Corporate Personality Scale. In subsequent chapters we apply this measure to provide answers to a number of challenges in Reputation Management.

6 Measuring reputation

The Corporate Personality Scale

> Measuring reputation, existing measures, insights form various sources: culture, ethics, social responsibility, brand personality, the development of our scale.

Existing measures of reputation

Reputation can be and has been measured in many ways. There are a number of general measures of corporate reputation, many focusing on the ranking of corporations (Fombrun 1998). The most widely known is from the business magazine, *Fortune* which regularly polls business executives and analysts as to the reputation of leading companies. Such measures have been criticized because the criteria for assessment have no theoretical foundation, are overly focused on financial performance, and because the sample used for reputation surveys is narrow (executives and business analysts) and excludes important stakeholders such as employees and customers. In response, a number of measurement techniques have been developed, although most focus on only one type of stakeholder (van Riel and Balmer 1997; Fombrun *et al.* 2000). There are a number of specific measures intended to assess a particular market sector. For example, a number of rankings exist of business schools that is used by many applicants to short list their consideration of set of schools they wish to apply to. Trade magazines tend to run annual 'beauty contests' to decide the 'best' organization in certain fields.

America's most admired companies

As we mentioned earlier *Fortune*'s list of America's most admired companies are chosen from the 1000 largest US companies (ranked by revenues) and the twenty-five largest US subsidiaries of foreign-owned companies. The companies are sorted by industry and the ten largest selected from each industry to form fifty-seven separate groups. Companies that are ranked 11 to 25 are not eligible for evaluation, but their executives can vote for the top companies in their industries.

10,000 executives, directors, and securities analysts are asked to select the five companies they admire most, regardless of industry. The group choose from a list containing the companies that ranked among the top 25 per cent in the pre-vious year's survey; the list also included companies that rank below the first quartile overall but finished in the top 20 per cent of their industry.

To create the fifty-seven industry lists respondents are asked to rank com-panies in their own industry on eight criteria: quality of management, quality of products and services, innovativeness, long-term investment value, financial soundness, employee talent, use of corporate assets, social responsibility and overall company results. As these criteria reveal there is a heavy emphasis on commercial performance. That the respondents include only executives and analysts adds to a picture of a survey focused on known financial performance. The scope of the survey is fairly narrow and restricted to commercial organ-izations. For example if you are a medium-sized charity both the ranking method and the context are irrelevant.

The best companies to work for

Fortune also produces a ranking of the top 100 companies to work for. To select the 100 best in 2000, 234 candidates underwent considerable scrutiny: a survey of a randomly selected group of their employees (at least 250 employees per firm). Some 36,000 employees in that year completed a survey that evaluates trust in management, pride in work and the company, and camaraderie. Some 14,000 also provided individual written comments about their workplaces. The survey and comments accounted for two-thirds of the scoring. The remainder of the score was determined by each company's explanation of its philosophy and practices, and includes supplementary materials – employee handbooks, company newsletters, and videos.

There are some co-relation between the list of good employers and the list of most admired companies. For example Cisco Systems ranked fourth in the 1999 most admired survey and third in the 100 best companies to work for list in 2000. Southwest Airlines came seventh and third respectively in the same surveys. There is also some co-relation between overall size and ranking. For example in the same years Walmart Stores was the fifth ranked company in the most admired survey and the second ranked in the list of the 500 largest companies in the world, the global 500 list, also complied by *Fortune*. General Electric, who topped the most admired list was ranked ninth in the world for size.

In summary the most admired list is an indication of the relative ranking of success among America's leading commercial organizations. Neither the list itself nor the criteria used are relevant to any general evaluation of the reputa-tion of companies outside this context. While the scale is claimed to assess repu-tation, in reality it assesses only image and image among one group of stakeholders. The separate survey of employees is a step in the right direction but again it is designed to produce a ranking of organizations. This implies that it is both possible and desirable to compare organizations with each other. Even if such studies are made within a sector, for example to identify the best bank to work for or the bank best regarded by its business peers, the key question is, 'So what?' How can an organization use the results of the most admired survey to improve or indeed is that even the point of the study?

The Reputation Quotient

The Harris-Fombrun reputation quotient is a relatively new alternative to the most admired list. The quotient is calculated from a list of twenty attributes representing six dimensions (see Figure 6.1).

The Reputation Quotient uses a broader range of criteria than those in the Most Admired survey. The survey also involves employees, investors, and customers, rather than being limited to executives. In the 1999 list some of the same companies that feature at the top of the RQ rankings are the same as those in the most admired survey. For example Walmart was fifth in the 1999 most admired rankings and sixth in the RQ rankings. Home Depot came ninth and eighth respectively. However, General Electric top in the most admired list could only manage twelfth place in the RQ rankings.

In an analysis of the six dimensions shown in Figure 6.1 the originators suggest that ratings for products and services, workplace environment, social responsibility, vision and leadership and financial performance each contribute to emotional appeal which in turn creates reputation. The emotional appeal criterion contains three items, 'Good feelings about the company, admire and respect the company and trust the company a great deal'. Interestingly vision and leadership contribute negatively to emotional appeal and financial performance is non-significantly co-related. Being financially successful appears to dominate reputation in the eyes of the business community but reputation in the eyes of employees and customers appears to be unaffected by this dimension.

The RQ may be used with investors, customers and employees, although employees may be able to respond to questions about vision and leadership with more confidence than customers. However the measure is intended to be used with multiple stakeholders which is a significant advance. Other approaches have been specifically developed to help to understand the internal view, what we have labelled as identity.

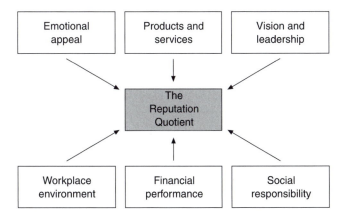

Figure 6.1 The Reputation Quotient.

The Rotterdam Organizational Identification Test (ROIT)

The ROIT questionnaire consists of a number of elements divided into six groups, van Riel and Balmer (1997) and Figure 6.2.

The key measure is that of the employees' identification with the organization, for example their feeling of belonging, acceptance and security. However the ROIT scale does not reveal the nature of corporate identity itself, more the inputs to and the consequences of that identity.

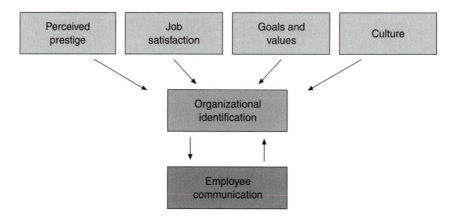

Figure 6.2 The ROIT measure of identification.

Source: Adapted from van Riel and Balmer (1997).

A new approach

One of our main contributions to the study of corporate reputation has been to develop a new scale that can measure reputation from the perspective of many stakeholders. We focused on employees and customers in our work as the two most important stakeholders.

The main issues in reputation measurement

Any measure of either image or identity that claims to be universal or generic, in other words it can be used to assess any organization, needs to be comprehensive and must not be context specific. To be either it is impossible to be direct, to test specific issues such as price and service quality, at least not without using a questionnaire that is unacceptably long. For example service quality could be assessed using SERVQUAL, product quality using another similar tool, price another, and so on. The measure must apply to large and small companies, to profit and to non-profit organizations. Most important it should be capable of use with as many different categories of stakeholder as possible.

The two most important stakeholders in any organization, from a reputation perspective, are employees and customers. This is because they are generally the two largest groups and the two who have the largest impact on the business. And it is also because Reputation theory holds that image, the external view and identity, the internal view are connected, Chapter 2. It follows that any measure of reputation should be capable of assessing both identity and image.

We began by looking at the various approaches that have been used in the past to measure what we thought were relevant to our objective of creating a reputation scale. In particular we were looking for how people describe or think about organizations.

The perspective of culture

A organization's culture embraces a number of aspects but a useful shorthand is 'how we do things around here'. A number of questionnaires exist to measure the culture of an organization (Xenikou and Furnham 1996) and a number of factors emerge that are highly likely to affect the way internal and external stakeholders view the organization: openness to change in a supportive culture, negation/resistance to change, the human factor in a bureaucratic culture, positive social relations in the workplace and task oriented organizational growth. Words that might be relevant to any list of adjectives to describe an organization include 'concern, aggression, creativity/innovation, supportiveness, dominance, risk taking, competitive, careful and socially responsible' (O'Reilly *et al.* 1991; Xenikou and Furnham 1996).

Chatman and Jain (1994)'s scale has seven dimensions labelled (with one or more indicative items that may be relevant to the assessment of both image and identity):

- innovation (risk taking, experimenting)
- stability (predictable, security)
- people oriented (fair, respect individuals' rights)
- outcome orientation (results and achievement oriented)
- easygoingness (calm, reflective)
- detail orientation (precise, analytical) and
- team orientation (collaborative).

Negative aspects of organizations

Organizations do have their dark as well as their light sides. Organizations can be 'controlling' to the point where they become totalitarian (Schwartz 1987). They can exhibit antisocial behaviour, that while not necessarily immoral, is typical of an organization given to insincerity and manipulative and negative actions (Daneke 1983). The 'sociopathic' firm described by Daneke can be populated by honest people, but the pressure of business can blind the organization as a whole to what is being done. Daneke argues that adverse corporate behaviour can include the following:

- socially questionable activities, despite the small costs of being socially responsible;

- a myopic focus on short-term profit at the expense of long-term viability;
- a failure to learn from mistakes, including a tendency to cover up rather than correct the cause of any problem;
- a general atmosphere of irresponsibility that breeds a poor image among stakeholders but which feeds off that same image.

Sociopathic firms build walls that insulate them from government regulation and which inhibit them from learning from their environment. Attempts to regulate their behaviour may fail and may actually embed the anti-social behaviour into the organizational culture.

At the time of writing one of the world's largest businesses, Enron, had just collapsed. Founded in 1986 in just fifteen years Enron grew to be America's seventh largest company, employing 21,000 staff in more than forty countries. Enron's core business was energy trading. Enron had to admit it lost $586 million, instead of the massive profits claimed in its trading statements. Clifford Baxter, a former senior executive of Enron, committed suicide apparently leaving a suicide note that he could not stand the pain of the scandal. Employees alleged that Enron encouraged them to invest their savings in its shares despite senior executives knowing about the firm's real plight. Employees lost billions of dollars because their pension scheme was heavily invested in Enron's own stock and they were prevented from cashing in their holdings when the share price fell. Enron's auditors, Andersen, revealed that some of its employees destroyed a number of documents related to its handling of Enron's accounts.

Enron had provided millions of dollars to finance George W. Bush's 2000 election campaign. The British political repercussions of the Enron collapse centred around whether Labour's sponsorship from the company had led to a change in government energy policy.

Whatever the truth that emerges over the coming years there is no doubt that Enron, its auditors, those who regulate corporate affairs and politicians as both law makers and fund raisers will have to reconsider the probity of a system that could allow such a scandal with hardly a whisper of advance warning. Those working within Enron and their associates may not have seen what was happening as wrong and this is really the dark side of any organization, behaviours that appear deviant to the external observer but not to those inside the organization. We sought to capture this dimension of corporate personality in our scale.

Kets de Vries and Miller (1984) identified five different styles of 'neurotic' behaviour exhibited by organizations which will be present in all organizations to a greater or lesser extent. When they become exaggerated they become neuroses, promoting aberrant behaviours that society or individuals find unacceptable. They link these behaviours back to the fantasies of key organizational members, particularly those of dominant senior executives. The five types of neurotic style are labelled paranoid, compulsive, histrionic, depressive and schizoid. Table 6.1 summarizes some of the characteristics of such organizations.

Kets de Vries and Miller link the personality of the organization to its behaviour. For example, paranoid firms are more likely to copy than to innovate. Stereotypes react differently to a changing environment; the compulsive

Table 6.1 Neurotic styles and their characteristics

Neurotic style	Characteristics
Paranoid	Cold, rational, unemotional, suspicious, defensive
Compulsive	Meticulous, dogmatic, obstinate, inward looking, rule bound
Histrionic	Craving for excitement, unable to focus, superficial
Depressive	Loss of interest, unable to experience pleasure, pessimistic
Schizoid	Indifferent to praise or criticism, aggressive

organization would find it more difficult to survive significant change, as its focus is internal. The compulsive type shares some of the characteristics of the totalitarian organization mentioned earlier, with an emphasis on the domination of employees.

Lloyd (1990) presents a more positive perspective of the corporation, the 'nice' company, where 'niceness' is manifest in empathy towards society, good corporate manners, and industrial neighbourliness. This contrasts with companies who might be motivated in the first place by a will to survive but in the second by greed. They bully, paying suppliers late. Their unethical behaviour becomes institutionalized but sanitized with labels such as toughness and shrewdness.

Retail and store image

There has been a long tradition of assessing corporate image in the retail sector since Martineau (1958) coined the expression 'the personality of the retail store'. (Interestingly the metaphor was dropped in favour of the term 'store image' in the work that followed.) Various reviews followed aiming to describe the factors that could contribute to a store's image (Lindquist 1974; Berry 1969). Many of these are objective dimensions such as price and quality of merchandise (see for example Table 6.2) and are probably better seen as causes of image rather than as image itself. Other studies have tended to devise image criteria that are specific to the retail sector being studied rather than criteria that are relevant to all businesses (Davies and Brooks 1989).

Table 6.2 Retail image criteria, after Berry (1969)

Rank	Criteria
1	Price of merchandise
2	Quality of merchandise
3	Assortment of merchandise
4	Fashion of merchandise
5	Sales personnel
6	Location convenience factors
7	Other convenience factors
8	Services
9	Sales promotions
10	Advertising
11	Store atmosphere
12	Reputation on adjustments

The reputation perspective

Markham (1972: 62) was early in suggesting the use of a 'personality' scale to compare the reputation of a company with that of its competitors. He used bipolar scales with items such as extrovert–introvert, efficient–inefficient, dishonest–honest, flexible–rigid, slow–fast, inventive–conventional. A number of descriptors appear frequently in the reputation literature, for example social responsibility and innovation. Bernstein (1986) described how comments by focus groups of managers can be captured along a number of dimensions including integrity, innovation, social responsibility, reliability, and imagination. Marwick and Fill (1995) show how the perception of different stakeholders can be compared along dimensions including quality, reliability, professionalism and cooperativeness. Openness emerges as a issue in ethical quality (Kaptein 1998). In the 1999 Yankelovich Partners Survey, the elements of a superior reputation were indicated as 'trustworthiness, high quality products and services, and reputation for innovation' (Winkleman 1999).

The emphasis within the reputation perspective has been on scales that are used to rank competing organizations. The most prominent is that from *Fortune* and similar scales used in surveys by the *Financial Times* and *Management Today*. The *Fortune* approach has been used as a starting point by Flatt and Kowalczyk (2000) who asked respondents to map fifty-four cultural attributes on to the eight attributes of the *Fortune* factors in order to explore the correspondence between the two constructs, although they did not do this in the context of named firms.

Brand personality

As we argued in Chapter 4, one way to understand the complexity of a brand is to use a metaphor. The most commonly used metaphor in branding is that of brand as person, the personification metaphor (King 1973; Hanby 1999). We pretend that the company is a person and draw parallels from our better understanding of people, including here that an organization, like a person, can have a personality. Typically the research approach used to assess brand personality is qualitative in nature. Whichever approach is used the process will normally start with a qualitative phase, where a small sample of customers or employees are asked to talk in general terms about the organization. During such unconstrained interviewing the important issues that need to be researched are revealed – at least in theory. The problem is that respondents are not always clear why they are satisfied or dissatisfied with an organization. It is also unlikely that any qualitative approach can guarantee to cover every possible issue.

Projective and other qualitative techniques

Reputation is a complex phenomenon, and measuring it is unlikely to be easy. Respondents to any market research are likely to be unfamiliar with the idea of thinking about a company's reputation. A standard technique in market research is that of 'projection'. The respondent is asked to pretend, to play a game, by, for example asking them to assume that the company being researched has 'come to life' as a human being. 'What newspaper would this person read? What car would he/she drive? Where would he/she go on holiday? If you were giving this person an annual appraisal what would you say to him/her? How old would this person be? What gender?' If the answers to these questions were, 'the *Financial Times*; a Jaguar; the Maldives; tell them to recognize that not everyone is rich; thirty-five years old; female', then you deduce what kind of image this company has. If the answers were 'doesn't read one; travels by public transport; stays at home; tell him to get a life; fifty-five going on seventy-five; male', then a totally different picture is evoked.

Another technique is to give respondents three organizations, say Microsoft, Apple, and IBM and to ask them if all three came to life as people which one would be the odd one out and why? The approach has the benefit of identifying what words or phrases people use to distinguish between organizations.

No qualitative technique can claim to be comprehensive or foolproof. It is unlikely that many respondents will be involved in the labour intensive process and the outcomes will be limited to the views of a small group. Even within the group there will be ideas that do not emerge on one occasion that might on another and so the results may not even reflect the views of the interview group. Qualitative research methods tend to be less popular among managers in America and Britain but very much the norm in countries including Italy, France, and Finland. The advantages are in the breadth of ideas that are produced rather than in their ability to provide a comprehensive view. Conversely the issue with quantitative research is that it can be too superficial because such research often relies upon a limited number of relatively simple questions.

Previous qualitative work has provided a wealth of words and phrases that could be useful in developing a Corporate Personality Scale. For example in Chapter 4 the following were identified in the context of brands of hair shampoo: natural, gentle, relaxed, quiet, conservative, active, sociable, young, cheap, happy and curious.

Quantitative measures

A number of attempts have been made to establish a more quantitative approach to measuring brand personality. Batra *et al.* (1993) started with the idea that the five dimensions of human personality could also apply to the personality of brands. They used Anderson's (1968) 555 human personality traits as a source, and three pairs of adjectives such as 'old' or 'young', 'masculine' or 'feminine' 'upscale' or 'downscale', added from the retail store personality literature. Their work identified seven factors assessed by thirty-five items. Another author to adapt a human personality scale into a brand personality scale was Biel (1993). He used twenty-eight personality descriptors, including 'family-oriented', 'responsible', 'rugged', 'peaceful', 'masculine', 'leader', 'gentle', 'feminine', and 'fancy'.

The Aaker scale

Aaker (1997) derived a generic scale to measure brand image. She used the personification metaphor and her scale for brand personality consists of

Table 6.3 The items and dimensions of the Aaker's (1997) scale

Sincerity	Excitement	Competence	Sophistication	Ruggedness
Down to earth	Daring	Reliable	Upper class	Outdoorsy
Family oriented	Trendy	Hard working	Glamorous	Masculine
Small town	Exciting	Secure	Good looking	Western
Honest	Spirited	Intelligent	Charming	Tough
Sincere	Cool	Technical	Feminine	Rugged
Real	Young	Corporate	Smooth	
Wholesome	Imaginative	Successful		
Original	Unique	Leader		
Cheerful	Up to date	Confident		
Sentimental	Independent			
Friendly	Contemporary			

forty-two items. These describe the personality of a brand along five dimensions, labelled: sincerity (11 items), competence (9 items), sophistication (6 items), excitement (11 items) and ruggedness (5 items) (see Table 6.3). The scale was developed from a much larger list of possible items drawn from the psychology literature, previous scales and original, qualitative research. The final scale was tested and re-tested on large samples of (American) respondents who were asked to assess the personality of product brands such as Diet Coke and Levi jeans, but also service and corporate brands such as MTV, Kmart, and CNN. In her questionnaire respondents were asked to imagine that the product, service, or corporate brand being assessed had come alive and to assess its personality on a five-point scale from strongly disagree to strongly agree.

The original work was sponsored by Levi-Strauss and Levi jeans was used in the research as a main example in developing and testing the scale. The ruggedness dimension is the weakest of the five and one that is associated with jeans (Keller 1998). There could be other dimensions more useful in assessing corporate personality. Limiting the number of dimensions to five could be taking the personification metaphor too far (human personality is held to have five main dimensions, the Big 5, see later). There is no theoretical reason why five dimensions should describe brand personality, indeed the more factors the more useful the scale, as brands are unlikely to be as similar or as homogenous as humans in their personality traits.

Aaker's scale contains a number of colloquial expressions (small town, outdoorsy) and words with specific meanings within American culture (cool, Western) which could be culturally specific (Samiee and Jeong 1994). For example, the term 'small town' appears in American English dictionaries, where it is defined as provincial or unsophisticated, but not in British English dictionaries. Other items may represent different ideas to respondents. For example 'original' might imply 'the first' to an American but 'unlike others' to those taught traditional English. The one major issue with any branding scale is that it is not designed to work with both customers and employees, let alone other stakeholders.

The business-to-business perspective

Reputation is important in a business-to-business context where the 'atmosphere' between organizations is seen as shaping the nature of transactions (Hakansson 1982: 21). Positive atmospheres are harmonious, are based on trust and cooperation (Ford 1997; Nielson 1998). Similar descriptors are common in the marketing channels' literature, where creating trust is seen as having an image for honesty and empathy (Kumar, Scheer and Steenkamp 1995).

The human personality perspective

Organizations are composed of people and so human personality should be a useful starting point for measures. A consensus is emerging that human personality can be described using the 'Big 5' dimensions, of extroversion, agreeableness, conscientiousness, neuroticism and openness to experience (Costa and McCrae 1992; Barrick and Mount 1991). The labels given to each dimension vary between authors, as do the items used to identify them.

Agreeableness reflects trust (Costa and McCrae 1995), something that is often used in assessing the reputation of companies. The dimension has also been labelled likeability, friendliness, social conformity, or love. It is negatively associated with aggression and arrogance (Barrick and Mount 1993). Extraversion is frequently associated with being sociable, gregarious, assertive, talkative, and active (Barrick and Mount 1991). Hogan (1986) sees extraversion as having two components, *ambition* (initiative, surgency, ambition, and impetuous) and *sociability* (sociable, exhibitionist, and expressive). Openness to experience has been interpreted as intellect and culture in the context of human personality (Barrick and Mount 1991; Digman 1990). Some traits that are associated with this dimension include: being imaginative, cultured, curious, original, broadminded, intelligent, and artistically sensitive (Barrick and Mount 1991) and a need for variety and unconventional values (McCrae and John 1992). Conscientiousness has also been labelled conformity or dependability. Some researchers claim that conscientiousness reflects mainly dependability, and as such, being careful, thorough, responsible, and organized (Barrick and Mount 1991). Digman (1990) also provides evidence suggesting that in addition to those traits, conscientiousness involves volitional variables, like hardworking, achievement oriented, and persevering. Many of the items associated with the dimensions of human personality appear relevant as descriptions of organizations.

It is worth pausing a second to consider the theoretical underpinnings for personality scales, either for humans or for brands. There are none. What psychologists have done in deriving their personality tests is to take the words or phrases we commonly use to describe human personality and put them into groups that have a similar meaning. There are literally thousands of words that can be used to describe human personality. All that the Big 5 does in assessing human personality when testing an applicant's suitability for a job, for example, is to use those words that have been found to assess the greatest differences between people in earlier research. There is no theoretical reason either why a relatively high or low score on any dimensions can be taken to mean anything other than that the person being tested is different from the average of everyone that has been tested earlier. Psychologists use norms to compare a subject's scores against to paint a picture of that individual. Studies have shown that certain personality dimensions are useful predictors of certain types of behaviour or success in certain activities. But quite often the results of studies aiming to associate even the most intuitively obvious associations, for example conscientiousness with success in a job, produce unclear or even conflicting results.

What a brand personality test will do then, but what it will *only* do, is provide a number of measures. If a database of measurements is available then the image of one brand can be compared against many others and it may be useful to know that its personality is very different from the average for other brands on one or more dimensions. Whether this is meaningful or useful depends upon whether that any dimension is associated with something important. For example if only one particular dimension co-relates with customer satisfaction, then exploring how to improve the brand's score on that dimension will be useful.

The Corporate Personality Scale

The development of our scale to measure both internal and external perspectives of reputation is described in detail in a number of academic publications, the first of which for example, Davies *et al.* (2001) offers a more technical description of its evolution, one that would not be appropriate to repeat here. What follows is an overview of the development work that continues to this day.

The approach we adopted to create a scale to measure both image and identity was similar to that used in human personality research and by Aaker (1997). We looked for traits derived from everyday language where a trait is defined as any distinguishable, relatively enduring way in which one object differs from others (Guilford 1973: 23). An organizational trait will also reflect that which is used or useful to distinguish one organization from another or which differentiates between the views of people about the same organization. This definition is similar to one definition of organizational identity as that which members believe to be central, enduring, and distinctive about their organization (Albert and Whetten 1985).

Pilot study

In a pilot phase we assembled nearly 100 items (words such as hardworking, concerned, arrogant, prestigious, leading) chosen from various sources but concentrating on those that appeared in more than one (such as innovative, competent, reliable, trustworthy and socially responsible). We used existing scales to identify possible descriptors of corporate personality. We refined and extended this list using focus groups and personal interviews asking respondents to describe organizations that they had worked for or of which they were customers. We content analysed the mission and vision statements of *Fortune* 500 companies' websites to assess which items appeared in material that is concerned to express 'corporate character' or 'personality'. We analysed the copy used in corporate advertising to ensure that we had reflected the main themes used to promote corporate image. We distilled all of these into what appeared to us to be a number of groups that previous work implied might be used to describe the personality of any organization. This produced a list of 114 items that appeared to describe organizations from both employee and customer perspectives.

We piloted a questionnaire on staff and students at two universities to screen the resulting list of 114 items. In the questionnaire respondents were asked to imagine that the organization they were assessing had 'come to life' as a human being. They were then asked to rate each word or phrase on a five-point scale from strongly agree to strongly disagree. Included in the student sample were a substantial number whose native language was not English, as we wished to eliminate any culturally specific items. Many of the interviews were conducted face to face, again to identify why any item might be retained or eliminated.

The resulting data was subjected to factor analysis with varimax rotation. Factor analysis is a mathematical technique that can be used to identify and understand any underlying 'factors' within, in our case, a longer list of words describing an organization. In practical terms it groups together words that produce a similar response in a survey, implying that the words or questions are measuring the same thing. Varimax rotation indicates that the factors being sought do not correlate with each other; in the jargon they are orthogonal. In total ninety-three items were retained after this phase. Many of the items that were eliminated were from the human personality literature such as 'patient', 'devoted', 'logical', 'outgoing', 'respectful', 'conscientious' and 'mature'.

Main study

Surveys were then conducted of the image and identity of nearly 50 business units of ten business organizations: three industrial services companies, four retailers, one bank, one manufacturer and one financial services company. The companies were chosen to include product and service providers, organizations representing high and low levels of customer involvement and both business to consumer and business-to-business markets. In each case customers were only surveyed if they had a close knowledge of the company (they were actual, not potential customers). As we were particularly interested in the customer interface in the context of Reputation Management, employees were interviewed only if they had a role that involved regular customer contact. The data from all surveys were pooled (including that from the pilot) for the final analyses. In total 4626 responses were obtained, of which 2565 were customers and 2061 customer facing employees.

Full data analysis

The database was factor analysed for all respondents and separately for customers and staff using Varimax rotation. It is important that the same factors we identified are relevant to both customers and to employees. The objectives of factor analysis are always to represent the data in as few dimensions as possible (parsimony) while identifying factors that are meaningful. Five major factors and two minor factors emerged from the retained items, the last two with only three items each.

We called the seven factors (in order of importance): agreeableness, enterprise, competence, chic, ruthlessness, machismo and informality. We selected labels that appeared to us to capture the essence of the items that constituted each factor. The Cronbach alpha measure was used as the main measure of reliability and the figures for the individual dimensions were: 0.93, 0.91, 0.91, 0.86, 0.80, 0.62, 0.60 respectively. Reliability is concerned with how coherent a scale has been produced. A perfectly coherent scale would consist of the same word repeated say 10 times and would have an alpha score of 1. In other words the response pattern to each item in the scale is the same. Researchers try to obtain a high score for the Cronbach alpha statistic without producing scales of synonyms that have no breadth or colour. The first five factors had reliabilities above the normally accepted critical point of 0.7 (Nunally 1978). They were then subjected to trait analysis (each factor was re-analysed using factor analysis and non-orthogonal rotation to subdivide the factor into any useful components). Items loading on to more than one trait were eliminated. The lists of factors and traits and our naming of them are shown in the figures below.

Each factor was retested using confirmatory factor analysis. This is a further test of the coherence of the scale, this time aiming to identify whether each item contributes something uniquely to the scale. In each case measures of fit (GFI, AGFI, and NFI exceeding 0.95) showed that the measures were acceptable statistically (Hulland, Chow and Lam 1996; Schumacker and Lomax 1996; Jaccard and Wan 1996). The five main factors contain fourteen facets and, with the addition of machismo and informality, the core scale consists of sixteen facets in total and forty-nine items. Tests of reliability are used to assess whether a scale is fit for purpose. In our case the results were very encouraging.

Further tests were made. Factor congruences levels for each factor were acceptable for the database divided randomly, and by gender. This means that the factors gave a similar response for people of different gender or ones randomly chosen from the list. The factor structures were compared for the customer and employee data and found to be the same. In other words both groups would describe organizations using the same words. The goodness of fit

Table 6.4 The seven dimensions of corporate personality

Agreeableness	Enterprise	Competence	Chic	Ruthlessness	Machismo	Informality
Cheerful	Cool	Reliable	Charming	Arrogant	Masculine	Casual
Pleasant	Trendy	Secure	Stylish	Aggressive	Tough	Simple
Open	Young	Hardworking	Elegant	Selfish	Rugged	Easy going
Straightforward	Imaginative	Ambitious	Prestigious	Inward looking		
Concerned	Up to date	Achievement oriented	Exclusive	Authoritarian		
Reassuring	Exciting	Leading	Refined	Controlling		
Supportive	Innovative	Technical	Snobby			
Agreeable	Extrovert	Corporate	Elitist			
Honest	Daring					
Sincere						
Trustworthy						
Socially responsible						

measures for the staff and customer data were similar with slightly better fit for customer data on competence and ruthlessness.

Satisfaction

Reputation and customer satisfaction have been seen as interlinked (Anderson and Sullivan 1993; Anderson and Fornell 1994: 253; Andreassen and Lindestad 1998: 82). Any valid measure of reputation should be able to identify such linkages. For both employee and customer satisfaction was defined as overall satisfaction with the organization, rather than with any aspect thereof (e.g. Wanous and Lawler 1972: 96). The four-item measure included both emotional and rational dimensions (Oliver 1997; Naumann and Giel 1995: 253) and the same items were used to assess the satisfaction of both customers and employees. The satisfaction measure yielded a Cronbach alpha of 0.85 overall with a higher figure for staff (0.9) than for employees (0.8). The CFA fit indices were above 0.95 for GFI, CFI, and NFI.

Each of the seven dimensions of corporate personality correlated significantly with satisfaction for both staff and customers. Agreeableness and competence were the two most strongly correlated dimensions. Stepwise regression showed that all dimensions contributed significantly to explaining the variation in the satisfaction data for either staff or customers or both. Chic did not add significantly to the explanation of staff satisfaction, while enterprise did not add significantly to the explanation of customer satisfaction. Agreeableness and competence accounted for the majority of variation in both cases.

At the level of the individual organization, the dimensions varied in their relative importance in explaining satisfaction. For example in the case of one fashion retailer, chic was the most important dimension in explaining customer satisfaction, while in the case of a department store it was competence. Generally agreeableness was the most important dimension, being the dimension explaining the most variation in the satisfaction data for twelve of the fifteen organizations.

Discussions with stakeholders

The results of our work were discussed with the managers, employees, and customers of the organizations we surveyed as a further test of face validity for the factors. The process often took the form of a workshop where groups were presented with the overall profile for an organization and asked to interpret the results. Respondents could relate to each dimension and the personality

Table 6.5 Correlation with satisfaction

	Agreeableness	Enterprise	Competence	Chic	Ruthlessness	Informality	Machismo
Staff	0.665	0.486	0.659	0.316	−0.243	0.062	0.376
P<	0.000	0.000	0.000	0.000	0.000	0.003	0.000
Customer	0.572	0.301	0.543	0.340	−0.194	0.051	0.290
P<	0.000	0.000	0.000	0.000	0.000	0.005	0.000

profiles and the results prompted a large amount of feedback. The overall scores for agreeableness and ruthlessness and the scores for the individual items defining them tended to create the most comment. Respondents were asked to suggest explanations for any high or low scores. Predominantly the explanations centred on examples of micro behaviours by employees. If an organization's culture can be defined as 'the way we do things around here', then the measures appeared to reflect the respective cultures of the organizations we had surveyed.

The seven pillars of corporate personality

The dimensions of what we can call 'corporate personality' reflect, inevitably, the content of scales established in the disciplines we consulted for our original list of items.

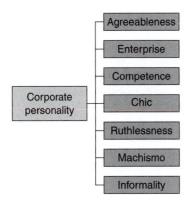

Figure 6.3 Scale to assess internal and external views of reputation.

Agreeableness

The importance of agreeableness reflects an emphasis in the branding and reputation literatures on trust and social responsibility. The result sheds light on the long-standing debate as to whether organizations should seek to be socially responsible, as their primary economic role is to make returns for the shareholders, who may wish to be philanthropic with their own money but on their own terms (Friedman 1970; Mulligan 1992).

That socially responsible is closely associated with trustworthy within the dimension of agreeableness, and agreeableness correlates strongly with satisfaction, indicates that being seen to be socially responsible is something that enhances the reputation of an organization. It is not now an option for profit seeking organizations. Being seen as a good corporate citizen helps build the intangible asset that is reputation. A good reputation in turn helps to attract and retain both employees and customers. It makes any stakeholder more forgiving, more willing to ignore any mistake. Social responsibility is now an essential aspect of corporate character. It is associated in the scale with being honest, sincere and trustworthy. In other words being socially responsible adds to a reputation for integrity.

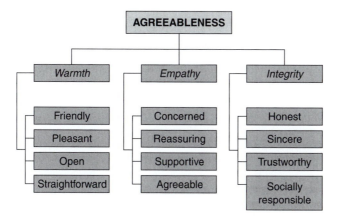

Figure 6.4 Agreeableness.

Agreeableness is also a key dimension of human personality. It is seen as the antithesis of being aggressive and arrogant in the human personality literature (Barrick and Mount 1993), but in the organizational context both of these traits load into a separate factor, labelled here as ruthlessness. The similarity of the dimensions identified for organizations suggests the potential for an organization to be seen as more agreeable if it hires customer facing employees with a high score on the equivalent human personality dimension.

Enterprise

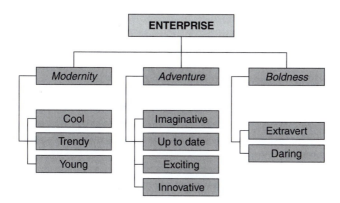

Figure 6.5 Enterprise.

The dimension of enterprise echoes the human personality dimension of extraversion but the enterprising organization is also seen as innovative and exciting, the former trait being frequently mentioned as a positive indicator of corporate reputation. The association of being seen as young with the factor (together with the items of cool and trendy labelled here as the modernity facet) is also interesting. It appears that if it wishes to be seen as enterprising the organization may be advised to employ younger rather than older people as customer facing staff, an observation that raises issues of ageism and equal opportunities in employment.

Competence

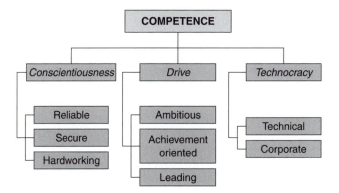

Figure 6.6 Competence.

The competence dimension is almost identical to the dimension of the same name in Aaker's (1997) brand personality scale, even down to the facet level. The same dimension appears relevant to both corporate and individual brands and to identity as well as to image. Competence was also the second most useful dimension in explaining staff and customer satisfaction. The dimension is clearly relevant to both contexts. Organizations should consider this dimension carefully for both their corporate and product images.

Ruthlessness

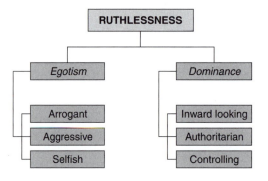

Figure 6.7 Ruthlessness.

Ruthlessness is the one negatively valenced dimension identified here. It correlated negatively with both staff and customer satisfactions but more strongly with the latter. It reflects the individual items identified in previous work in the organizational behaviour, particularly in the concept of organizational totalitarianism (Schwartz 1987) and in the reputation literatures, but the items and the dimension are not apparent in the product branding literature. As in human personality, organizations can have less desirable aspects to their corporate personalities. Inward looking, the opposite of extraversion in human personality helps to describe a different concept in the context of an organization. Employees often associated high scores on both facets with the way individual managers behaved towards them. Customers not surprisingly tended to focus on examples of behaviours by customer facing employees.

Chic

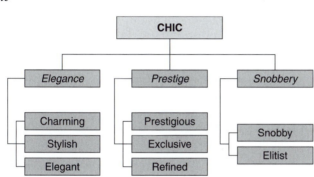

Figure 6.8 Chic.

The Chic dimension was relatively important for some of the retail organizations in our survey. The dimension is very similar to that labelled as sophistication in Aaker (1997). One particular item in Aaker's scale 'feminine' was however seen as sexist by a number of respondents to our survey and did not load within any factor defined here. The same underlying idea is probably underpinning both chic and sophistication measures. In the context of an organization, the dimension contains more emphasis on prestige. Both employees and customers of the companies we surveyed appeared to value their associations with a prestigious organization. There is a less attractive side to the dimension, that of snobbishness. Organizations that wish to emphasize chicness in their image need to be concerned that this does not alienate those potential customers and employees who do not wish to be seen themselves as snobbish.

Machismo and Informality

We have chosen to retain two minor factors, machismo and informality, even though they were not strongly defined and did not explain much of the variance in the data set. Machismo is similar to Aaker's weakest factor, ruggedness,

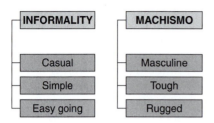

Figure 6.9 Machismo and informality.

and the latter could have been over-defined in the original work because of the emphasis on the Levi brand in the empirical research. In work within other cultures other factors, such as peacefulness and passion, have been identified as more important than ruggedness (Aaker *et al.* 2000). In identifying dimensions of corporate, brand or human personality the factors that emerge are to an extent pre-determined by the items included in the original source list. In our case this reflected the content of a number of literatures and the results of original qualitative research, but this does not guarantee that potentially useful dimensions have not been excluded. Any resulting dimensions are also merely an aggregation of words that are used (by customers and employees) to describe corporations. In different cultures different dimensions of personality may also be more or less important. It is then essential in our view that seemingly minor factors are not ignored as they may prove to be useful in other contexts.

Stakeholders saw both machismo and informality as relevant when the data were presented to them. Both dimensions appeared to have face validity. The idea of a more 'informal' organization evokes a picture of a company that allows its employees to 'dress down' and to address each other and customers informally. Interactions between customer and employee are rule bound. Businesses such as Swedish furniture company Ikea emphasize their informal culture in their corporate advertising. As a result, staff might be seen as more approachable. Machismo reflects a different type of organization, one that is tough with both its staff and with customers. In our survey an organization in the construction industry scored high on this dimension.

The scale has been shown to be reliable for both customers and customer facing employees of a diverse sample of organizations. As such it offers potential for comparing the image and identity of organizations, something that has been lacking in the reputation literature and specifically in the context of exploring linkages between image and identity. The data offers a basis for comparison between the image and identity of organizations in similar or different sectors. Linkages between image, identity and other variables such as the loyalty of both employees and customers can now be explored.

The scale was retested in ten other organizations. The same factors emerged indicating that the factors we originally identified are robust. In practice we tend to use a larger number of scale items in our work with organizations but the same seven dimensions emerge each time. We are also working to translate the scale into different languages and to use different methods of presenting the scale items. Finally we have used the scale to assess the views of other stakeholders, suppliers and investors. In each case the scale has proven a useful and reliable measure.

Using the scale

One of the more effective ways of presenting the main findings of any study are to use the type of diagrams in Figures 6.10 and 6.11. These are the results

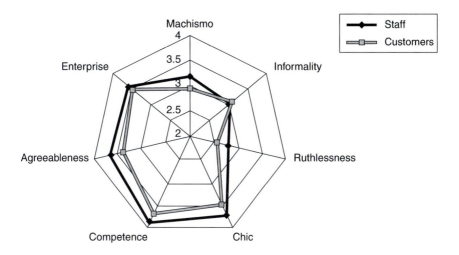

Figure 6.10 The Corporate Personality Scale applied to a service organization.

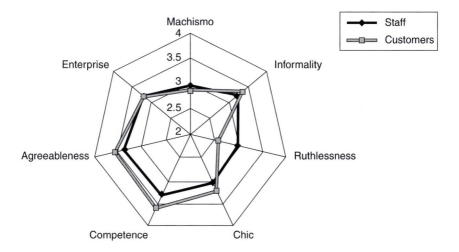

Figure 6.11 The Corporate Personality Scale applied to a similar organization.

of work with two European service organizations in an identical line of business. Despite being in the same business sector, their personalities are very different. In particular, in the first example, Figure 6.10, the profile as seen by staff is generally superior to that seen by customers. In the second the reverse is true.

In both diagrams the scores for each dimension are the average for the factors on the 5 point scale. Thus an average of 3 indicates a score in the middle of the scale, 4 high and 2 low.

If image and identity co-vary, in other words they move together, and one affects the other then one of two things could happen, either the customer and staff profiles will average over time or one will follow the other. It would be more logical if the staff view led the customer view. If this is the case then in the first example the customer view will improve and in the second it will go down. The same effect would occur even if the two views affected each other.

Summary

There are many ways of measuring corporate reputation. We feel that we have improved upon what was already there by developing a scale that can assess both internal and external views of reputation simultaneously. What is important in the scale is not so much the individual items but the 5 main and two minor dimensions. As work in this area develops others will find different and perhaps better words to describe the 7 dimensions but they are unlikely to find a very different set of dimensions to describe corporate personality. Because the scale contains the same items for both image and identity direct comparisons can be made between the two. Thus if image and identity do affect each other then managers can assess their situation and do something about it. How this is done will form the content of the next chapter, an extended case study of one organization.

7 The management of image and identity

An extended case study to illustrate the management of image and identity.

The Corporate Reputation Chain

The main purpose of this chapter is to use the Corporate Personality Scale and the Corporate Reputation Chain to illustrate how reputation is managed using a study of one of the organizations we have worked with. The chain, Figure 7.1, represents an ideal, a series of linkages that should be present, but all too often in our experience are not. At the heart of the chain are the key elements of image and identity.

Two of the more important questions in the management of corporate reputation are 'Who are you?', the question most likely to be asked by an external stakeholder and 'Who are we?', the question most likely to be asked by an internal stakeholder. The first question concerns the external image of the organization. The second concerns the way employees view the organization they work for, its identity (Chun 2001).

Identity and image as we have seen are believed to be linked, either through their mutual dependency on factors including the company culture, mission, and strategy (Hatch and Schultz 1997), or because they share a common core

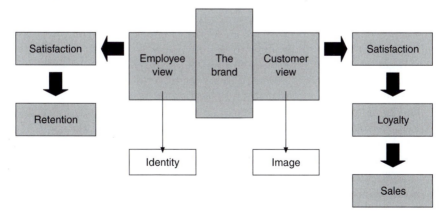

Figure 7.1 The Corporate Reputation Chain.

(Fombrun 1996) or because any gaps between what a company is and what it is seen to be, can be a source of concern (Davies and Miles 1998). The picture such ideas present is of organizations needing to and trying to make the way customers and employees see them as similar as possible, while at the same time being seen in as positive a way as possible. As the aim of any commercial organization in promoting such initiatives is to improve company performance both financially and in terms of employee and customer satisfaction, there should be evidence that harmonizing image and identity is beneficial to both. The second purpose of this chapter is to explore such 'harmony' between image and identity in the context of a single organization, a relatively large retail business. By 'harmony' we mean two things, whether there are demonstrable linkages between image and identity and whether and how an organization is managing such linkages. This chapter provides a useful overview of how we see the application of the chain in practice and how reputation can be managed as a consequence. Some issues are picked up again in later chapters. The heart of the study is a survey, of employees and customers, using the corporate personality questionnaire explained in the previous chapter.

The context

The organization featured in this chapter is one of the world's largest retailers. It achieves a high ranking both nationally and internationally in surveys of reputation. Its main product area is that of everyday products (fresh and packaged food, toiletries, paper products). The company operates globally but the data we present here is from their British operation. In that country they manage over 300 stores each trading under the same corporate name.

In the last fifty years there has been a dramatic change in the structure and nature of British retailing. Fifty years ago independent retailers dominated the market. Today the market is dominated by a limited number of multiple retailers. They are highly centralized (decision making is at a head office level; stores are similar with similar or identical product ranges) and their buying power means that they can obtain preferential prices from suppliers. This in turn means a cost and price advantage over the smaller independent stores. This trend is particularly obvious among 'superstore' retailers, companies selling a wide range of everyday products from relatively large stores, typically of 3–4000 square metres in size. Although not as physically large as hypermarkets, the main retail format in Continental Europe, superstores sell a full range of food, including fresh produce, everyday items such as toiletries and, increasingly, other non-foods such as clothing and electrical products. The stores are quite similar in design and layout to North American grocery stores, but a marked difference from North American stores is in the strength and role of own branded products. British retailers of everyday products sell a substantial proportion, some 30 to 40 per cent of sales, of products under their own names, so called own brands. What is also different about their operations is that the pricing strategy for these own branded products is not, as it is in many countries, cheap and cheerful. At times own brands are sold at higher price points than the brands marketed by manufacturers. The reputation of the retailer is such that customers trust products with the retailer's name on the package much as they would any manufacturer's brand.

To any newcomer to Britain the stores of the main superstore operators would appear very similar. They have a similar size and layout. The product range is similar. Prices are very similar. Collectively the six largest grocery chains account for more than 60 per cent of the market (a situation that has prompted investigations by the Competition Commission and its predecessors). Their market share collectively has grown quickly as they have all moved to build new stores mainly on the edge of towns or in the suburbs of the large cities. Whereas in the past shoppers might not have much in the way of a choice of superstore locally, it would be normal for anyone travelling say to work in a city centre to drive past five or six superstores and to have two or three within easy reach of their homes. There is talk of 'superstore saturation'.

There is little obvious difference between what the main retailers sell and how they sell it other than the name above the store. In such circumstances it is important commercially for each retailer to retain some positive and differentiated image in the minds of customers and potential employees. The company we focus on here had experienced strong sales growth against both the entire market but also against its nearest competitors. Figure 7.2 shows its sales growth indexed against its nearest rivals in a sector that was showing strong overall growth in itself. The company naturally wanted to see this continue and believed that this was possible by managing its identity and image.

Managing values

During the period of the study, we were able to talk with senior management about the phenomena we were investigating. In their view, what we were assessing in our survey of employees was closely associated with the culture of the organization and this had been changing. One informal survey of store managers fifteen years earlier, had included the question, 'If you had not become a retail store manager, what career would you have liked to follow?' The two most common responses had been the police and the armed services. In a similar

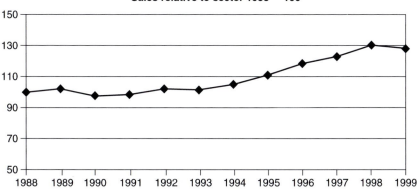

Figure 7.2 Sales performance.

survey at the time of our study the answers were more varied and included 'starting my own business' and 'sales'. (However there was still a high proportion citing the services and the police.)

These responses paint a picture of a middle management cadre who value a structured environment and one where people look to be told what to do and then do it. However the company wanted to change and to evolve a less centralized, more responsive culture, one that was more customer oriented. Companies can have one or more of a number of orientations, towards sales, product, operations or the market (Lynch 1997). A market orientation is more likely and more likely to be effective, where market growth is low and there is little fundamental difference between the offerings of the leading competitors. This is the situation in superstore retailing in Britain (Liu and Davies 1995). A market orientation is not a guarantee of profitability but is advocated as a general philosophy in the search for improved market performance (Kohli and Jaworski 1990; Narver and Slater 1990). An extreme form of market orientation is customer orientation, one where the company is organized to find out how the customer would like the business to operate and then endeavours to make profit from whatever the customer wants. Such an orientation requires a high degree of contact between customers and customer facing employees, and the empowerment of these employees to adapt to the needs of customers, rather than necessarily stick to a set of centrally defined rules. It is a cultural issue as well as a strategic one (Slater and Narver 1994). A checklist of market orientation is shown in Figure 7.3. When assessing themselves against the list managers of this retailer would typically rate their company as being only 70 per cent market orientated, believing instead that the main focus in the organization in recent years had been on operations and within this on logistics, in other words ensuring that products were in stock and on display.

Their self-ratings were even lower on a second checklist designed to assess customer orientation, Figure 7.4. While managers felt that staff had a stake in the business through a highly successful share scheme, they did not feel that customers had much influence on the way the business was run. Staff had to work within a clear set of guidelines. Indeed a change of senior manager during the time of our study led to a greater emphasis on 'conformity'. One of the issues identified in the discussions that followed was that managers of large stores spent very little time with customers. Even when they did, the contact was often centred on managing a complaint rather than understanding what cus-

---

- There is direct customer contact at many levels in the organization.
- Market research on who the core customer is and on the market structure is widely available and acted upon.
- Managers receive and act upon regular customer satisfaction surveys.
- The company is responsive to customer complaints and suggestions.
- The company image is regularly monitored.
- Aspects of quality relevant to the marketplace are regularly monitored.
- The company conducts regular surveys of competitive prices and services.
- Rewards within the organization are based on performance with customers.

Figure 7.3 A checklist to measure market orientation.

- The business is led by someone who is a fanatic about the customer and able to model the desired behaviours.
- Customer facing employees are empowered to react to what the customer wants.
- Employees have a stake in the business (usually share or other form of ownership).
- Employees feel trusted to run the business.
- Customers are regularly asked for ideas as to how the business should be run.

Figure 7.4 A checklist to measure customer orientation.

tomers might value in their store or want to see changed. The main points of contact with customers was with checkout staff and those who ran the counter service sections, the bakery, delicatessen, and fish counters. They were among the lowest paid staff in the organization and many would not see their role as providing feedback to management as to how the business might change.

Nevertheless the retailer's senior management wanted a change to a more customer friendly culture, one where power was more widely distributed. To help to manage such a cultural change, the company had defined a set of corporate values and promoted these through training and by introducing a new employee magazine designed specifically to promote the new values.

Training included a video featuring a checkout operator, the role with the most customer contact in most retail organizations. The opening scenes showed her in her personal life and having an argument with her boyfriend. Later, at work, she treats customers in an off hand way because she is still absorbed by her own personal problems. Her *alter ego* then sees something of her customers' own private lives and the day-to-day problems that they have had to contend with. An elderly woman, clearly less than affluent, had taken her husband out for a meal where the quality of the food had been unacceptable. A man had waited at home to receive delivery of an expensive electrical item, only to find it damaged. Her own attitude changes and, despite her own problems, she endeavours to bring a little happiness into the lives of her own customers. She is rewarded in the video by an improvement in her own personal life, when her boyfriend appears, flowers in hand. The values the video promoted include those of empathy and friendliness showing the interaction between customer satisfaction and employee satisfaction with relevant background music. Responsibility for promoting these values was vested in the human resources function. What was interesting to us was the similarity between this value set and that being promoted outside the company by the marketing function and labelled as the company's brand values (see Figure 7.5).

The two functions in the company were working towards a similar set of 'values', one inside and one outside of the company. They wanted energy and innovation to be valued inside the company and for innovation and modernity to be associated with their corporate name in the marketplace. Inside the company they wanted the principle of looking after staff, so that they would look after customers to be valued and at the same time they wanted to be seen by customers as being friendly and helpful. Inside the company they were looking for trust and respect between employees. The final line in the marketing department's statement on brand values was that in projecting the list of

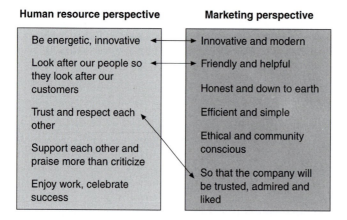

Human resource perspective

Be energetic, innovative

Look after our people so they look after our customers

Trust and respect each other

Support each other and praise more than criticize

Enjoy work, celebrate success

Marketing perspective

Innovative and modern

Friendly and helpful

Honest and down to earth

Efficient and simple

Ethical and community conscious

So that the company will be trusted, admired and liked

Figure 7.5 Internal and external values.

values, the company would be trusted, admired, and liked. But the company's management had not been consciously working on making the two sets of values similar. They had been aiming intuitively to align the two but now realized they needed to make the process more overt.

The research stage

Our study was concerned primarily with the more formal measurement of what was happening within the organization. To assess image and identity in a quantitative way so that we could explore the harmony between image and identity, we used the Corporate Personality Scale described in Chapter 6. Respondents were asked to imagine that the organization 'has come to life as a human being' and to rate the company persona on a five-point scale from strongly disagree that the item described the persona to strongly agree. Many of the adjectives used to describe the company values are included in the questionnaire.

A number of other questions were added to the questionnaire, including four designed to assess satisfaction, details of employee's length of service, respondent demographics, frequency of shopping for customers and measures of customer loyalty. We aimed to assess which aspects of image and identity were co-relating with the satisfaction of customers and employees respectively.

We measured the identity and image of the organization by surveying a random sample of up to fifty customers exiting from each of eight stores (total sample 385) and a sample of a similar number of customer facing employees from the same stores (total sample 367). The choice of customer facing employees was made, as it appeared logical in assessing whether image and identity were harmonized, to analyse identity from the perspective of those most in contact with customers. To assess the most pertinent managerial perspective of identity, 327 middle managers were surveyed. They were predominantly store or regional managers. For customers, the interviews were conducted in person with shoppers leaving the stores to ensure both a high response and that the respondents were actually customers of the retailer. For the eight stores financial and other performance data were obtained such that any co-relations between image identity and performance could be identified.

Results

The first test assesses whether the scale is relevant to the context we are examining. Table 7.1 shows the co-relation coefficients between the measure of satisfaction and the scores for each of the seven factors for each of the three groups in our study. Most co-relations are very high and all were significant at above 95 per cent levels of confidence other than machismo.

There are some marked similarities and differences in the pattern of data between the three columns, particularly between the store manager data and the data for customer facing employees and customers. Agreeableness is the dimension of corporate personality most highly correlated with satisfaction in each of the three groups. Store employees appear to be more concerned with all seven dimensions than are the customers and store managers. Store managers showed less concern with enterprise whereas customers and customer facing employees appear to value this dimension. Store managers have to achieve specific weekly or monthly targets based upon a balanced scorecard. So it is interesting to see how competence is not in fact highly correlated with satisfaction. This says a lot about the pressure of being constantly evaluated by their store's sales performance. All three groups are dissatisfied by ruthlessness.

If there is any causal linkage between image and identity, particularly between the views of customer facing employees and customers, then any gaps between the two might be of concern. This may be critical on any dimension of reputation that correlates highly with customer satisfaction. The average scores for each dimension of image and identity are shown in Table 7.2 and Figure 7.6. (Our scale has five points, thus the maximum average mark is 5 and the minimum is 1.) The views of managers and customer facing staff are similar but they differ from those of customers. Customers saw the company as more informal and agreeable but less ruthless, competent, and enterprising. Agreeableness is highly correlated with satisfaction and the overall scores are similar for each of the three groups (see Tables 7.1 and 7.2). The small gap between customer and employee scores for agreeableness may not then be an issue.

Table 7.1 Co-relation of corporate personality dimensions with satisfaction of customers and staff

Factor	Store employees (367)	Customers (385)	Store managers (327)
Agreeableness	0.703	0.593	0.538
Enterprise	0.580	0.458	0.235
Competence	0.477	0.407	0.281
Ruthlessness	−0.293	−0.160	−0.260
Chic	0.455	0.366	0.129*
Informality	0.207	0.185	0.137*
Machismo	0.199	0.081**	−0.091**

All are significant at 0.01 level but * at 0.05 level, **not significant at 0.05 level (2 tailed test).

Table 7.2 Average scores for each personality dimension

Factor	Staff (367)	Customers (385)	Managers (327)
Agreeableness	3.52	3.68	3.67
Enterprise	3.29	3.08	3.63
Competence	3.89	3.69	4.23
Ruthlessness	3.02	2.59	3.03
Chic	3.09	2.83	2.75
Informality	3.05	3.49	2.84
Machismo	2.95	2.63	3.26

However the gaps between the scores for enterprise and competence (the second and third most highly correlated dimensions with satisfaction) are more obvious issues. In both dimensions, the internal, identity, scores are higher than for the external view, of image, and if identity and image do co-vary then image could well improve as the staff demonstrate that they are 'reliable, hardworking' and that the experience for customers is 'exciting'.

However it may be that customers do not appreciate that staff are working well and hard, either because they do not see the work behind the scenes, or that what the customer values is not actually being delivered by staff. Customers rated informality more highly than did staff, who do not see their employer's style as 'casual and easygoing'. It is possible that staff views and attitudes could affect customer views and reduce the latter scores.

As informality is not highly correlated with satisfaction then this may not be as important an issue as with the ruthlessness scores. Staff score the company much higher than do customers but if customers start to sense the same behaviours that create this impression among staff, then customer satisfaction may

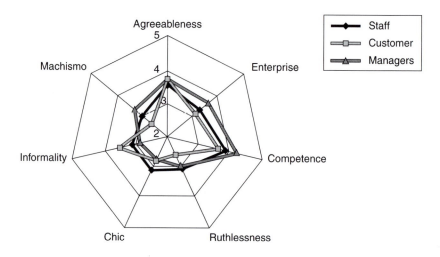

Figure 7.6 Average identity and image scores.

well fall. Much depends upon whether there is a causal relationship between image and identity as implied in the reputation literature.

A statistical technique called stepwise regression was used to assess the main drivers of satisfaction for each of the three groups in our study. The technique aims to explain as much of the variation in the satisfaction scores as it can, but using the least number of the seven personality dimensions to do so. It excludes any variable if it does not add to an understanding of the variation in satisfaction and is therefore useful in identifying which variables are the most important in explaining satisfaction. The most important are likely to be the ones actually driving satisfaction. Agreeableness emerged in each case as the most important dimension of corporate personality, accounting for 48 per cent of the variation in satisfaction among staff, 35 per cent among customers and 32 per cent among managers. Combining agreeableness with enterprise, 52 per cent of the variation in Employee satisfaction and 39 per cent of that in customer satisfaction are explained. No other personality dimension added significantly to the explanation of satisfaction for this organization.

Branch data

Because we gathered data from eight different branches we can gain some insights into any causality between satisfaction and image and identity by examining differences between branches. Table 7.3 shows the outcome of stepwise

Table 7.3 Satisfaction of drivers at branch level

Branch	Whether staff or customer	Rank order of dimension	Dimension explaining satisfaction	R square
A	Staff member	1	Agreeableness	0.62
	Customer	1	Agreeableness	0.46
B	Staff member	1	Enterprise	0.44
		2	and Ruthlessness	0.66
	Customer	1	Agreeableness	0.34
		2	and Informality	0.42
C	Staff member	1	Enterprise	0.49
	Customer	1	Agreeableness	0.36
D	Staff member	1	Agreeableness	0.55
	Customer	1	Agreeableness	0.44
E	Staff member	1	Competence	0.43
		2	and Agreeableness	0.53
	Customer	1	Agreeableness	0.54
F	Staff member	1	Agreeableness	0.46
		2	and Chic	0.56
	Customer	1	Agreeableness	0.30
G	Staff member	1	Agreeableness	0.49
	Customer	1	Agreeableness	0.32
		2	and Chic	0.41
H	Staff member	1	Agreeableness	0.70
		2	and Enterprise	0.80
	Customer	1	Enterprise	0.27

Table 7.4 Average scores of the seven factors at branch level

		A	B	C	D	E	F	G	H
Staff	Agreeableness	3.43	3.73	3.64	3.45	3.66	3.41	3.44	3.23
	Enterprise	3.27	3.37	3.27	3.31	3.42	3.16	3.25	3.23
	Competence	3.94	4.01	3.90	3.79	4.04	3.83	3.89	3.53
	Ruthlessness	2.96	2.87	3.00	3.02	2.93	3.15	3.15	3.15
	Chic	2.88	3.10	3.11	3.08	3.16	3.03	3.19	3.17
	Informality	2.98	3.23	3.07	3.15	2.94	2.98	3.01	3.07
	Machismo	2.85	2.81	2.90	3.01	2.99	3.02	2.93	3.17
Customer	Agreeableness	3.68	3.81	3.56	3.68	3.76	3.68	3.58	3.64
	Enterprise	3.28	3.10	2.94	3.20	3.34	2.87	2.96	2.96
	Competence	3.81	3.73	3.65	3.74	3.73	3.59	3.68	3.56
	Ruthlessness	2.64	2.59	2.57	2.52	2.62	2.54	2.64	2.57
	Chic	2.89	2.82	2.72	3.02	3.06	2.74	2.67	2.76
	Informality	3.41	3.51	3.48	3.51	3.47	3.61	3.26	3.66
	Machismo	2.78	2.53	2.59	2.68	2.77	2.47	2.53	2.69

regression for each store, between the average satisfaction of staff and customers and the seven dimensions of corporate personality. Only the dimensions that were retained in the model are shown.

Agreeableness was the most significant predictor of staff satisfaction in most branches except branch C and D. In particular, agreeableness explains 62 per cent of the variation in satisfaction at Branch A and 70 per cent at Branch H. Branch H was located in a down-market area and its average agreeableness score is the lowest among the branches (Table 7.4). In other words, differences between the levels of staff satisfaction in the eight stores can be explained by differences in their rating of the personality dimensions. Ruthlessness, enterprise, and competence were important in some stores.

Considering customer satisfaction, agreeableness is also one of the best factors to explain satisfaction in seven of the eight branches. Enterprise was also important. Chic and informality were important in some branches. However the importance of agreeableness is highlighted yet again.

The relationship between identity and image was also tested at the level of the branch through co-relation, Figure 7.7. Customer and employee scores correlated significantly ($R^2 = 0.518$). In other words if customers marked the store high on one variable and low on another then so did employees. The R statistic measures the amount of variation explained by the co-relation. Its maximum value is 1 where 100 per cent of the variation is explained. In this case 52 per cent of the variation between image and identity is explained by the co-relation. In other words if image is driven by identity, the customer view depending on the attitude of staff and the behaviours this promotes, then half of the store's image is down to the view of staff.

In reality, the two views might well depend upon another intervening variable, for example the store design and all we can claim at this stage is that we cannot disprove that image and identity are linked. There is then some support for the idea that image and identity are linked. The relative importance given to each is similar for each branch. However, it is still difficult to be sure of any causality.

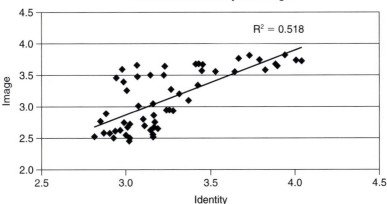

Figure 7.7 Correlation of identity and image.

Financial performance

There was a significant relationship between the year on year sales growth for each store and the average customer satisfaction scores (p = 0.038) explaining 43 per cent of the variation in the data. There were no significant co-relations between financial performance and any individual dimensions of corporate image. There were however co-relations between average customer satisfaction in each store and average customer agreeableness (p = 0.008), enterprise (p = 0.001), and chic (p = 0.007). This implies that satisfaction drives performance and it in turn is driven by image as we proposed in our model of reputation, the reputation chain, Figure 7.1.

Employee satisfaction did not co-relate with financial performance, but did with various dimensions of identity, averaged for each store, agreeableness (p = 0.01), informality (p = 0.008), enterprise (p = 0.082) and negatively with ruthlessness (p = 0.058). There was no clear co-relation between employee and customer satisfaction, which is odd as the maxim of 'happy staff equals happy customers' is intuitively attractive and forms a key component of many models of service effectiveness (Heskett *et al.* 1997). However the data did contain one outlier and if this data point was removed then a significant co-relation did exist (p = 0.1). Any link is likely not be direct, as we suggest in our model. Other links in the chain have to be in place for there to be any statistical linkage between staff and customer satisfaction. We return to this issue in a later chapter.

Image then co-relates with performance, but only via customer satisfaction. It is satisfied customers that create profitable businesses, but an analysis of image can indicate why one business is more profitable than another. In this case the answer is often that one branch is seen as more 'agreeable' than another.

Traits of agreeableness

The Corporate Personality Scale contains seven dimensions. The more extensive dimensions (our Big 5) can be subdivided into a number of traits. The most
important dimension is that of agreeableness. This has three traits labelled:
warmth (friendly, pleasant, open and straightforward), empathy (concerned,
reassuring, supportive and agreeable) and integrity (honest, sincere, socially
responsible and trustworthy). Correlations were made with each trait to identify
what within agreeableness was driving satisfaction.

At the level of the individual respondent, satisfaction correlated slightly
higher with integrity and lower with warmth. For customers, the co-relations
were almost identical in significance. For managers, warmth was slightly below
the other two facets in significance, Table 7.5. All co-relations were significant
(at $p < 0.001$). Using stepwise regression, integrity and empathy accounted for
48 per cent of the variation in staff satisfaction, 37 per cent for customers and
24 per cent for managers. Warmth would appear to be somewhat less important
than either empathy or integrity. However at the level of the eight stores, the
average staff views of warmth ($p > 0.000$) co-related more strongly than for
empathy ($p = 0.001$) and integrity ($p = 0.009$) with satisfaction. For customers
the co-relations were similar ($p = 0.008$, 0.012 and 0.018 respectively), with
empathy being more important in explaining differences between the average
satisfaction scores for each store. Stepwise regression confirmed the importance
of warmth in the staff data, where the facet explained 89 per cent of the difference in satisfaction scores and also in the customer data where it explained
59 per cent of the difference in satisfaction scores, averaged for individual
stores. So while warmth was not the most important facet for individual customers, differences in warmth scores explained the differences in average customer satisfaction between stores. Clearly managers of less well performing
stores would need to focus on warmth, while the company as a whole would
need to focus on empathy and integrity to raise the average customer satisfaction levels for all stores. (How they should do so became the focus of workshops
that we discuss later.)

Customer loyalty

Included in the questionnaire were a number of measures of customer loyalty,
the possession of a store loyalty card, the frequency of shopping at the store and
whether the store was the main store used to buy everyday products. 75.6 per
cent of customers had a loyalty card from this retailer. The benefits to the
shopper included a small refund (of about 0.5 per cent) of the value of their

Table 7.5 Co-relation coefficients for facets of agreeableness with satisfaction

	Warmth	*Empathy*	*Integrity*
Staff	0.575	0.655	0.619
Customers	0.466	0.549	0.542
Managers	0.432	0.451	0.464

purchases. T-tests, comparing the variation in satisfaction scores for those with or without a loyalty card, revealed that those with a loyalty card were significantly more satisfied than those without (p = 0.001). There were also differences in the scores on two of the seven personality dimensions, enterprise (p = 0.043) and competence (p = 0.012).

Interestingly loyalty card schemes were becoming less popular with retailers at the time of the study in the UK market, as many retailers had them and customers tended to carry more than one card. Our data indicated that there was still mileage in such schemes if targeted at less well performing stores as a part of an initiative to improve a store's overall image.

Satisfaction scores also differed with patronage. Seventy-seven per cent of shoppers said that the store we interviewed them in was the one they shopped at the most; 23 per cent said that they patronized that one equally or they patronized a competing store more. The more loyal shoppers had significantly higher satisfaction scores (p < 0.000). Satisfaction also differed with shopping frequency. Eighty-three per cent said they shopped at the store once a week or even more frequently. They were more likely to be satisfied (p = 0.004). Their scores for agreeableness and competence were also significantly higher (p = 0.01 and p = 0.04). For two of the three facets of agreeableness, the significance levels were higher still, warmth p = 0.002 and empathy p = 0.02.

Loyalty appears to be more associated with satisfaction than with image, apart from shopping frequency, where the key facet of warmth was strongly associated with shopping frequency. In many ways this final finding summarizes the picture that emerges from our study. Image is not closely linked to behaviour. Image is more associated with satisfaction and, most probably, satisfaction drives customer behaviour (loyalty) which in turn drives financial performance.

In terms of actions that could be taken by the retailers' management, much of this is covered in the next section, but it is interesting to compare the data for the best and worst performing stores in our sample. The only significant difference in the two sets of loyalty data were in the possession of a loyalty card. Only 58 per cent of the customers interviewed at the worst performing store had one, compared to 73 per cent at the best performing store. Loyalty and performance are of course a function of the way a store or any business for that matter is performing against its competitors and we do not have comparative data on the marketplace in general. However the stores' managers cannot affect their local competitors directly. They can only work on improving their own stores, ensuring the retention of existing customers and attracting those whose current loyalty is with a competitor but who happen to have visited their store. The way forward for them is clear from the data. Certain actions need to be identified from the image and identity data. Improved performance on these will enhance customer image, thereafter satisfaction and loyalty. Encouraging customers to adopt a loyalty card would be one way forward, but it is unlikely that customers will adopt them unless they feel better about the store.

Staff loyalty

Staff loyalty was assessed by the number of years employees had spent with the company. This is a crude measure of loyalty but it identified a number of interesting points. For all store employees' length of service co-related, in particular, with enterprise and competence followed by informality (negatively) and chic. It also co-related with satisfaction. In a stepwise regression these four accounted for 83 per cent of the variation in length of service. When only shop floor employees were considered there were no such co-relations; in other words the longer standing employees also tended to be those who had been promoted to supervisor or manager and it is not surprising for example that their satisfaction scores were higher. There was no co-relation between average length of service at each store and business performance. Indeed the worst per-forming store had one of the highest average length of service figures.

Management workshops

In a second stage and following the customer and employee surveys, the results of the surveys were presented to teams of middle management. They were asked to consider what changes should be made, largely within the company's stores to improve identity and image, taking into consideration that certain of the seven dimensions of both co-related more strongly with satisfaction and financial performance. Large gaps between customer and customer facing employee scores for agreeableness and ruthlessness became their main focus. In particular low scores from staff for the words 'supportive' and 'concerned' within agreeableness and high scores among staff for 'authoritarian' and 'con-trolling' within ruthlessness were seen as most worrying.

Their immediate reactions were to discuss whether the new corporate values were being promoted as effectively as possible. Questions were asked as to whether staff actually did feel supported. A more fundamental issue was whether the orientation of the company was appropriate. In the previous twenty years the company had undergone a major transformation in the design and location of stores and in the range of products they sold. Out of stocks had been a major concern, but this was now much better managed. While the company undertook a great deal of market research and had accumulated an enormous amount of information from the data that had been generated after the introduction of its loyalty card, most of the changes in operations had been driven by the company. The culture was still 'top down' of everyone waiting until their line manager had told them what new direction to follow. Some favoured a more customer oriented approach and one where customer facing employees had more discretion in how the business was run, with less emphasis on controls and more on setting objectives.

Tables 7.6 and 7.7 list some of the ideas that emerged from the managers' workshops to improve image and identity. Most constitute changes in micro-behaviours among employees. Almost all represent quite small changes in what the company did or in the way they did them for the benefit of customers. For example, having staff permanently assigned next to changing rooms would have been seen by managers as a generous allocation of a scarce resource, but the customer would expect such service as this was the norm in specialist clothing shops.

Table 7.6 Ideas from the workshops for changing identity

Agreeableness	Ruthlessness
Promote a non-blame culture	Introduce a reward system at lower levels
Recruit or produce well-trained staff	Coach more than train
Ask rather than tell, when dealing with staff	Be flexible over company rules
Listen rather than talk when dealing with staff	Allow people the freedom to make mistakes
Celebrate success at a local level	Employ less confrontation
Celebrate birthdays	Treat all people the same/equally
Introduce a 'fun' day	Spend time to talk to staff
Listen more to staff problems	Build on what people enjoy
Try to create a group who are willing to lead in changing culture	Empower employees
Be more consistent in dealing with staff	Ask; don't tell
Deliver promises	Provide feedback on values
Recognize staff more (thank and praise)	Introduce a staff forum
Recognize significant achievement formally	Introduce problem solving teams
Live the company values personally	Promote joint decision making
Spend quality time with employees getting to know people	Share knowledge
Promote support between management and employee and employee to employee	Give staff confidence
Identify and respect personal interests	Appraise more than criticize
Ask staff to identify needy causes	Explain the reasons and background to decisions
Empower and trust employees more	Live the company values yourself
Promote better community relations	Lunch together, party together
Be more sensitive about personal issues	Give immediate recognition if anybody is doing a good job
Become less task driven	Empower staff within a framework of goals
Work alongside the people	Don't use formal titles such as Mr
Listen more to staff suggestions	Dress-down days
	Treat them as you would like to be treated

Table 7.7 Ideas from the workshops for changing image

Agreeableness	Ruthlessness	Enterprise
Ensure changing rooms are staffed	Employ more approachable staff	Use seasonal promotion – back to school
Introduce full length into changing rooms	Link better between food and non-food products	Improve lighting, mirrors carpeting, music, space
Have a separate checkout for non-food	Improve stock control	Promotions such as a fashion show
Provide more space in browsing zones	Use external opinion to improve	Merchandise branded goods better
Provide bagging services	Use feedback from market research more	Avoid constant changes
Considering the needs of elderly people more	Ask the customers more often	Have a separate identity for clothing staff
Spend quality time with customers	Don't have too much stock in the aisles	Provide activity for kids
Ask customers what should we do to improve?	Create separate shop for non-foods	Get staff to wear clothes we sell
Local community sponsorship	Introduce trolley-free zones	Play background music in certain parts of store
Tell the local media what we do	Link events and promotions (e.g. computers for schools/ school uniform)	
Train in empathy skills	Introduce a suggestion box	
Recruit knowledgeable staff	Trolley park	
Be more honest with customers	Have a specific bag for clothes	
Trust staff opinion – ask staff what is 'selling'	Allow time for personal selling	
Tell customers what we do, such as our measuring and altering service	Employ trained professional expert staff in key areas	
	Tell customers about refund policy	
	Introduce spacious, not cramped, aisles	
	Train checkout staff in handling products	
	Send brochures/samples to schools and attend open evenings	

Lessons

There was evidence at the start of our research that the company were trying to harmonize their image and identity. Values that map on to the dimensions of reputation that they were working with included 'friendly, helpful, supportive and trust' that emphasize agreeableness, and on 'innovation' which suggests enterprise. Our work certainly confirms the benefit for the company to focus on agreeableness. It is the dimension most highly co-related with staff and customer satisfaction, which in turn co-relates with loyalty and sales growth. The company were trying to align identity and image but not in a purposeful way at the start of the project. The use of the management workshops helped to focus their attention on a number of practical actions that they could introduce to promote company values both inside the company and to customers.

There do appear to be linkages between internal and external perspectives of reputation and to commercial performance, but these latter linkages are via satisfaction. Certain aspects of reputation satisfy customers and staff. It makes intuitive sense if the same aspects that satisfy staff also satisfy customers. In this example agreeableness is clearly something that is important to both groups. We believe that this is the key to achieving harmony between the two. It is not enough to promote the same values inside and outside the organization, unless what are called 'values' are actually valued by stakeholders. In this example we have used measures of satisfaction to demonstrate that indeed the company's chosen values are generally the most appropriate ones. While the management were emphasizing agreeableness they were also featuring enterprise, which is also highly co-related with satisfaction.

At the same time, management had similar ratings for the various aspects of reputation. It is not surprising perhaps that the organization we were studying has faired relatively well in its market. In later chapters we return to some of these issues within other organizations, ones where performance is not as good as here.

In summary this company appeared to be succeeding because what satisfied and motivated customers in its reputation also satisfied employees. There were links from image to satisfaction and from satisfaction to relative financial performance. In addition to image and identity being in harmony staff had a logical reason through a share scheme to be motivated to satisfy customers.

8   Managing the Reputation Chain

What is satisfaction, its antecedents and consequences, why it co-relates with image and identity, mission and vision, what is identity and culture, can culture be managed, internal marketing and the customer facing employee, organizing for managing reputation?

In Chapter 7 we illustrated how an organization can use an approach to managing corporate reputation that involves harmonizing image and identity. We also illustrated how reputation links to financial performance. In describing how the case study company went about managing its reputation we also illustrated the scope of Reputation Management in that it involves coordinating the roles of two traditionally separate functions, human relations and marketing. But that is not the end of it. Other stakeholders, suppliers, and the financial markets, for example, will also need to come within the remit of Reputation Management. This implies an interface with finance and purchasing. The company in Chapter 7 used a new staff magazine and training packages to implement its new approach. Two other functions are immediately involved, internal communications and training. Thus a change in reputation requires the coordination of much of the organization's work, and reputation affects the company's financial performance. If changing reputation involves changing the values of the organization, then Reputation Management is a long-term and not a short-term matter.

Reputation encompasses a wide range of business activities. It can affect financial performance and is concerned with managing aspects of the business that cannot be changed quickly. In our view reputation has to be seen as a strategic issue and not a tactical one. At its heart is the harmony between identity and image. Both work via satisfaction to affect the organization's performance either as a social or financial system or both. Satisfaction is therefore a key concept in the reputation chain, Figure 8.1.

Customer satisfaction has been argued earlier in this book to be an important driver of commercial performance. In Chapter 1 we discussed the service profit chain which argues that there are linkages between customer and employee satisfactions (Heskett *et al.* 1994) and that one creates the other. The maxim of happy staff equals happy customers. The same idea is a cornerstone

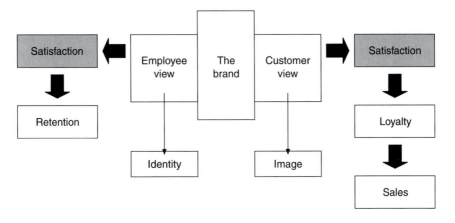

Figure 8.1 The Corporate Reputation Chain.

of the business excellence model, Chapter 1. In this chapter we examine this idea of a causal linkage from employee to customer satisfaction (if you want satisfied customers start with satisfied employees), reject it and present our own ideas as to how organizations can approach their management of customer satisfaction and business growth using the reputation chain. First then what really is satisfaction and how can it affect business performance?

What is satisfaction?

Satisfaction is an important but woolly concept. It is defined in various ways. The most definitive source sees it as similar to the way service quality is defined, the difference between what we expect and what we receive (Oliver 1997). For example if we expect a provider to offer a high level of service and they do not, we are dissatisfied. If we expect an organization to behave badly but they treat us well we are likely to be satisfied. So it is not the absolute performance of a business or its products that matters most, it is the performance relative to what we expect from them. To others, satisfaction is defined as the cumulative evaluation of what a company provides over time, thus one bad incident can be ignored if the sum total of previous experience is still positive (Anderson *et al.* 1994). This definition of satisfaction is similar in approach to our definition of reputation.

In the reputation chain we are concerned with employee as well as with customer satisfaction. An issue is what aspect of the organization's performance is the customer or employee thinking about if asked to rate their satisfaction with the organization. Satisfaction has been subdivided into economic and non-economic aspects (Geyskens, Steenkamp and Kumar 1999). In the first, the employee will be concerned about levels of pay, the customer with relative price and value for money. With non-economic satisfaction, it is the overall contentment with the relationship that is at issue for both employee and customer. The two aspects co-relate but they are subtly different (Geyskens and Steenkamp

2000). If we are unhappy with the financial side of our relationship with an organization this will affect our overall attitude towards it and it will affect our overall view of the company.

In a business-to-business environment, Andaleeb (1996) sees customer satisfaction as the 'overall positive affect' reflecting the overall contentment with the business relationship. This type of definition captures both the economic and the non-economic, psychosocial views (Gassenheimer *et al.* 1994). The down side of satisfaction includes feelings such as frustration, things that inhibit or that raise problems or conflicts (Ruekert and Churchill 1984). The latter researchers argue that satisfaction in a business-to-business relationship is multi-dimensional, comprising satisfaction with (1) products, (2) financial considerations, (3) social interaction, (4) cooperative advertising programmes, and (5) other promotional assistance.

Thus different authors in different contexts appear to agree that satisfaction can be thought of as an overall feeling of satisfaction, or satisfaction with a number of important issues. It can be subdivided into economic and non-economic satisfaction. The two interact, for example, if we trust a company we are more likely to see its products as giving us value for money.

In our work we have adopted the definition of satisfaction as being the overall and cumulative effect of the respondent's evaluation over time, as we are not concerned with employee and customer satisfaction due to a single incident or aspect, but the way such stakeholders feel about the organization generally. This will be modified by each individual experience but will not change radically as a consequence of any one experience unless that experience represents a crisis. This definition is compatible with the view that reputation is formed through an accumulation of our reactions to the experiences we have with an organization.

Antecedents of satisfaction

There are a number of antecedents and consequences of satisfaction that have been identified that are not directly concerned with reputation, but which are relevant here. Businesses tend to try to influence each other and their own employees through the exercise of power. Power is the potential for one party to get the other to do something it would not otherwise have done. It can be exercised in two very different ways, coercively or non-coercively. Coercive power is in essence the approach of 'I say; you do ... or else'. An example of the use of non-coercive power would be 'This idea has worked for other companies. If you try it will work for you'.

In a business-to-business context, research has consistently shown the use of coercive power by one organization to be negatively related to the satisfaction of another (e.g. Simpson and Mayo 1997). On the other hand, the use of non-coercive power has been found to be positively related to the satisfaction of recipient organizations (e.g. Gaski and Nevin 1985).

Academic research consistently identifies a positive relationship between the view that another organization is cooperative and our satisfaction with that organization (e.g. Johnson and Raven 1996). If an organization sees its supplier, for example, as working with it in a mutually beneficial way then its satisfaction with that supplier will be higher than with one who adopts a more transactional approach.

Empirical studies also consistently support a negative relationship between conflict and satisfaction. Conflict can have a number of facets, our negative feelings (anger, hostility) or the cause of the conflict (an incompatibility of objectives for the relationship). The rationale to argue a negative causal relationship between conflict and satisfaction is that 'disagreements tend to block achievement of the firm's goals, eliciting frustration, and thereby cause feelings of unpleasantness about the partnership' (Anderson and Narus 1990).

Trust in a business-to-business context is positively related to satisfaction (e.g. Andaleeb 1996), and is seen to be an antecedent of satisfaction. In other words 'trust' by employees or customers is a necessary step on the way to creating their satisfaction. Trust is usually seen as having two components, honesty and benevolence, and exists when one believes one's partner to be honest and benevolent (Larzelere and Huston 1980). Benevolence means that we believe the other party has our best interests at heart; that they see the relationship between us through our eyes as well as through their own.

In Chapter 6 we showed how in both business-to-consumer and business-to-business markets, image acted as an antecedent to customer satisfaction and identity to employee satisfaction. In the general business-to-business literature trust, honesty, and benevolence are seen as key antecedents of satisfaction with a business relationship. In our work agreeableness (our equivalent to trust, honesty, and benevolence) is better correlated than any other factor with satisfaction.

Zeithaml *et al.* (1990) in the context of SERVQUAL (see Chapter 1) argue that there are a number of dimensions of service quality: access (Can the customer obtain the service easily?); credibility (Can you trust the company?); knowledge (Does the supplier understand the customer's needs?); reliability (Is the service dependable and consistent?); security (Is the service free from risk?); competence (How knowledgeable and skilled are staff?); communication (Is the service well explained?); courtesy (Are staff considerate and polite); responsiveness (Are staff quick to respond?); and the tangibles associated with the service (buildings, uniforms). Credibility and courtesy echo our agreeableness factor and reliability reflects our competence factor. The outcome that researchers in service quality are concerned with is service quality, rather than satisfaction, but the definitions of the two as we saw earlier are very similar if not identical. The PIMS approach has it that relative perceived quality is the main driver of market share that in turn drives profitability. If we liken perceived quality to customer satisfaction then the inputs to service quality and our image factors are providing the same role.

Image drives customer satisfaction (you can call it service quality, if you wish). Image and identity (our trust in the organization) is affected by the behaviour of that other party (if there is conflict or abuse of power it will be negatively affected).

Consequences of satisfaction

In our model we argue that customer satisfaction is linked to sales growth and therefore to financial success. Intuitively, having satisfied customers leads to a profitable business but the linkages between satisfaction and profit may not be quite as simple as this implies. For example if a company were to give its products away for free it would satisfy its customers, whose expectations would be exceeded, thus meeting the main definition of satisfaction, whilst bankrupting the company, and dissatisfying most other stakeholders. Another issue is the relative satisfaction achieved by a company. If your satisfaction rating is 99 per cent but your competitor next door achieves 100 per cent then you will still lose. Down the road is another business whose satisfaction ratings barely reach 20 per cent, but they have no competitors and they still win.

Many companies boast that they achieve say 99 per cent customer satisfaction ratings. This begs the question satisfaction with what or because of what? When customers who have defected to another supplier are asked whether they were dissatisfied, why, and whether this caused them to switch, many claim to be have been perfectly satisfied. We believe it is vital to understand why a customer is satisfied. Only then will it be possible to manage the business to maximize customer retention.

In Chapter 7 we showed that satisfaction in the case of the retail company was associated with loyalty. Customers with loyalty cards reported higher satisfaction with the company. More satisfied customers shopped more frequently and were more likely to have the store as their main source of everyday products. Loyalty may act as an intermediate step between satisfaction and sales growth.

In summary the outcomes from, or the consequences of, customer satisfaction are the determinants of business success. No business can survive if it does not satisfy its customers. If the business requires repeat orders to survive then having dissatisfied customers will be an early sign of decline. Even those who have captive customers or who sell products or services where there is little or no repeat purchase will suffer in the long term, if customers do not receive something that they feel is worth what they paid for. Few businesses survive for long if they dissatisfy too many customers.

Satisfaction linkages

Does having satisfied staff mean having satisfied customers? Intuitively this sounds likely and is a feature of both the service profit chain and business excellence models of business success (Chapter 1). In our database at the time of writing we have large sample data on staff and customer satisfaction for nine different organizations and smaller samples for a number of other companies. Figure 8.2 shows the co-relation between the average staff and customer satisfaction scores for those companies for which we have large data sets. Those organizations with high average staff satisfaction scores tend also to have high average customer satisfaction scores (our scale ranges from 1 to 5 and so an average of 3 is neither satisfied nor dissatisfied). The co-relation is positive but barely significant. Quite clearly the relationship is far from being as simple as 'happy staff equals happy customers'. One organization for example has a very high staff satisfaction but a middling customer satisfaction.

Many of the companies we have worked with operate in divisions or through a branch network and we can treat each part of the organization as if it were a

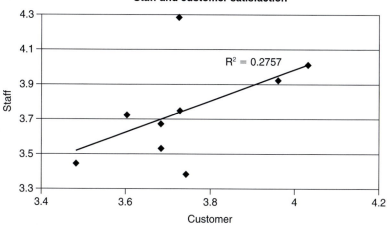

Figure 8.2 Average staff and customer satisfactions.

separate business. If we do this and plot average staff and customer satisfactions against each other again, the picture is even less clear, Figure 8.3. There is an almost random co-relation between staff and customer satisfactions. The idea that staff satisfaction causes customer satisfaction is immediately called into doubt. As is often the case, the devil is in the detail.

Figure 8.4 shows a co-relation between the average satisfaction scores of staff and customers for eight branches of a financial services distributor. Figure 8.5 provides a similar analysis of data from a food retailer. In the first case there is an inverse co-relation between staff and customer satisfaction (albeit one that is

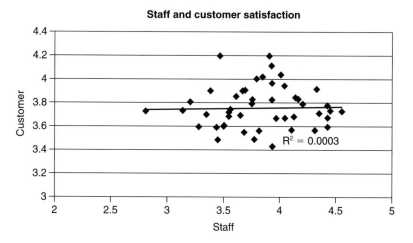

Figure 8.3 Average staff and customer satisfaction for individual business units.

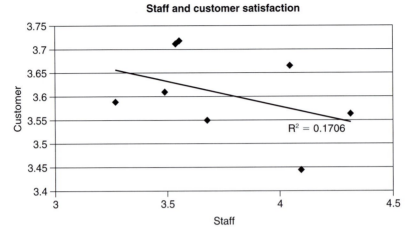

Figure 8.4 Average satisfaction at business unit level for a financial services distributor.

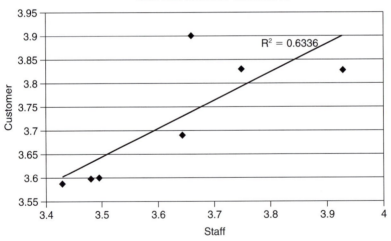

Figure 8.5 Average satisfaction at business unit level for a food retailer.

statistically non-significant), in the second the expected positive co-relation, one that is statistically significant.

In Figure 8.6 the same approach is used to show that the financial services example is not unique. The data are from the branches of a fashion retailer. This time the co-relation is statistically significant. The first and third of the three diagrams in this series are the more interesting in that they present a completely opposite picture from that which we might expect. Are these aberrations, the exceptions that prove the rule? Or is the rule wrong?

Naturally we spent a great deal of time debating Figures 8.4 and 8.6 with the

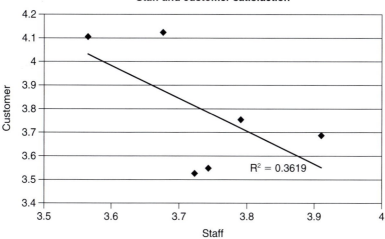

Figure 8.6 Average satisfaction at business unit level for a fashion retailer.

senior managers of the organizations that we were working with. Our shared view was that the idea of a negative relationship between staff and customer satisfactions was not credible. There would be no sense in arguing, for example, that staff take satisfaction from dissatisfying customers. The consensus was that different things were driving the satisfaction of staff and customers and thus they were disconnected. Our conclusion is that staff and customer satisfactions are not inherently interlinked. The key insight came from asking the question, 'Why *should* staff and customer satisfactions be co-related?' Only if there is a reason why staff should take satisfaction in having customers that are satisfied is it understandable that customer and staff satisfactions are co-related.

We went back to the organization whose data is shown in Figure 8.5 to try to discover whether there were reasons why their staff should take satisfaction from having satisfied customers. In their case there was a widely adopted stock option scheme. Even junior staff were able to profit, to the extent of four or five years' salary, by investing in the employee share scheme over time. Second, what co-related in the company's personality profile with customer satisfaction also co-related with staff satisfaction. Third, the firm used a balanced score card to report market performance, including the results of mystery shopper surveys, to all staff. The score card for each store was presented as a 'steering wheel' in the corridor connecting the staff room to the store. Staff were being constantly reminded about what the customer thought and expected and about the performance of their store in meeting customer needs.

In the organization represented by Figure 8.4 we were able to identify a reason for the strange inverse relationship. The number of processing errors made by staff was used as a key measure of branch performance. Errors caused additional work for the head office and for the organizations for whom they acted as distributors. In branches where the error rate was low the staff satisfaction levels were higher than in branches where the error rate was high.

However customers were adversely affected by the diligence of staff in ensuring that errors were reduced. The time spent in a branch would be longer and customers could become frustrated by what they might see as unnecessary bureaucracy. If the staff were less diligent the customers would receive a better experience and be more satisfied. Thus error rate acted as an intervening variable between staff and customer satisfactions. It affected staff satisfaction negatively and customer satisfaction positively, making it appear that the two satisfactions correlated negatively.

In the fashion retailer the explanation for the odd relationship between staff and customer satisfaction was less clear. One suggestion was that branches that were more attractive to customers attracted more shoppers and became busier. The retailer was experiencing a decline in its overall sales and profitability and was reluctant to increase its staff levels. Staff in branches that were increasing sales would have to work harder and would become less satisfied. In branches that were declining staff became less busy and more satisfied with the easier time they experienced. Whatever the true explanation, there was clearly no effective incentive for staff to be motivated by satisfying customers and there could have been a significant disincentive.

Staff satisfaction and retention

Our database allows us to examine a number of co-relations between satisfaction and two variables that are indicators of staff retention. For the twelve companies for which we had good age data, there was a significant positive co-relation between age and satisfaction in six cases. For the nine companies for which we had good data on the number of years the employee had been employed, there were significant positive co-relations between years employed and satisfaction in three cases but significant negative co-relations in three other cases. Older respondents then, generally appeared to give more positive responses to the satisfaction questions, and so the negative co-relations are even more startling. We can conclude that having satisfied staff is no clear guide to their retention.

Again there was nothing obvious to explain our findings. When we talked with each company there were a number of separate explanations. In one, major changes in the way the company functioned were blamed. Employees who had known 'better' times were dissatisfied because their terms and conditions had worsened, while those who had joined more recently had known no difference. In another, a merger between two competing companies had gone wrong and established employees could not adapt to the fusion of two different systems. Employees who had joined since the merger were unaware of the issues that more established workers saw as fundamental problems.

The only generalization that suggested itself was that if an organization undergoes significant change, especially change that is not liked by employees, then the idea that satisfied staff mean longer retention is unlikely to be relevant as the longer standing staff will be less satisfied than those who join after the change and who do not experience a shift in working practices.

In the case study in Chapter 7 there was a positive co-relation between staff satisfaction and retention but only if the views of managers and supervisors were included. In an analysis of the data for shop floor staff, there was no positive co-relation between retention and satisfaction, implying that long employment without promotion can be a cause of dissatisfaction. If employees that have been with you for many years have not been recognized in any way, then it makes sense that they would not be as satisfied with their employer as someone who has joined recently. Yet again we were finding holes in given wisdom.

Customer satisfaction and loyalty

For five companies we had data on frequency of customers' visiting the business. In each case there was a strong positive co-relation between customer satisfaction and frequency of visit. For one retailer (Chapter 7) we obtained data on whether customers possessed a loyalty card and whether they were loyal to the store they were interviewed in. There was a significant difference between the satisfaction scores of those with loyalty cards and those without and between those who were loyal to the store and those who were not.

Loyalty again can be conceptualized in a number of ways, and the possession of a loyalty card, when many customers have more than one, is not exactly evidence of fidelity. But if loyalty is conceived of as being a propensity to patronize one business more than others, in other words repeat purchase rate, then it is clear that satisfaction is linked to loyalty and loyalty to performance.

Harmonizing image and identity

Chain effects

Our data challenges the idea that staff and customer satisfactions are necessarily linked. If management want them to be linked then they need to forge the linkages. They cannot and must not assume that the links are present. In fact it could be disastrous for a business to raise wages and thus raise staff satisfaction in the expectation of a rise in customer satisfaction. However we would support the idea of a chain effect that links employee attitudes with those of customers. Our view is that the chain needs to be formed first by management action. It cannot be assumed that any of the links in our reputation chain will exist. It can be assumed, from our work, that there is benefit in forging a strong chain with each link in place.

Linking between image and identity has been argued to be associated with the mission and vision of the organization and the strategies and policies of senior management (Hatch and Schultz 2001). We would not argue with this view, but from our experience matters are more complex. In summary our views are that harmonizing image and identity involves three aspects: symmetry, affinity and connection.

Symmetry

The way an organization is seen by employees and customers must first be from within a similar framework. For example in the typical large manufacturing companies such as Procter and Gamble, Unilever and Mars there are many brands, most of which would not be immediately associated by the consumer with the parent company. To use an analogy, the employees of such companies will not see the organization through the same set of glasses as will the consumer. It is unnecessary for the internal identity of Procter and Gamble to be the same as the external image among the users for its brands. To Procter and Gamble the brand image is all important. We use the word 'users' here because if we use the word 'customer' then this might evoke the idea of the retail buyer as the customer of the consumer product manufacturer. Here it is important for the dimensions of image of the company supplier to be symmetrical with the identity dimensions of the supplier's customer facing employees.

When there is a need for image and identity to be seen in the same way, then symmetry exists if the dimensions used by the internal and external stakeholders are the same. For example, if two of the dimensions of corporate personality are seen by employees as describing the company but another two are seen as relevant by customers then symmetry is absent. Take the example of a high tech company developing new electronic components. If the dominant internal identity is that of a technical nature, but the customer wants advice and support as to how to reduce its costs, then symmetry will not exist.

Affinity

Affinity follows from symmetry, but for affinity to exist, it is not enough for stakeholders to see the corporate personality in the same way. What satisfies them must also be the same. There must be an emotional linkage between the internal and external stakeholders, such that what they value in the corporate brand is the same. For example the retailers of electronic goods are often criticized by female customers as being patronizing towards them, in explaining the technical aspects of the products to them as if they were speaking to a juvenile. Female customers cannot understand why the retailer does not address their concerns, about functionality and design. At the same time the (mainly male) shop assistants cannot understand why the customer is apparently ignorant of, or indifferent to, the importance of the technical aspects of the product. The two perspectives clash. The typical shop assistant values technical content, the customer functionality and ease of use. Their perspectives are asymmetrical and they do not share the same affinities.

In our context we correlate satisfaction with the scores for the seven dimensions or the sixteen facets of corporate personality to identify which dimensions and facets appear most relevant in explaining the satisfaction of both main groups of stakeholders. If agreeableness, for example, correlates with customer satisfaction but not with employee satisfaction then no affinity exists. Some mismatch is possible but not an obvious difference in what satisfies both groups.

Affinity is at the heart of our model of business effectiveness. Affinity is concerned with the emotional attachments that stakeholders have with an organization. The problem for organizations is that understanding the feelings of customers and employees involves two hurdles. First, management has to be comfortable with the idea of the feelings of their staff and customers (let alone other stakeholders such as suppliers) as being highly relevant. (We have seen the eyes of many a manager glaze over when we start talking about 'feelings'.

After all it is the actual quality of products and services that matters.) Second, the organization has to be comfortable with the idea that you can measure 'feelings', (which are inherently subjective in form) and in an objective way, that is meaningful and actionable.

If two people meet and discover that they have interests in common, they tend to get on. If customers find an organization with which they feel they share the same interests and values, then they also 'get on'. Managing affinity is about aligning the values of customers with those of customer facing staff. In our work we have assessed what stakeholders value in an organization by asking stakeholders to rate their satisfaction with the organization and to see what in the organization's personality co-relates with this measure of satisfaction. An organization where affinity is high will have the same rank order or importance of dimensions co-relating with the satisfactions of the stakeholders it seeks to bind to itself emotionally.

Connection

If affinity is concerned with the emotional linkage between employee and customer, connections are the logical reasons why employees should want to see their customers satisfied and why customers would want to patronize the business. Earlier we challenged the intuitive idea that satisfied staff means satisfied customers. That there is no logical reason for such linkages to exist will have come as a surprising finding to some. We do believe that the two *should* be linked but that management must provide a logical reason for this to happen. In some organizations customer facing employees are constantly under threat of losing their jobs if their customers become dissatisfied and go elsewhere. We are talking about sales personnel here in particular. It is common practice to reward sales staff with a financial incentive for meeting or exceeding a sales target.

However this approach is less common in organizations such as retailing, banking, entertainment, and fast food where the customer facing employee does not 'sell' but, as we have argued, does influence the customer's loyalty and patronage and thus the sales of their employing company. Why it is logical to give sales staff a financial incentive to keep customers happy, but not customer facing employees just because they do not sell, is a bit of a mystery. Part of the answer is that most customer facing employees do not make, and cannot make, an easy connection between what they do and the loyalty and patronage of the customer. Even among sales staff, studies indicate that salespeople who have an inherent difficulty in linking what they do to actual sales achieved (e.g. those selling transport services such as Federal Express) are less motivated than those who can see a sale deriving directly from their actions (e.g. those selling office equipment) (Doyle and Shapiro 1980).

When neither managers nor customer facing staff can see the logic of linking sales achieved to staff remuneration, then other, more general approaches must be used. There is a great deal of evidence that when employees feel they have a stake in the financial performance of the business they will focus more on those activities that enhance sales and reduce costs. At its extreme the stake becomes ownership, and this does not only apply to small businesses. Some businesses,

such as cooperatives or partnerships, are owned by those who serve its customers. The John Lewis Partnership in Britain and Nordstrom on the West
Coast of the USA are in the same line of business, department stores, and offer
different ways of promoting employee-to-customer connections. John Lewis is a
partnership where the employees 'own' the business (Bradley and Taylor 1992).
Nordstrom has a raft of employee incentives (profit sharing, savings plans and a
stock purchase plan) that encourage employees to see the business as partly
'theirs'. Both retailers have acquired reputations for above average customer
service.

Of the two retailers, John Lewis is the more unusual organization. It has a
chief executive (chairman) with the same power and authority of any CEO, but
the role involves ensuring that the aims of the company's constitution are met.
A Central Council acts as the Partnership's 'parliament'. Staff elect 80 per cent
of the 100 or so members. They in turn elect a central board that is responsible
for commercial activities. The Partnership has its own newspaper, in which the
chairman is required to answer questions from the partners (the staff) about
his running of the business. None of this is obvious to the customer, who just
sees a well-run department store, where staff attitudes appear to be different
and usually better than the norm.

Customers too need a logical as well as an emotional reason for completing
the reputation chain. If the company's products and services are not seen as
providing value for money, then talk of a reputation chain is irrelevant. We
would agree with the PIMS paradigm (Chapter 1) that it is perceived rather
than actual quality that is at issue here. That is where reputation can overlay a
less than leading quality product with an added value that will promote an
image for quality, one that may be undeserved but one that is real enough. In
the services sector, one critical effect of reputation is to precondition both customer and employee into expecting a positive interaction. Because the customer in part determines the service experience, then an expectation that all
will be well ensures a positive outcome. (However too high an expectation that
cannot be met by the provider will create the perception that service quality is
not good enough.)

The linking role of mission and vision

The song 'It's not what you do, it's the way that you do it' sums up our view on
the role of mission and vision statements in the management of corporate reputation. There are opposing views as to the value of trying to 'manage' the identity and culture of an organization. Some see mission and vision as the glue that
connects and links identity to image (Hatch and Schultz 2001). We see the
process of visioning as just as important as the mission and vision itself and the
way the two are communicated and embedded into the organization as key.

What is it?

So what is meant by a company mission and vision (M&V) and how might it
affect identity and image?

As we described in Chapter 1, a company's mission and vision is said to indicate 'corporate character' (Campbell and Tawaday 1990) or 'personality' (Want 1986). The main elements that mission and vision statements have in common are: purpose (why the company exists), strategy (its commercial rationale), values (what the senior management believe in) and behaviour standards (policies and behaviour patterns that guide how the company operates) (Campbell and Tawaday 1990). They answer the questions: 'Who we are, what are we trying to do, who do we serve, who or what determines our success?' (David 1989; Klemm *et al.* 1991; Muckian and Arnold 1989).

Values, behaviour standards, and ideas such as 'who we are' are the most difficult to encapsulate in a mission and vision statement, because they are about less tangible matters. For example the mission and vision statement for Manchester Business School at the time of writing included the following section:

> Inside the school, we work in a lively, bustling atmosphere where ideas can be shared openly without the hindrance of internal boundaries. We strive to be honest and friendly in our dealings with each other. Our aim is that, right from day one, new arrivals feel supported and recognized and work as part of one large team to achieve the school's shared goals. As a result, the spirit of Manchester Business School will be one of mutual support, confidence, trust and pride. We also value and rely upon those who have studied with us. We aim to remain helpful to them in their careers, supportive and concerned for their futures as they are for ours.

The section paints a word picture of an organization, but having the words is not enough; living the values implied by the words is essential. The MBS mission and vision statement was derived from a series of group debates involving staff from all levels. The resulting statements were crosschecked with other groups in presentations to all staff and to other stakeholders. The process took eighteen months. Even after that time staff could not always recall the main content and sometimes thought that the mission and vision statements contained other than it did. The main messages in the mission and vision were introduced into other forms of communication to constantly remind those who had evolved a picture of what they wanted to be as to what this was. Mission and vision statements have to be aspirational. Otherwise they merely reflect and institutionalize the status quo, or are too bland to have any effect (Davies and Glaister 1997).

Applying the idea of mission and vision internally is not easy. In one survey only about half of the companies contacted felt they could claim that 'the mission vision and values are understood by all employees, most of whom believe in them strongly' (Opinion Research Corporation International 1999). In our experience the real figure is considerably lower than half.

In summary, it is the process of visioning and the communication of the mission and vision content that is more important than the vision itself. Well managed and well communicated a mission and vision or rather the process of creating and debating one, can work to change an organization's identity. But it is no quick fix.

Once an organization has an agreed mission and vision statement, what else should it do with it? We have implied that internally marketing the mission and vision is important but should it be communicated externally? We believe it should. Potential employees will be interested to understand whether you are 'their kind of company'. Other stakeholders could be similarly concerned. One of the problems will be the sheer length of any comprehensive mission and vision statement, in that it is unlikely to be read by all stakeholders if it appears to be long. A summary or strap line can be useful to capture the essence of an organization's character. It is important that a mission and vision statement is clear and concise and not something that adorns the CEO's wall and is ignored by staff. Many organizations encapsulate their thinking in a limited number of punchy 'principles' such as these from Nike:

1 Our business is change.
2 We're on the offensive all the time.
3 Perfect results count – not a perfect process; break the rules; fight the law.
4 This is as much about battle as about business.
5 Assume nothing; make sure people keep their promises; push yourself push others; stretch the possible.
6 Live off the land.
7 Your job is not done until *the* job is done.
8 Dangers: bureaucracy; personal ambition; energy takers v. energy givers; knowing our weaknesses; don't get too many things on the platter.
9 It won't be pretty.
10 If we do the right things well we'll make money damn near automatic.

The Nike principles say much about the company and its style. They paint a picture of 'the way things are done around here', what the organization is about and its culture. Outsiders reading the list would also gain an impression of the type of corporate brand Nike represents. The picture is of an organization that would score high on machismo and perhaps lower on other dimensions of corporate personality. (Notice for example the absence of any mention of the customer let alone the community or the individual employee.)

Positioning the organization using mission and vision

In Chapter 4 we discussed the idea of positioning, the marketing or branding idea that people see competing products or services in a mind map where each is compared with the rest. The idea has been used by us to compare the content of mission and vision statements or similar material in the websites of *Fortune* 500 companies (Chun and Davies 2001).

Mission and vision or equivalent statements were downloaded from the websites of companies in three business sectors, including commercial banks. Many of the websites had sections that were not entitled mission and vision but which were very clearly designed to communicate 'purpose, strategy, values and behaviour standards'. Occasionally the mission and vision statement appeared as part of the annual report and accounts section or within a message from the CEO. The labels used to identify them by companies varied widely, for examples, for the Bankers Trust the text selected was labelled 'values and goals'. National City bank used the term 'our management principles' to label the material selected.

The mission and vision material was content analysed to count the number of words associated with different aspects of corporate image. As the material was American English the framework of Aaker (1997) rather than our own was used to structure the analysis. Aaker's framework, Chapter 6, has five dimensions: competence, sincerity (similar to our agreeableness), excitement (similar to our enterprise), ruggedness (similar to our machismo) and sophistication (similar to our chic). Mission and vision material was found within the websites of twenty-one banks.

Words associated with 'competence' dominated the content of the banking sector data. 108 (57 per cent) of the 189 keywords identified in the twenty-one company statements analysed were associated with competence, 49 (26 per cent) with sincerity, 21 (11 per cent) with excitement and 11 (6 per cent) with ruggedness. No words associated with sophistication were identified. Only one bank, MBNA, was strongly associating itself with ruggedness. The number of words associated with each bank on each dimension was used to construct a positioning map indicating the relative impression that the content of the mission and vision statements might offer the visitor to a website. Figure 8.7 uses the data on the three main dimensions of competence, excitement, and sincerity.

The majority of the banks are clustered around competence. This reflects the inclusion by all the banks studied of at least one word associated with the construct in their mission and vision statements. Five banks shared exactly the same coordinates in Figure 8.7, Boston, Wachovia, Regions Financial, State Street Corp., and First Union. Competence was the most dominant construct in their mission and vision material. Two banks had relatively distinct positions. MBNA not only used more words associated with ruggedness, it also emphasized excitement more than any other bank. BB&T's mission and vision section contained the largest number of the words in the Aaker framework, 54 (29 per cent of the total), of which 23 were associated with sincerity, positioning them closest to this construct. Bank of America is positioned mid way between excitement and competence. It and BB&T had by far the largest number of relevant words but within relatively large mission and vision sections.

Potentially at least the content of a mission and vision statement can position the organization. In this case it is unlikely that too many customers or potential employees would search each website looking for mission and vision material in the way we did. However the analysis does indicate that mission and vision statements do have quite different content and that this can affect the impression that a reader would have of the organization. They can be used therefore to affect any stakeholder's view of an organization.

Next, can identity be 'managed'. But before we try to answer that, here is a case study to illustrate what is identity?

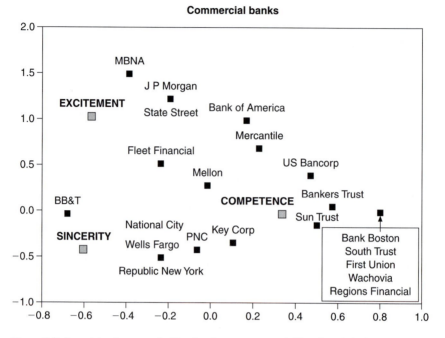

Figure 8.7 A positioning map indicating how commercial banks might be seen as different from their mission and vision statements.

What is identity?

A sense of identity: the Co-operative movement

The global Co-operative movement has its roots in the new manufacturing towns of Northern England in the late nineteenth century, and in one town in particular, that of Rochdale. Rochdale was typical of its era. Historically a centre for the textile trade its population grew rapidly as thread and textile manufacturing became mechanized and demand for manufactured goods boomed. In 1801 its population stood at 14,000, by 1841 it was 68,000. Nearly half were working people employed in textile manufacturing (Cole 1994). The industrial revolution had made paupers of the independent weavers and spawned a new breed of worker, semi-skilled and employed by mill owners.

Divisions in society became increasingly obvious. Only the privileged few could vote. The Church of England, by then in decline and attended more by the ruling classes, still retained the right to tax everyone. (Ballots in the town to abolish the Church rate were eventually responsible for its abolition nationally.) Schooling was the privilege of the few until the growth of Sunday schools, but the teaching here was still primitive. Traditionally the privileged classes had seen it as their duty to support the poor during periodic famines and the inevitable rise in food prices that went with such times. This changed with the industrial revolution and mill owners appeared to reject any philanthropic aspect to their role. The government of the time rejected calls for a minimum wage. Trade unions were illegal until 1824, but public protests against food prices and wages became common. The Chartist movement (named from their six point charter) was formed to demand the right to vote for all (at least for all men). The resulting Reform Act of 1832 still excluded the majority of the population from voting, adding to popular discontent. The Poor Law Amendment Act of 1834 ended the rights of the poor to payments during hard times. Instead they were to live in workhouses. Repeal of the amendment became a working-class cause. The merchants, who were demanding changes to the Corn Law that ensured that cheaper imported food was largely blocked from the market, joined the workers in their protests against the government. Political and economic power was still in the hands of the landed gentry who were concerned to minimize any price competition from cheaper imports of agricultural products.

Common at the time in retailing were the systems of Truck and Badger. Truck was a system whereby mill owners paid staff in tokens that could only be redeemed in their own factory shops, where food was generally overpriced. Food was also allegedly adulterated to increase the mill owners' profits even further. Badger shops traded for credit at extortionate rates of interest.

In 1817 mill owner Robert Owen published his thoughts on a different way of organizing the workplace. Fundamental to his thinking were the ideas of improving the workers' environment and giving them a stake in the business. Capitalism would be replaced by a 'Co-operative Commonwealth'. William King modified Owen's thinking and extended it to the operation of retail business. Although often linked with socialism, Co-operation is not allied to communism, where the means of production and distribution are owned by the state. In a co-operative, instead of capital being invested by owner/shareholders, the business is funded and owned by those who work in it and those who buy from it. In a retail co-operative those who buy the merchandise share at the end of the financial year in any surplus in proportion to their purchases (the dividend or 'divi'). Investors receive an interest on their capital but do not otherwise share in the profits.

After a number of false starts elsewhere (at least one in Rochdale itself) a group styling themselves the Rochdale Pioneers opened their first cooperative store in Toad Lane, Rochdale in 1844. They bought food at wholesale prices and sold it to themselves and to others who wished to become members at competitive retail prices. Any customer who became a member would receive a share of the profit (or surplus as it was called) at the end of the year in proportion to the total value of the purchases they made in the store.

The founding committee, many of whom were weavers, established a number of principles:

- democratic control, one member one vote and equality of the sexes;
- open membership;
- a fixed rate of interest payable on any investment;
- pure unadulterated goods with full weights and measures given;
- no credit;
- profits to be divided pro-rata on the amount of purchase made (the dividend);
- a fixed percentage of profits to be devoted to educational purposes;
- political and religious neutrality.

None of the principles were that new, but their combination within a single creed was to revolutionize retailing and manufacturing both in the UK and worldwide. All the ideas had their roots in the writings of other radicals and in the circumstances of the time. Indeed the main principle behind co-operation, that of self-help, reflects the lack of any state or other support for the majority of workers in the Victorian era, the lack of political power for the masses and the reality of real power of the mill owners over their employees.

There were only twenty-eight founder members of the Rochdale society in 1844. By 1849 there were 390 members, by 1860, 3500. Shops based upon the same principles flourished in other towns. In 1863 the various retail societies created their own wholesale society, which eventually became the Co-operative Wholesale Society, the CWS (known today as the Co-operative Group), (Carr-Saunders *et al.* 1938). The CWS entered manufacturing in 1872. New businesses proliferated, funerals, travel, insurance, ophthalmics, farming and banking. The Rochdale concept was copied around the globe, albeit with varying success, as far a field as America, (Lazo 1937), Japan, South America, Scandinavia and Italy. These initiatives survive and sometimes prosper today particularly in Scandinavia and Italy (FDB, NKL, SOK, Tradeka, and Coop Italia).

If you worked for the Co-op or you shopped there you had a clear idea of what the Co-op was. It was a business you had a stake in. You were probably a member sharing in the surplus at the end of the year through the 'divi'. If you were an active member you could share in managing your co-operative alongside the professional managers. In its heyday in Britain in the 1950s the Co-op was the largest food retailer, farmer and funeral provider. But the abolition of resale price maintenance and the growth of centralization in all types of business, fuelled the expansion of other business formats (Davies 1993).

Many of the hundreds of smaller societies failed and were absorbed by the CWS or other societies, placing burdens on their own finances. The dividend was scrapped, and replaced by trading stamps. A useful form of saving for members had disappeared. The Co-operative College was retained to train staff but education for members generally was no more. There was no need; the state provided a better option. Some say that as society has moved on, the cooperatives have had their day, that they have served their purpose.

Today, many reading this book will not know of the Co-op's origins and be less than aware of what makes it different. In Britain membership has become dominated by employees, rather than by customers. Stores sometimes do not display the Co-op logo and most no longer promote membership overtly. In other countries the Co-ops are little different from any other business in the way they are seen. The Co-ops have lost market share in almost all of their markets, to businesses that did not exist in 1884, large centralized multiple retailers, businesses with shareholders. Other forms of mutual organizations, building societies or savings banks have failed or have become limited liability companies with shareholding replacing membership. One of the strongest identities in commercial life had gone from nothing to dominate its areas of activity in many countries only to fall back, at times to obscurity. Why is this? Isn't a strong and differentiated identity and image enough? Obviously not, an organization needs to have an identity that is for its time and of its time to survive commercially.

In 1844 there was a need for something like the Cooperatives. The alternatives at the time were too self-seeking and often corrupt. There was a greater sense of self-help and community than exists today. To succeed, an organization needs an identity that is in tune with the needs of its stakeholders. The principles established by the Rochdale Pioneers have not always been brought into the modern era in a meaningful way.

Identity is what holds a group together, the corporate glue, a sense of belonging, the informal and formal sets of rules that we abide by, an understanding of who can join. Identity is socially constructed. It does not exist but is created through our interaction with other organization members. It may be formalized in part by a company history, rule books, terms and conditions of employment and documents such as the mission and vision statement, but it is still difficult to encapsulate in any formal way.

National identity is easier to illustrate than corporate identity. We feel we belong to a nation because we are born in the country, speak the language, and have strong emotional ties to others who live there. We reinforce that identity by supporting our national teams, by paying taxes to support our institutions. We have our own literature, art and media. We differentiate ourselves from the members of other nations and we have a clear idea of why we are different. We are proud to belong to our nation. We swear an oath to protect it and its institutions. We learn certain rituals, a national anthem, and celebrate certain days with symbolic meaning. We learn about our history and traditions. We may profess a certain religion that is associated with our country.

At the level of an organization rather than a country, if we say, 'We are a bank', this implies certain social practices that are institutionalized. 'We are the XYZ bank', implies we have certain practices that set us aside from other banks. 'We are the largest XYZ bank', implies a certain role or status within the organization. Each element builds our sense of who we are. Identification is about belonging to a group, the blurring of self-concept into the group norms, the acceptance of their rule sets and norms.

The process of identification is the stages we go through to in adopting an identity. This can also develop a sense of affinity. However our sense of identity and the power of the identification process that binds us together may also blind us to some uncomfortable realities about our country. It may not be acceptable to criticize an overbearing bureaucracy or the stranglehold of a dominant religion or political party. We may even believe in what appears to outsiders to be totally unacceptable. We may not allow ourselves to see the dark side of our society. Nationalism may blind us to less acceptable aspects of our society, extremism, intolerance, sexism and inequality.

There are parallels in our identification with an organization as an employee and our national identity. We have our own traditions and history. We may have our own language, the jargon and acronyms that we use to communicate with each other. Our sense of identity is reinforced by having our own sports teams, a works band, an annual outing, a Christmas party and a uniform. A uniform may be officially defined as with a retailer, the armed services, the police or the fire service, or it may be informally defined, the white shirt, the dark blue suit, the absence of bright colours. In the same way there will be darker sides to our organization and what it stands for that we are uncomfortable in facing. If we work for a tobacco company, or one marketing alcohol or armaments we will tend to rationalize what others may find unacceptable. We might work for the sociopathic firm described in Chapter 6 but we will be unlikely to voice our concerns and may not even see *our* firm as deviant.

True identity it is said is revealed in a crisis. We can be told that the organization is moral, trustworthy, and dependable in internal communication, only to find that once the chemical spill has contaminated and killed, that we seek to avoid our responsibilities.

We learn about the company identity and culture formally through formal training and informally by working there. One CEO described the role of his trainer as the 'keeper of the company myths and legends'. The trainer's role with new employees was to provide a sense of identity. Informal rules are the most difficult to identify for the new employee. One suggestion is to set out to break as many informal rules as you can in the first week or so! You will soon find out what is acceptable and accepted.

Companies tell their histories in their communications to new and prospective employees. The problem with all history is that it is usually written from the perspective of the winners. It is a sanitized and orderly view of the past. Try writing your own 'history', explaining your career progression, and see how difficult it is to remember the truth, let alone tell it. That is why some claim, somewhat tongue in cheek, that myths are more real than history. Myths romanticize the past deeds of the company's heroes. They recall personal battles and scandals that are often more illuminating about the company than any official history.

Culture

Identity and culture are similar ideas in an organization and one complements the other. While identity is more intangible (how we see ourselves), a shorthand definition of culture would be 'the way we do things around here'. But culture is more complex. It has a number of characteristics (Williams *et al.* 1993). It is learnt, an input as well as an output, partly unconscious, historically based, commonly held, rather than shared and heterogeneous.

When we join a new organization we are socialized into it. We are educated into the culture; we learn the culture. The new arrival sees culture as an input, shaping his or her values, attitudes, and beliefs relevant to the workplace. But it acts as an outcome; the attitudes of long-standing employees are a consequence of their actions. We may not even be conscious of our culture until someone analyses it from outside. It can therefore be very difficult to communicate to others in an objective way. In the Mars organization everyone clocks in to work and clocks out before going home. The philosophy is that because the shop floor, who produce the products, need to do this, so must everyone else. However, at the time one of us worked there, this also shaped an attitude that if you stayed late this symbolized that you could not do your job in the time available. This was not a written maxim, nor anything official. It just became part of the culture to get your work done during normal working hours. Another of us worked for the communications company, BT. Here the symbolism of working hours was very different. Working long hours was seen as a sign of dedication.

Cultures can be based historically upon the assumptions, strategies, and structures of their founders. In the case of the Mars company, the family is still very much at the helm and their values and ways of doing things are an important influence on the business. Organizations can have more than one culture. For example the ways of doing things and treating people in marketing, manufacturing, and finance might be very different, due in part to different contexts. Extraversion and creativity may be seen as desirable traits in one part of the firm but not in another.

Culture is then heterogeneous and we have tried to emphasize the importance of customer facing employees in shaping reputation rather than the role of all employees. Even within a specific group there will be heterogeneity. As we have shown, different branches of the same organization will have slightly different identities that are linked to different sets of micro-behaviours, in other words to modifications in, or aberrations of, the same culture.

There are many ways of identifying differences between cultures and typologies of cultures. In this book we will aim for consistency and use the same labels as we do for the dimensions of corporate personality to identify, in the final chapter, the main characteristics of organizations with each of the seven dimensions as dominant.

Managing culture

The sales manager of a pharmaceutical company had a problem with one of his sales staff. Pharmaceutical 'reps' did not sell directly to anyone; their main role was to influence doctors to prescribe their employers' products. They had limited time to achieve their goals and many products to feature. Normal practice was for the company to give their representatives a list of priorities. The list would change and so in one period one product would be given the status of 'first detail', meaning the sales person would be expected to at least promote that product. If time permitted the rep would also talk about other products on second or third detail and so on.

The manager's company specialized in manufacturing and marketing 'generic' drugs, copies of products invented and marketed originally by other companies, but whose patent protection had expired. They tended to sell on price rather than on innovation. The sales manager was concerned about one of his team. As he explained to a friend, 'Bill's product knowledge is poor. He knows everything there is to know about our best selling lines but nothing about the products we are putting on first and second detail to promote them to doctors. Worse, his personal presentation is poor. He's worn the same raincoat for years. He looks more like a down and out than a salesman at times. It's embarrassing when I go with him to visit a doctor. Frankly he is boring. He goes on and on about how good our leading lines are. The doctors have heard it all before!'

'So what's the problem?' asked the friend, 'Get rid of him'. The sales manager smiled, 'The real problem', he explained, 'is that Bill is our most successful salesman. He has built up a tremendous market share for us in his territory. My problem is that I need to keep him!'

The company management were trying to control the way their customer facing employees were dealing with their customers, the doctors, rather than setting them targets that reflected the company goals and then letting them decide how to meet them. Management was keen to promote their latest look-alike products but the company made its money from more established lines. Perhaps the more pedantic approach of Bill was the right way forward and other ways should be found to introduce new products. It would be difficult to get the rep to change his ways.

This small case study illustrates how difficult it is to 'manage' culture. There are two main models of organizational change: step change and evolution. In the first, a crisis or other event such as a takeover provides management with an opportunity to make major changes quickly. Management 'unfreeze' or unlock the company, introduce change and then freeze working practices in the new mould. Generally management tries to promote constant but more evolutionary change and a culture of continuous improvement. One way of changing attitudes, and therefore identity, is to market internally.

Internal marketing

Too much time and money is spent marketing to customers or potential customers and too little marketing is done to employees, particularly customer facing employees. Such employees are referred to as 'brand ambassadors'. They should be engaged intellectually but also emotionally with the brand they are representing and often selling.

The role of a marketing function in a service organization must include communicating a strong sense of (brand) values internally. Customer facing employees must be trained in how to provide consistent standards that match the customer's ideal of what the service brand's personality should be. They should understand what these values are and why it is important that they should be manifest. The customer facing employee is the equivalent in the services sector of the advertisement that is used to brand a consumer product. They are both the medium and the message for the customer, yet they are often marketed through rather than marketed to. By this we mean to refer to the trend towards the industrialization of the services sector.

In many businesses (fast food would be a prime example) it is possible to identify a number of stages in the customer service experience and set standards for each. The acceptable queue is so long, the acceptable time taken for an order to be served is so long and these imply other standards for cooking and other supporting activities in the back room. This, operations management, perspective is fine as long as the customers do not mind having a process imposed upon them. But have we gone too far in forcing processes on to customers that they do not want? Is the layout of the typical supermarket right? Perishables are displayed first and the (heavy) items of soft drinks and alcohol last in the route the customer has to take, resulting in the crushing of the produce in the bottom of the trolley. Are computerized answering systems customer friendly? The typical computerized phone system invites us to press endless combinations of buttons to filter us into one track or another, when all we want is to talk to a human being.

Employees become cogs in the corporate wheel as the organization tries to reduce costs. Employees are taught that they have to smile. They have to ask whether they can offer help. They have to refer any complaint to a customer services manager. Fine, but how about their understanding why or being committed in their hearts to what the customer wants, agreeableness? General Patton is credited with saying that if 'you have them by the balls, their hearts and minds will follow'. He was referring to his enemies and the way he wanted them treated and not to his front line troops to whom he was an inspirational leader. A feature of the ruthless organization is that managers act and behave towards their employees much as Patton did towards his enemies, believing that their job is to bully or coerce employees into being submissive to customers. A better model is where customer facing employees actually want to provide service and the customer, recognizing that they do, joins in the creation of the service experience to their mutual satisfaction. Managers need to win the hearts and minds of their front line troops.

Organizational footnote

Reputation is not a business function but there are functional implications from the ideas in this chapter. The most obvious is the relationship between human relations and marketing. Essentially for our thinking to work these two must operate in tandem. They must not be two separate silos as we have seen too often in practice. In one company internal and external communications were separate departments and part of separate functions. Internal communications was a part of human resources and external communications part of marketing. In another, Chapter 7, the two functions of HR and marketing were working on corporate values but separately. Even when the two functions are combined they often lack the strengths or budgets to achieve what is needed. We return to this issue later.

Lessons

The reputation chain lays out a series of links between the customer and the employee. Key stepping stones are customer and staff satisfactions. These link to image and identity. We have argued that three elements need to be present to harmonize the last two mentioned: symmetry, affinity, and connection. Ways of linking them include developing a shared mission and vision and marketing this to all stakeholders. The way to manage external image is to focus on internal identity. Identity and its close relation, culture, can be managed, but with difficulty, as we shall see in the next chapter.

---

9 Reputation and business performance

> Traditional views of the link from reputation to performance, evidence of direct and indirect links using the reputation chain and the corporate personality measure, the links between image and performance, between other aspects of reputation and success measures, putting a value to reputation, what to invest in.

Not every organization that is concerned about its reputation is also concerned with profit or business performance. However many do share such concerns and the aim of this chapter is to explore and clarify the links between reputation and business performance.

The existing paradigm

What has excited management about reputation to date are the apparent linkages between reputation and commercial performance. However these linkages have often been demonstrated between traditional measures of reputation, such as the *Fortune* America's most admired survey, which reflects the financial success of the companies being ranked.

A crisis or some other major cause of a downturn in profitability will certainly create a reduction in reputation among peer group managers. Profits slump following a crisis and the company becomes 'less admired' by its peer group, Figure 9.1. So in this circumstance financial performance and reputation must be linked.

But, more generally, we believe that there is little or no evidence that a good showing in a reputation ranking based on measures of financial performance can usefully explain positive financial performance. We believe that the reverse is true, that good financial performance creates a good image among peer groups and that this creates a good position in traditional rankings. Some companies, for example those involved in tobacco, will under perform their financial performance in the rankings but this merely reflects the general concerns about such an industry. A high ranking also reflects historical performance rather than future performance.

A sudden decline in financial performance is probably the best way to ensure

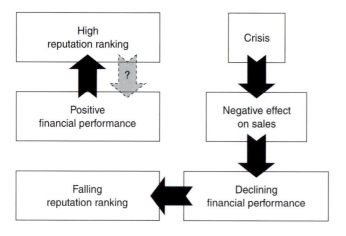

Figure 9.1 Reputation rankings and financial performance.

a fall in ranking (Figure 9.1) as it will be regarded as a crisis. Such links are clear. What is needed is a better understanding of the general links between reputation and commercial performance.

Differentiation and brand strength

As we outlined in Chapter 1, both the marketing and strategy literatures emphasize differentiation as a source of competitive advantage. 'Differentiation' means that the organization has something distinctive in its external image that is valued by its customers. If the organization and its products are seen as distinctive, then the customer will have difficulty in comparing prices. There will be little or no price competition in the market and an opportunity, if costs can be controlled, of making above average profits in the market, the objective of business strategy.

Figure 9.2 presents the results of studies of the image of four fashion retailers that illustrate what differentiation means and the possible links to performance. One of the department stores (the one labelled as store D) scored relatively well on the dimension of chicness. This dimension was the second most highly correlated dimension of corporate personality with customer satisfaction (after agreeableness) for its customers. The ladies fashion chain (store C) outscored its rivals on the dimension of agreeableness but also on enterprise, a dimension that correlated strongly with both staff and customer satisfaction for their particular business. Store C also scored highly for informality, a dimension that was also valued quite highly by its customers, compared to the importance of this factor for the customers of the other retailers. The two stores not mentioned thus far (A and B) scored unremarkably on virtually all dimensions. They lacked any distinctiveness, other than one that was rated quite highly for informality, unfortunately a dimension that was not valued strongly by their own customers. Stores C and D both scored above the norm on dimensions that were valued by their customers.

Fashion store images compared

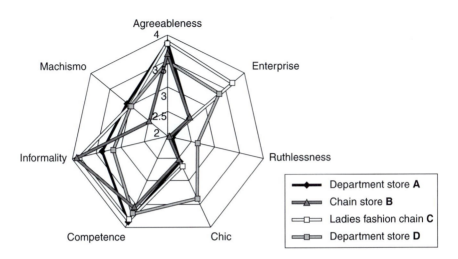

Figure 9.2 Differentiation and brand strength.

In Chapter 4 we talked about the company as a brand and about what was meant by a strong brand. Being a strong brand means having a strong image, stronger than your competitors. It means scoring more highly on at least one of the key dimensions that matter to customers. In this example, the two retailers C and D are clearly stronger brands than either A and B. The ladies fashion chain (store C) and the more chic department store (store D) were growing their sales at the time of our surveys, and continued to do so afterwards. The department store labelled A and the chain store labelled B were both losing market share and continued to do so.

This example illustrates the general lesson that being distinctive in a positive way pays dividends. There is a clear message here for Reputation Management: emphasize what is both distinctive and valued by your customers; harmonize what is valued by customers with what motivates customer facing staff internally and you will succeed.

Using the reputation chain

In Chapter 8 we discussed the links between customer and employee satisfaction, or the lack of them, and the need to have an emotional as well as a rational link between the two if the two are to be linked. We dealt with the employee side of the reputation chain and the customer side as far as loyalty. In this chapter we try to get to the heart of the relationship with sales growth.

The links from the core brand or reputation of the organization to sales and other financial measures of business performance are, in our experience, unlikely to be obvious and their nature will vary from company to company. The links from image to sales growth may for example not be direct. In our

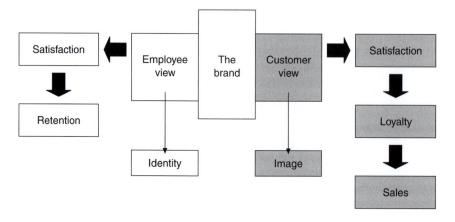

Figure 9.3 The Corporate Reputation Chain.

experience there is often one, key, intervening variable, customer satisfaction (Figure 9.3).

Our measure of reputation is that of corporate personality and we have defined a number of dimensions to this, which in turn have a number of facets. One obvious question is whether there is a dimension or a facet thereof that is generally important, particularly in driving customer satisfaction. Table 9.1 lists the co-relations between the scores on the seven main dimensions of corporate personality from the individuals we have interviewed and their satisfaction. The maximum value of a co-relation coefficient is 1.0. All the co-relations are statistically significant but some are stronger than others. The data is for all surveys we had conducted at the time of writing.

The patterns of co-relation with satisfaction between employee and customer views are similar. Agreeableness and competence rank as the two strongest drivers of satisfaction. Chic appears to be more important for customers and ruthlessness more negative in its effect on employees.

Examining the two main dimensions in more detail the two main dimensions can be divided into three facets each, agreeableness into: warmth, empathy, and integrity and competence into: conscientiousness, drive, and technocracy.

Table 9.1 Co-relation coefficients of personality dimensions with satisfaction (all companies)

Dimension	All	Employees	Customers
Agreeableness	0.611	0.665	0.572
Competence	0.613	0.659	0.543
Enterprise	0.432	0.510	0.338
Machismo	0.342	0.376	0.290
Chic	0.323	0.316	0.340
Informality	0.032	0.062	0.051
Ruthlessness	−0.180	−0.243	−0.194

Table 9.2 Co-relation coefficients of the personality traits of agreeableness and conscientious with satisfaction (all companies)

Facet	Employees	Customers
Warmth	0.571	0.488
Empathy	0.598	0.494
Integrity	0.604	0.474
Conscientiousness	0.621	0.481
Drive	0.547	0.454
Technocracy	0.516	0.400

Table 9.2 shows how the facets of agreeableness and competence correlate with employee and customer satisfactions.

The differences between the co-relations are not huge but there are subtle differences between the satisfiers for customers and staff within the two main drivers of satisfaction. Customers are looking more for empathy, for companies that see things through their eyes. They value warmth more than technocracy. Staff value integrity and conscientiousness with empathy a close third. It would appear from this that integrity is more of an issue for staff than for customers. This finding could have a number of explanations. The one that we find most convincing is that staff do not always get treated with integrity whereas customers probably expect this at least from the kind of organizations we have surveyed, which tended to be large and well known.

The picture changes dramatically at the level of the individual organization. Table 9.3 illustrates this with data from four retailers. The first three all sell textile products (clothing, etc.) and are direct competitors. The last is a food retailer (but a company in the same business sector as the first three). All the data are for customers and the sample size is given for each study.

What drives satisfaction differs from one company to another. Competence is more important for retailer 1, chic for retailers 2 and 3, and agreeableness for the food retailer, retailer 4. So while in general agreeableness and competence are the most important dimensions of corporate personality in driving satisfaction, these drivers vary by company and probably, given the importance of Chic in textile retailing, by sub-sector.

Table 9.3 Co-relation coefficients of personality dimensions with satisfaction: four retailers

Dimension	Retailer 1 (219)	Retailer 2 (431)	Retailer 3 (232)	Retailer 4 (385)
Agreeableness	0.425	0.423	0.196	0.602
Competence	0.508	0.420	0.330	0.440
Enterprise	0.397	0.418	0.401	0.463
Machismo	0.307	0.310	0.158	0.171
Chic	0.439	0.476	0.467	0.347
Informality	0.000	0.108	0.103	0.185
Ruthlessness	−0.068	−0.132	−0.036	−0.156

Driving commercial performance

Beware of mathematical co-relations, because they do not necessarily demonstrate causality! While this is true, we have few alternatives to explore whether one thing influences another other than co-relations of one form or another. But what is also needed, to be convincing, is some rational explanation of why one variable might influence the other that can add credibility to the raw mathematical relationship. For example the co-relation between smoking and lung cancer is quite low statistically but we believe the two are linked in reality because of evidence that cigarette smoke contains chemicals known to cause cancer in experiments on animals. However this does not mean that everyone who smokes will develop lung cancer nor that non-smokers will be immune to the disease. There are other factors that influence whether people who smoke develop lung cancer.

To try to get a clear picture of links between reputation and commercial performance, in our work we have often been able to assess different parts of the same organization, for example different branches of a bank or a retailer, or different regions of the same business. What we can then do is to co-relate the *relative* image or identity of these different parts with their relative commercial performance. As the different branches of a bank or retailer are similar to others in the same company, if differences in reputation correlate with differences in performance in the same overall business, we can be fairly sure that there are real links between the two (as long as there is a logical explanation to underpin any statistical co-relation).

For example, in the following sections we present data on a retailer with ten branches. The ratio of sales to employee co-related with the average customer scores for each outlet for integrity. In other words in branches that the customer rated higher for integrity, sales assistants were selling far more goods. The mathematical co-relation appears to have face credibility when one considers why salespeople in a fashion retailer would achieve higher sales if they are honest with their clients. Claims that 'madam looks wonderful in that', or that the assistant 'has one just like that' herself or that the item is 'the hottest thing we have had in for years' *may* be true but rarely sound so. Good and honest advice may lose the odd sale of a garment (that would probably come back as a return anyway), but is more likely to retain the customer in the longer term. Few shoppers have the time these days to trudge from shop to shop in search of a collection of clothes and many might value a shop where they can get informed help to put together a selection of items. You would only do this in a branch that you could trust. Instead of buying one garment, shoppers who trust the retailer might buy four or five.

Generally the links between image and customer satisfaction are more convincing (Figures 9.4 and 9.5) than the direct links between any personality dimensions and commercial performance. In the example in Figures 9.4 and 9.5, the company is a fashion retailer. There are significant co-relations between the scores for each store from customers on the two dimensions of competence and informality. In other words the stores that were rated higher for these two dimensions of corporate personality in their image achieved better ratings from customers for satisfaction.

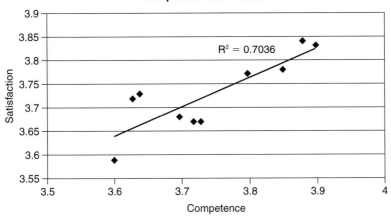

Figure 9.4 Average customer competence and satisfaction scores: fashion retailer.

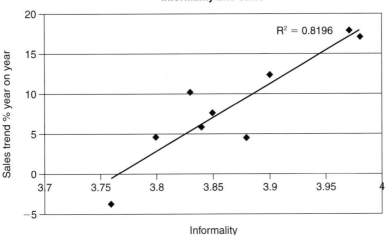

Figure 9.5 Average customer informality and satisfaction scores: fashion retailer.

Again some qualitative insights are needed to explain how these two dimensions of corporate personality can be so influential. The target group for this retailer is the younger shopper, eighteen to twenty-five-year-old single females and young mothers on a budget. The positioning of the business is overtly on price with bargain rails and special offers a feature of the store. The ambience is generally relaxed with pop music in the background. Staff are mainly female and mainly part time employees. The company would be seen as a follower of fashion, rather than a leader. Informality would appear to be important here because the core customer would not be overly confident, yet at the same time the customer appears to want competence which implies a more formal approach. In reality this often means little more than having adequate staffing, your size in stock, and a good choice of product. Those stores who were more on the ball in these areas were growing.

Figure 9.6 shows a very different picture in another fashion retailer. Their positioning was for the older more conservative shopper with a customer base that tended to be less well off. Here there is a clear co-relation between sales growth and enterprise (modernity, adventure, boldness), but it is negative. Branches of the retailer that were seen as more enterprising were in decline, while some that were seen as less enterprising were growing. The core customer did not want to have an experience that was too 'trendy, daring, and imaginative'. The retailer's buyers and store managers were trying to attract younger, more affluent shoppers (by featuring lines that were more attractive to such shoppers). In doing so, in some stores they were dissatisfying their core customers.

Liu and Davies (1995) found that two aspects of a retailer's marketing mix co-related with success in positioning a retail business: staff training and store design. In this example the stores that were under-performing tended to be the better-presented branches where the shopper was more likely to be faced with a more fashionable image. This was being done to try to attract new customers, but what it appeared to be achieving was to turn off the existing customer base who found the stores too 'with it'.

Figure 9.7 shows data from another competitor, a department store, where enterprise co-relates strongly with actual sales growth but now in a positive direction. The core customer is different. She is looking for quality as well as value, for something different and she is able to pay for distinctive quality. The retailer had lost its way somewhat in the market, lost touch with its customers, and lost market share. However some of its stores were seen as more enterpris-

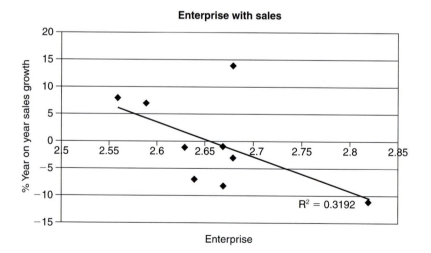

Figure 9.6 Average customer enterprise scores and sales growth: fashion retailer.

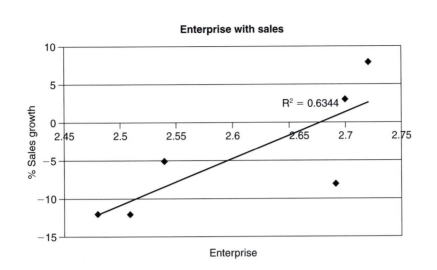

Figure 9.7 Average customer enterprise scores and sales growth: fashion retailer.

ing than others, even though they were selling the same merchandise. In this example it was difficult to see any explanation from differences in store design. The main difference appeared to be in the staff. There was some evidence in the data that the stores that were performing less well employed staff who were older. The average experience of a workforce should co-relate positively with its performance. In this case it appeared to be a disadvantage. It could be that the retailer benefited from having younger staff, as this gave their stores a younger, more modern image.

Figure 9.8 tests this idea and it would appear that the average age of staff does affect the customers' perception of the modernity facet (cool, trendy, young) of the store. (Staff age was measured on a five point scale.) As

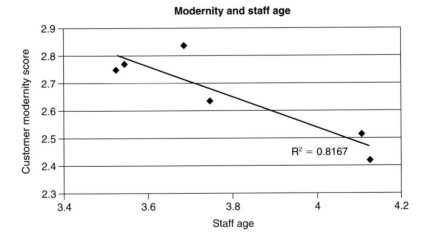

Figure 9.8 Average customer modernity scores and average staff age: fashion retailer.

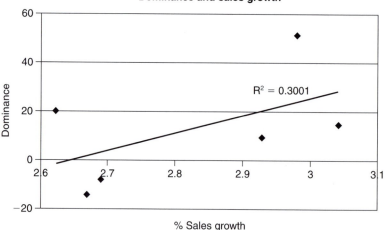

Figure 9.9 Average customer dominance scores and sales growth: construction
company.

enterprise co-relates with financial performance, then lowering the average age
of customer facing staff would appear to be a positive step, albeit one that
would be difficult to implement without damaging at least the staff view of the
company.

As we said earlier, what correlates with sales growth differs markedly from
organization to organization. Figure 9.9 shows one of the more remarkable relationships in our database, a construction company where sales growth co-
related positively with dominance (inward looking, authoritarian, controlling).
Regions of the company where staff and customers saw the organization as
more dominant were growing faster than regions where the scores on this,
apparently negative, dimension were lower. The co-relation is not very strong
due to the small number of regions in the company, but there is an explanation
of the relationship that suggests that it is valid.

In the construction industry business is often obtained by sealed bid. The
norm is to bid low and to try to make a profit by negotiating hard with the
client and by controlling costs once the contract has been awarded. In particular companies would seek to make as much margin as they could on the
inevitable changes to the original brief that would be needed once the project
was underway. Being domineering is probably then the norm in the industry
and even expected by customers. Customer satisfaction did not co-relate negatively with dominance.

The company operated under a different name in another part of the
country. The image and identity of this part of their organization was much
softer. However the sales per employee was only a fraction of that in the harder,
more ruthless part. The company management had realized that their culture
was sometimes quite ruthless and were concerned about it. They were trying to

change to a more agreeable approach both internally, in the way employees treated each other, and externally, in their approach to managing customers. This was in our view a risky strategy as the better performing parts of their business were the more domineering.

Is there a direct link between image and performance?

The co-relation of image with performance is not always direct. In the next example the financial performance of a food retailer was not well co-related with the most salient aspects of its reputation and the relationship appears to be very much via satisfaction. The company is that described in Chapter 7. Figure 9.10 shows the co-relation between customer satisfaction and sales growth for the stores we measured.

Figure 9.11 shows the co-relation between customer satisfaction and one of its main drivers, customer views on agreeableness. The co-relation is again quite strong. However when agreeableness on its own is co-related directly with sales growth the result is not very convincing (Figure 9.12). It is easier to argue that the relationship between agreeableness and sales runs via satisfaction.

In this example chic also co-relates with customer satisfaction (Figure 9.13). After discussion with the company's managers the view was that agreeableness reflected the customers' view of the staff they came into contact with while chic reflected their view on the store design. A good or a new store design would also have a positive effect on the staff. Together, agreeableness and chic explained the majority of the variation in sales trends between the stores.

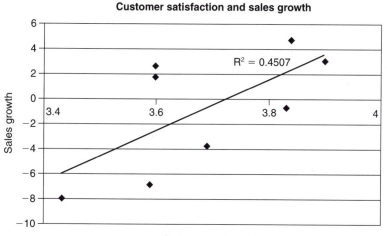

Figure 9.10 Average customer satisfaction and sales growth: food retailer.

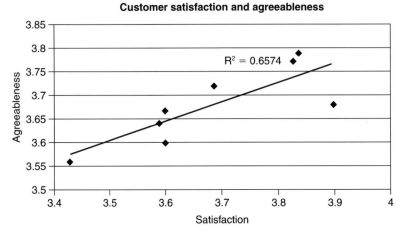

Figure 9.11 Average customer satisfaction and agreeableness: food retailer.

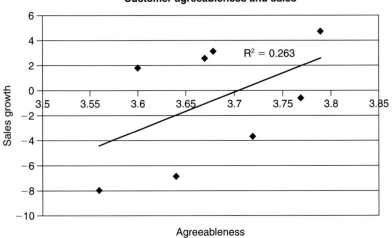

Figure 9.12 Average customer agreeableness and sales: food retailer.

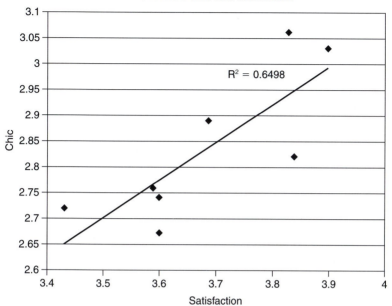

Figure 9.13 Average customer chic and satisfaction: food retailer.

Lessons from the inevitable exception?

Any research project needs one or two exceptions that 'prove the rule'. In this case the 'rule' is that customer satisfaction is the link that drives sales. In reality any exception weakens such a theory, and in one company we have worked with we found a negative co-relation between customer satisfaction and business performance (Figure 9.14). The trend line is statistically significant and the example can be used to support the idea that customer satisfaction is not always linked to commercial performance.

There are a number of possible explanations. One is to challenge the way we measure reputation and performance by comparing data on different branches. In any business a general rise in customer satisfaction should be good for trade. When you measure at branch level you are treating each branch as a separate business, which has its advantages in trying to understand what drives success in that business until you come across an apparent anomaly like this. However another explanation is that what we are seeing in Figure 9.14 is not an anomaly, that it is possible to have negative co-relation between sales growth and customer satisfaction.

What we believe was happening here was that sales growth was affecting satisfaction and not the other way around. When the branches of this company, a distributor of financial services became busier and sales grew, staff levels were not increased. As sales grow, unless the management increased the capacity of

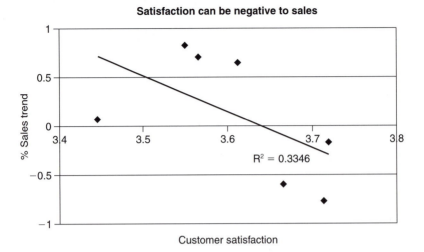

Figure 9.14 Customer satisfaction reducing as sales increase.

the growing branches, then customers would experience greater delays in being served. Eventually, customers will become frustrated enough to leave. Think of a fashionable restaurant. It is difficult to get a table. You queue to get in. The service is slow (unless that is you are a regular customer who tips well), but the food is good. The average satisfaction rating for the restaurant is only modest, despite the fact that it is busy. Eventually custom drifts away to a rival restaurant. What management have to be aware of is that sales growth is not a good leading indicator of future success. Satisfaction and reputation are better indicators of what will happen in the future, after any growth has slowed. Unless customer satisfaction can be maintained at the higher levels of business achieved, then customers will drift away.

We have found other examples of no, or negative, co-relations between satisfaction and sales growth, but none so marked as the one in Figure 9.14.

Loyalty

In the previous example loyalty, measured by how frequently the customer visited the branch, and satisfaction, correlated. Those who visited most frequently had a much higher satisfaction level than those who visited infrequently.

In Chapter 7 we discussed the loyalty issues for a large food retailer. Most customers had a loyalty card and they were significantly more satisfied than those without such a card. There were also differences in the scores on two of the seven personality dimensions, enterprise and competence. In this and other studies, shoppers who said that the store we interviewed them in was the main one they shopped at had significantly higher image. Those who said they shopped at the store more frequently, were also more likely to be satisfied.

In one fashion retailer the average satisfaction scores among those shopping there most frequently were 10 per cent higher than for those shopping less frequently. Scores on key dimensions of personality were also higher. In our experience loyalty, satisfaction, and sales growth link together, but not always in the way management would wish. Yet again the issue becomes one of trying to make such links work rather than assuming that every organization has them.

How much is improving reputation worth?

In the graphs in this chapter are examples of branches of businesses that were growing and declining in the sales they achieved. The differences were often very high. In one company we have worked with there was a 30 per cent difference in sales growth between the best and worst performing regions of the company. The differences we have found to date are generally around the figure of 12 per cent.

If the sales decline in the less well performing parts of the typical business could be turned into an average position, then this would be worth 6 per cent overall sales growth (half of the typical difference between the best and worst performing parts) but the figure could be higher, as much as 15 per cent. Image, the customers' view of the organization's reputation does not however explain all of the difference in sales growth differences between different parts of the businesses we have studied. In our experience the contribution from image explains about half of the difference in sales growth/decline. (We can judge this from the strength of the co-relation between satisfaction and performance.) The other half is due to market factors, such as an improvement or fall in the image of a competitor, or the arrival of a better competitor. So, typically, reputation is worth at least 3 and up to 7.5 per cent sales growth. Put another way, managers can expect to improve the sales of their organization by at least three per cent per annum merely by learning from what is already happening within their own organizations and acting accordingly. If the sales growth of the more successful parts of the organization can also be enhanced, by for example learning form the wider marketplace, then the potential from managing reputation will be higher. A round figure of 5 per cent sales growth overall appears to be a reasonable estimation to us as the potential annual gains from using existing ideas on how any firm influences its image.

We also know that a company can lose sales or value if it loses reputation. In the case of Exxon for example this was about 5 per cent of sales due to the issues surrounding the *Valdez* incident.

We would not wish to exaggerate the importance of reputation nor to add to the books offering instant but ethereal advice to business managers as to how to 'fix' their organizations. Realistically we would expect organizations that are improving their reputations to be adding up to 5 per cent per annum sales growth that they would not otherwise achieve. Organizations that are indifferent to their reputations are risking much but again realistically, some 5 per cent of sales loss per annum appears to us to be the figure that managers should work with.

If we are right then how much should companies be willing to invest in reputation? In Chapter 2 we used a device of suggesting that a company give up its name and lease it back to estimate the capital value of reputation. Reputation we concluded is worth up to a year's turnover, particularly for a pure service business. Taking two figures, 5 per cent sales growth and, say, 50 per cent of turnover as a capital equivalent, we can speculate how much organizations should be spending on Reputation Management. If reputation is the equivalent of a capital asset then it will depreciate if it is not invested in. If a 5 per cent sales growth can be obtained with no increase in cost other than that associated with enhancing reputation, then assuming a modest (for a service business) 20 per cent margin on sales it is worth one percentage point on profit. Assuming a return on capital of 20 per cent as a target, then if the value of reputation is worth half a year's turnover, the maximum we should spend on reputation is 10 per cent of turnover before it becomes unprofitable to invest more. If the profit on sales is 5 per cent then a 1 per cent uplift (20 per cent improvement) would be worth no more than a capital investment of 5 per cent of turnover, a lower figure than the 10 per cent implied by the capital asset calculation. Thus a crude budget for reputation would be some 5 per cent of turnover. This is very similar to the budgets of consumer goods manufacturers for their advertising, expenditure designed to enhance the image of products, rather than organizations.

The reputation toolkit

So what would you choose to spend such sums on? The following list is not exclusive, nor is the order meant to indicate any priority but it is a summary of the ideas we have covered thus far.

- **Tangibles** (building design, refurbishment, colour schemes, furniture, signage)
- **Mood** (lighting, sound, smell, heating)
- **Training** (especially for customer facing employees)
- **Communicating values** (induction training, mission and vision, internal communication, external communication)
- **Corporate identity** (logo, letterhead, signage)
- **Culture management** (training for managers to identify appropriate micro-behaviours)
- **Recruitment** (paying extra for staff who are likely to espouse the desired values)

Figure 9.15 The reputation toolkit.

Different organizations would want to allocate budgets with differing priorities depending upon their situation. However that is not to say that any of the elements in what we have labelled as the reputation toolkit, Figure 9.15, can be ignored. In one department store we have worked with, the company had spent £20 million on refurbishment only to find that its identity and image were not as good as they should have expected from this level of investment in tangibles. One shopper captured what had happened brilliantly with the words, 'a facelift with the spirit unchanged'. The company had forgotten to spend money on its staff. We have more to say about the detail of Reputation Management in the last two chapters.

In summary

We have found too many links in the organizations we have worked with between aspects of reputation and commercial and financial performance to be able to question that reputation and performance are linked. What is equally clear is that such linkages are not easy to generalize about and not easy to predict. The linkages implied by the reputation chain diagram are not always there. Neither are they always present in the way logic would have us expect. What the diagram does is to provide a framework, a starting point from which to test what happens in any organization so as to learn and move forward.

Reputation as an asset is worth about half a year's turnover. Improving reputation using only what the company should already know is worth up to 5 per cent per annum sales growth. It is probably worth investing 5 per cent of turnover each year in Reputation Management, given its importance.

It is, we repeat, in aiming to achieve an improvement in reputation and performance, the role of management to ensure that the links in the reputation chain are in place and are the most appropriate.

10 Challenges in Reputation Management

Identity crises following a merger, symbols, symbolism, and visual identity, managing financial stakeholders' views, the benefits of measurement.

The purpose of this chapter is to illustrate how reputation is managed in the context of a number of typical challenges facing Reputation Management. We use the perspective of corporate personality and the reputation chain. We start with the problems that may occur when two organizations merge. We then explore how the personality framework can guide the development of a new corporate identity programme. We examine whether corporate personality can be a useful framework in assessing the perspectives of another group of stakeholders, investment analysts.

An identity crisis following a merger

Organizations can experience an identity and image crisis for a number of reasons, falling sales, the death or departure of a key individual, or a merger. Here we consider two examples of organizations that were created as the result of a merger. In both cases the most interesting group when considering the views of employees as to corporate personality, were those of the group who had joined since the merger. As expected there were also differences in view depending upon which of the merging companies the employee had worked in before the merger.

Mergers create gaps in organizational images and identities. It is possible that the image, culture, and identity of the two organizations merging together will have been significantly different. It is possible that external stakeholders will have seen significant gaps between the two companies in the past and will be confused as to the reputation of the merged entity. There will be a gap between what existed before and what is perceived now. Quite often such gaps are trivial. In the following examples they were not.

The effects of a merger

Some argue that there is no such thing as a merger, there is only always a takeover. One party comes to dominate the other. But what we are looking at here is the effect of the origins of employees on their view of corporate identity. In both cases we asked employees to assess their view of the merged organization and to tell us which of the original organizations they had worked for, or, whether they had joined the company since the merger.

Two cultures clashing

In our first example the two organizations had previously been fierce competitors, both selling into the same market but each offering different technical solutions to the same problem. Sales people from both companies were trained to point out to prospective clients the weaknesses of their opponent's technology. One company was originally European in its scope of operations, the other American.

Figure 10.1 shows the identity profile of the merged organization depending upon the background of the respondent. The company's managers had expected us to identify two different sub-identities but not a third, that of employees who had joined since the merger. In this case company A had acquired company B but our survey was in a country that had previously been a stronghold of company B. The identity of employees who had worked for the acquiring organization was less positive than that held by employees who had worked prior to the merger for their competitors. The identity of those who had joined since the merger was far more positive than for either of the two groups who had come together. They saw the organization as more competent, more agreeable, and more enterprising. Employees who had worked for company A

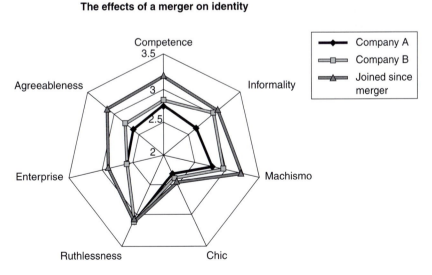

Figure 10.1 Identity by origin of employee.

saw the new organization as relatively informal. Interestingly the satisfaction levels of ex-company B employees co-related strongly but negatively with their scores for informality. Ex-company A employee satisfaction levels did not co-relate with informality. Their (American) culture had been more sales driven and less bureaucratic. Company B had been more systems and procedures driven, with a strong sense of having to be organized. Many of the sales staff in the merged company had come from company A and many of the finance and accounting staff from company B. It was not a marriage made in heaven.

Some employees had been made redundant after the merger but many more had left of their own accord and others were threatening to leave. The average satisfaction levels for the organization as a whole were the lowest on our database. However the main driver of satisfaction for all employees was agreeableness.

Those who had joined since the merger formed a rather separate group. You could argue that they would need to take a more positive view of their organization, as they had only recently joined a new company and would need to justify that decision to themselves (the merger had taken place about a year before our survey). Their view of the corporate identity offers a blueprint of what the company could become. The problem facing management was how to migrate the various cultures into a single and coherent unit.

The likely effect on customers

In this study we did not measure the image that customers had of the organization, but, assuming that we are right in our claim that identity and image interact, then the likely effect on the customer can be judged by comparing the identity held of the merged organization by those with regular face to face contact with the customers and those without (Figure 10.2). Particularly on the

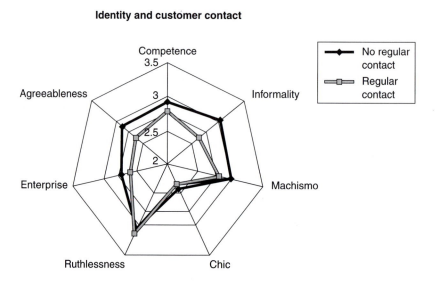

Figure 10.2 The identity as seen by staff with and without regular customer contact.

dimension of agreeableness, sales staff and service engineers with regular face-to-face contact with customers held a far more negative view of the company than did employees based permanently in head office and manufacturing. The effects on customers can only be imagined, but they were unlikely to have been positive. Sales and service engineers working away from head office were often vociferous in their comments about the remoteness of the head office staff they had to deal with. Some sales staff rarely visited the head office and did not know the support staff they had to deal with once they had obtained an order.

We included a number of extra questions in this survey. One asked whether staff felt confident about the future. On a five-point scale where a mark of one indicated strongly disagree and a mark of five strongly agree, the average mark was below two, indicating that staff generally had no confidence in the future, at least not one with their current employer.

Managing identity crises

We worked with the last mentioned company to help its management manage its identity crisis. The managing director closed the company for half a day. Staff were invited to participate in a workshop to identify how best to solve the company's problems. A senior director made an initial presentation painting a realistic and positive picture of the future for the company and of its current financial strength. We then shared the results of our survey, pulling no punches, with the staff. We divided them into groups and each group was given our data on one of the seven dimensions to examine in detail. They were to propose ideas as to how the organization should change to improve upon the scores. A volunteer from each group was asked to present their findings and recommendations. We distilled their ideas into a list of issues. The senior management team took these away and promised to circulate their responses to each issue on the list detailing what would be done on every point.

Is this always the same?

We had the opportunity of working with a well-known bank, formed as the result of a merger between two long established rival banks. We only interviewed managers for this study and analysed the data to see whether the same effect was apparent here, that is to say three identities in the same organization.

This time the identity held by those who had worked previously for either of the two banks that had merged was very similar. However the identity held by those who had joined since the merger was again quite different. They saw the merged business as more ruthless, less enterprising but slightly more chic and competent, in other words less favourably than managers who had been with either business prior to the merger.

We presented the managers we had interviewed with the aggregated results for their comments. Those who had worked for either bank prior to the merger were surprised to see how similar their views were of the merged entity. Those who had joined since the merger pointed out how alienated they felt within the new organization. In the discussion the realization emerged that there was a great deal of rivalry between two camps, representing the employees who had

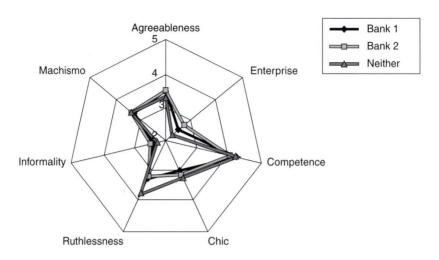

Figure 10.3 The identity of a bank formed by merger depending on a bank worked
　　　　　for previously.

worked for the two banks that had merged, including claims that one bank's
way of doing things was superior to the other, whereas in reality there was little
difference. New arrivals probably felt alienated because they did not see the
point of such rivalry and certainly did not share in the arguments about what
were often irrelevant matters. They were not members of either camp and this
could have increased their sense of alienation.

Lessons about mergers

There are some lessons that we can offer from the two studies. First, it is likely
that the employee groups in any two companies that merge will both have an
affinity to their old organization. They may well have different identities or feel
that they do. Management needs to assess and measure the identities of the two
merging cultures to understand the likely consequences *before* the merger takes
place. If the two cultures are similar it will be comforting to employees to be
told so. If they are different, then it will probably be useful to understand what
in the respective working practices are underpinning each identity, so that they
can be integrated or that one will be known to be replacing the other. Yet again
a training programme would seem a sensible way to smooth any merger, and
being open with employees who will have to face new challenges.

In both our examples those who had joined the organization since the
merger had a very different view of the corporate identity. Where did they get
this perception? In the first case we believe their view was close to the reality, a
company that was working reasonably well. The aggravation that surrounded
them came from the perception that all was not right from two groups of previously fiercely competitive employees who were now being asked to work as a

team. The same was true in the second case, but this time the newcomers had a less positive view of the organization as they appeared to be frustrated by the bickering of those who had lived through the merger. The example brings it home how important perception of issues rather than their reality really is. Perhaps the difference between culture and identity is that if culture is how we do things around here then identity is how we feel about that.

Symbols and symbolism

What sportswear company does a tick represent? Which fast food restaurant is suggested by an arch? It would probably insult you, the reader, if we noted that the first is Nike and the second McDonald's. Which retailer used the device of a giraffe poking its head through the front awning of its stores? More difficult this one but it was the Banana Republic. All organizations use symbols as part of their expression of themselves to their customers and to employees.

Symbols can become shorthand for information about an entity. The shape of a bottle tells us whether it is a sparkling wine, whether it is a hock or similar wine from Germany. Symbols can change their meaning over time. Car designs become rounder and rounder becomes more modern. BP changes the square edged shape of the canopies over its petrol stations in a multi-million pound global expenditure, in order to appear more modern. The typeface in a logo is changed subtly every ten years to keep it looking traditional rather than old fashioned. A more dramatic change signals a new direction.

Olins (1989) likened the use of corporate symbols to that of the need of a new country or a new regime to establish symbols and rituals. The Confederacy developed their own flag (their logo) and established a capital city (corporate headquarters). It had its own currency and army, which had its own distinctive uniform. Each of these has its own functional purpose but each has its own symbolic meaning. Olins invites us to think of France after its revolution against its monarchy, a new flag the tricolour, the Marseillaise, the metric system, a new calendar, and the new title of emperor for Napoleon, the Eiffel Tower, the Arc de Triomphe and the celebration of Bastille day. As he notes, countries 'celebrate their reality with pageants and national monuments whose symbolic value is infinitely more significant than their economic value'. His point is that companies do the same.

There are companies that are ruled by design, the classic case being the German AEG early in the twentieth century when Behrens was appointed to establish what became a corporate design paradise. Not only products, but also office exteriors and interiors and factories were all subject to the same corporate look.

The manufacturer-turned retail company Laura Ashley in its heyday was dominated by a design culture that was described as having a 'sense of nostalgia' and 'a brand new version of the past'. Laura Ashley herself searched secondhand shops for examples of Victorian designs that could be updated and used in clothes, materials, wallpaper and other items of personal and home adornment. Such extreme examples of the design led organization are rare and the issue for us here is to identify the role that design may have for any organization in expressing and managing its corporate reputation.

Design alone cannot work miracles and an over-reliance on it can be fatal. In the 1970s the Mars confectionery and food group identified the potential in Europe for the fast food culture that had been long established in America. It was clear that sooner or later McDonald's would arrive and Mars decided to pre-empt them with a chain of its own called Crocketts. The internal design aped the typical McDonald's look but in green rather than red. Staff waited patiently behind the counters in the first outlet in the town of Slough, near Heathrow Airport, and beneath the type of menu that was familiar enough to all Americans. The number of customers was low and the main customer base was from the Mars corporate offices nearby, whose employees had been given discount vouchers. Other citizens of Slough were more reluctant to enter. Many got as far as the door but left looking confused. Some left after ordering their meals, infuriated by the lack of cutlery and disgusted by the idea of eating hot food with their hands. To the more cosmopolitan businessperson this was obviously a hamburger joint but to the main target market it was something to do with the Wild West that they were not too wild about visiting. When McDonald's eventually arrived they benefited from a large number of recent American films that had helped explain to Europeans what a fast food restaurant was all about. To make sure they knew, McDonald's ran an advertising and PR campaign. They did not rely upon the symbolism of their restaurants.

Planet Hollywood is as much a museum of film memorabilia as a restaurant, serving typical American fare. It boasts a large display of movie and television memorabilia. The company's celebrity endorsers have included actor Arnold Schwarzenegger and sports stars such as Tiger Woods, André Agassi, and Joe Montana. But this did not save them from filing for bankruptcy in October 1999. The business has a heavy design emphasis. Restaurants often rely upon a design concept, but that alone is not enough to guarantee success.

Managing visual identity

The term 'corporate identity' is often used to refer to the visual identity of an organization, its trademark or logo, the design of its buildings and products, the colour, and the typeface and design of its logos. In this book we use the term 'identity' to refer exclusively to the way internal stakeholders, employees, view the corporate reputation. Aldersey-Williams (1994) defines what we will refer to as 'visual identity' as an expression – visual but also attitudinal – of a company's character. Munari (1999) explains that a trade mark can 'express force or delicacy, development, durability, flexibility, richness, stability, drive – each of these qualities has a suitable sign and colour'. He goes on to explain how simple shapes such as squares, triangles, and circles can be used to symbolize different attributes and, if they are modified, by for example stretching the basic shape, how they can be made to add different aspects to the character implied by the logo or trademark. The logo encapsulates and evokes the associations that we make with an organization. They can be extremely powerful in evoking the company or brand they are associated with and the associations we then make with the brand itself.

Try the following game at your next party:

Cut twenty familiar logos from the pages of colour magazines. Cut a piece of each logo, less than one tenth the total size will normally do, and avoid including any part of a strap line that might easily identify the company or brand. Mount each piece on to separate pieces of card and number each one. Give your guests each a paper and pencil as they arrive and ask them to write down the brand or corporate name each fragment represents. The British tend not to like such party games (even though they can be excellent ice breakers) through the fear of losing face if they cannot guess what is obvious to everyone else. The beauty of this game is that few people get any of the answers wrong.

This rather unscientific experiment conducted across a number of years demonstrates the power of the logo and explains why organizations are so devoted to them. It might also explain the mumbo jumbo that the design industry uses to make logos a panacea for any corporate reputation issue that a company may have. Great claims are made for logos to evoke attributes of corporate personality that are not always credible. Consider the following abstracted from a collection of corporate identity manuals, Carter (1978):

Andco's highly stylized A is a unique design that quickly communicates a great many feelings and attitudes about the corporation: strength, unity and modernity.

The functions of the ConAgra logo are to project the characteristics the corporation wishes to communicate about the organization: integrity, invention, dynamism.

Duquesne Light – the signature and symbol have been designed to present a strong, singular visual image and to reflect that Duquesne Light is a dynamic modern company supplying a clean and contemporary product.

Pitney Bowes – the trademark has been designed to symbolize several of the basic elements of the corporate personality ... (it) will attract attention and be easily distinguished and recognized.

And this, paraphrased to reduce the length of the piece, from a book about the development of a number of corporate logos (Aldersey-Williams 1994), where the designers are explaining the symbolism of their new logo to what had been the Nippon Life Insurance Company, now to be re-named Nissay:

The Nissay symbol is a meeting of two worlds – the traditional and the modern. The signature symbolizes the four directions of the compass, four elements of the universe and the four seasons. Within the square are the triangles, symbols of life or the metaphysical idea of the body, spirit and soul. The triangle is also the triangle of divinity of humanness and of nature.

The Nordic financial services group Nordea were so pleased with their new corporate logo that they took full-page advertisements in the business press to explain the symbolism of its different parts. The logo consisted of the company name, Nordea, with what looked like the spinnaker sail from the front of a sailing yacht to the right of the last letter. The advertisement explained that the first three letters in the name represented 'Nordic', which symbolized being 'easy, straightforward partnership', the last three represented 'ideas' indicating 'innovative, breaking new ground' and finally the sail shape implied 'dynamic', 'empowering possibilities'.

Expensive 're-branding' exercises are often criticized and lampooned in the media particularly in the likes of magazines such as Britain's *Private Eye* in what they call their 'Pseud's Corner'. They are seen as a waste of time and money. Others see them, as we have noted, as the focus of any Reputation Management. The reality lies firmly between the two extremes.

The rules

There are few generalizations that can be made about what must be included in any trade mark or logo. Some are simple, others complex. Some are logotypes such as IBM. Others rely upon a symbol such as the shell of the oil company of the same name. Whatever approach is adopted the 'rules' appear limited to the following:

> • **Be original** (scan the market place for similar designs and use of colour to avoid confusion)
> • **Ensure flexibility** (ask whether the logo will reproduce in colour and monochrome just as well and in all media, print, television cinema, website, hoarding, and whether it can be sized up and down easily)
> • **Try for symbolism** (despite the scepticism there are certain associations that will be made with certain shapes and colours)
> • **Ensure the logo is not culture bound** (if your company is international, or could be in the conceivable life of the logo, will it work equally well in different markets?)
> • **Check for unexpected symbolism** (what could the new logo represent, if someone wanted to interpret it negatively?)

Figure 10.4 A few rules for logos.

Corporate identity manuals can be a useful device in managing logos. They will define the logo, its precise shape and colour (normally using the internationally recognized Pantone system), the typeface and any options, and any issues such as whether the logo can be used reversed out, within a border, against any colour background. It may sound pedantic but there is a real danger of individual managers using slightly different typefaces, or colours to represent the logo. Once there are a number of clearly different representations of the same logo then confusion is possible and the professional look that is part of a well-coordinated programme will be missing.

Most organizations will work with a specialist agency to define their trademarks and logos. The usual rules apply for working with any agency. Give them a proper brief, probably one that defines the personality you seek and explain why and any gaps between where you are and where you wish to be. Invite a number of presentations. Be prepared to pay for any excessive work by the agencies. Select not only on the basis of creativity but also on the basis of whether you feel you can work with the chosen agency.

Typeface

Take a look at the very many typefaces that are available and that are used in different logos. The analogy of 'corporate handwriting' is relevant here. Ask yourself what type of writing your corporate personality would be expected to have. Figure 10.5 takes a fictitious business name, the International Vision Institute and presents it in different typefaces to illustrate how it is possible to imply a different character to the company merely from the typography used in presenting its name. The last one in the figure for example appears to evoke a more business like and cleaner image than the more fussy first choice, which might in turn suggest a more intellectual approach.

The International Vision Institute
The International Vision Institute
The International Vision Institute
The International Vision Institute
The International Vision Institute
The International Vision Institute
The International Vision Institute
The International Vision Institute

Figure 10.5 Different typeface, different identity.

A corporate identity programme

In 2000 Manchester Business School began a reappraisal of its identity and image. Surveys were conducted of students on the flagship MBA programme, on executive and research degree programmes, and of staff, both academic and support staff. Other surveys followed of potential MBA applicants in ten countries, of managers responsible for training and development in companies that had used the services of the Business School, and those who had not. What follows is the story of the development of a novel approach to a corporate logo, one that was defined by using the corporate reputation scale.

By the middle of 2000 marketing staff at MBS had identified those parts of the MBS personality that satisfied both staff and student stakeholders and in particular those aspects that they wished to feature in their corporate communications. Figure 10.6 is an abstract of the brief sent out to a number of agencies inviting them to present their ideas as to how they might interpret the brief in a new logo. For the previous decade, MBS had relied on a simple typographical form of logo with the letters M, B and S picked out in a red colour in the words Manchester Business School.

Extracts from the Manchester Business School corporate personality brief

Manchester Business School is seeking to update its corporate personality to more accurately reflect its strengths and aspirations. By corporate personality we mean the organized visual and verbal imagery to internal and external audiences. Our current personality is consistent across all media apart from the web, where a new web logo, strapline and creative feel was used as part of the launch of our new site. Agencies should be aware that other creative agencies may be used to apply corporate identity work in practice and therefore comprehensive corporate guideline manuals will be required.

Established in 1965, Manchester Business School was one of the first schools to offer a coherent long-term philosophy to management development, one based on real business problems and real business opportunities. Our practical project-based approach to learning is acknowledged throughout the world as the 'Manchester Method', developing managers with the hands-on experience required in an increasingly competitive and international arena.

A copy of a new mission and vision statements was included, the most relevant parts for the agency brief being the following:

Mission

> Our mission is to develop the business leaders of tomorrow, within a culture where undertaking original research and consultancy enriches and continually improves our teaching. We aim to pursue our mission locally, nationally and internationally and primarily to the activities of postgraduate and post-experience education and training.

Vision 2000

Our vision of ourselves is:

> Manchester Business School is seen, globally, as an academic leader, one of the top business schools. We pride ourselves on our innovation, in 'getting there first' to identify what senior managers will need to know and to do, not only today, but into the future. Our work is guided by an inclusive stakeholder approach, which reflects the views of our employees, students, business partners, peer institutions and government and community organizations.
>
> Inside the school, we work in a lively, bustling atmosphere where ideas can be shared openly without the hindrance of internal boundaries. We strive to be honest and friendly in our dealings with each other.

The brief continued with a summary of the research as follows:

The MBS personality

> We aim to promote the following aspects of our personality both internally and externally. We believe that a strong personality is not created through an advertising slogan but by many real illustrations and examples. The following brief then applies to all of our communications.

Agreeableness

We aim to promote actions and activities that demonstrate our sincerity in dealing with each other and with external stakeholders. In particular we need to provide evidence of our trust in each other, evidence to show that external stakeholders can rely upon promises we make and in our honesty. We need to demonstrate that when we deal with all stakeholders that we do so with their interests in mind.

Competence

We need to provide evidence of our leading rather than following markets and trends. We need to assure all stakeholders that we are reliable, that what we say we do. As a research driven organization, we are inherently innovative as a culture but we need to provide evidence of this and how it benefits external stakeholders. We need to communicate this externally and celebrate examples internally.

Enterprise

Much of what happens at MBS is exciting, but not always seen by us as being so. We need to provide evidence of how we excite those who come into contact with our organization. Specifically we need to demonstrate to ourselves and to our potential stakeholders that we are up to date and imaginative.

Areas of usage

We anticipate being fully advised by our agency partner, but key areas for consideration are:

- brochures
- advertising
- stationery
- vehicle decals
- corporate signage

In verbal briefings it was emphasized that the core value that MBS wished to encapsulate was that of innovation. As a research based school, stakeholders should expect new, perhaps even controversial thinking from MBS.

A number of agencies responded to the brief and a selection were short listed to present their thinking in more detail. As is normal in such a context, the ideas from agencies varied dramatically, including one suggestion that MBS change its name. Most focused on a relatively traditional style of logo, reflecting the more traditional aspects of a university and business school. One was very different. A relatively young company, Design Associates from Huddersfield in the north of England presented their thinking, not taking the hour or so as some of their competitors, but in minutes. They presented a green box-shaped logo and proposed that different areas within the business school would each create their own versions of the logo using this simple form as a base. Figure 10.6a shows examples from their presentation of the logo itself and 10.6b examples that were sketched during the meeting of how the logo might be used in different parts of the Business School.

Figure 10.6a The original green box design.

Figure 10.6b The original green box design with examples of its application.

The group of marketing staff, academics, and students who saw their presentation felt immediately that the agency had responded to the brief in an innovative and direct way. The approach was innovative, the main platform for the new direction the school wanted to go in. It was inclusive in that students and staff would be involved in creating their own variants of the logo. While Design Association's thinking was a good match to the brief, the group had to recognize some of the dangers of being so innovative. The agency were asked to work on the box and to 'give it more character'. Their second version was less plain and the marketers felt that there had been some progress. A number of group discussions were held to compare the 'green box' approach with the work of a more conventional agency. The green box researched far closer to the brief but was seen as somewhat risky, too trendy and lacking a corporate dimension that people wanted not to lose.

Design Associates were asked to provide some further evolution of their ideas to make the box appear less trendy and more corporate. Their response was to change the colour to purple and to suggest the addition of a strap line (Figure 10.7). The decision was made to go ahead.

In 2001 different departments within MBS met to evolve their own version of the logo, Figure 10.8.

The logo was also applied to signage within the building, for example to the coffee shop (Figure 10.9).

Figure 10.7 The final version of the logo.

Figure 10.8 The logo as modified for use by the school's Centre for Business Research.

Figure 10.9 The logo applied to signage.

Managing diverse stakeholder groups

In this book we focus on the two main stakeholders for any organization, its customers and employees but an organization has many stakeholders. For a public company, shareholders are the owners/stakeholders but they are not the only group that are concerned about the financial well-being of the company. The major shareholders in any company tend to be institutions rather than individuals. Both types of investor will have their advisers. Financial journalists will play a similar role in appraising the likely movement in the company's share price. Ask most executives what the primary goal is of an organization and the answer will often be 'survival' or 'sales growth' or 'profit'. Investors in corporations do not always see things in the same way. They are often concerned to see the price of the shares they own rise, so that they can make a capital gain.

Many CEOs will see their company's share price as their prime concern. Many will have salary and benefits packages that depend upon the share price rising. Relationships with investors, the stock market and with those who make their living as commentators and analysts are often the responsibility of the finance director who will try to put a realistic but favourable picture in front of external stakeholders. Given the choice many FDs would prefer to see their share price over, rather than under valued, rising rather than falling. It makes it easier to raise capital; investors are happier and analysts less inquisitive.

There are many ways to assess a company's share price, the ratio of price to earnings, the ratio of assets to shareholder value. There will be many examples of shares where it is difficult to explain the price on the basis of purely rational calculation. Markets, it seems, factor in their future expectations of the ability of a company to grow its sales and profit and therefore its real value as a company. Thus judgement forms part of the equation. We have done one study of the image of an organization held by external stakeholders, analysts concerned with the financial performance of that organization (Figure 10.10).

The analysts' view of the corporate personality contrasts with the senior

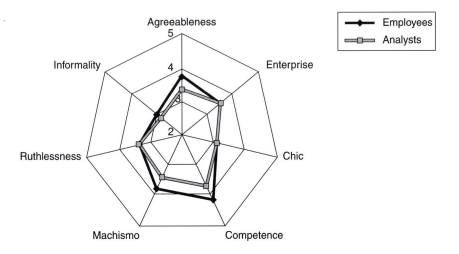

Figure 10.10 Internal and external views of financial management.

managers' view. They are subtly different. Employees see themselves as more agreeable, competent, and macho. Analysts appeared to doubt the sincerity of the company and their ability. It is likely that the company's share price would suffer as a result.

Specialist public relations companies exist whose role it is to ensure that such gaps in perception do not exist. What is clear is that, while they might be able to influence the external view directly, a better starting point might be inside the organization to identify what their managers were doing or not doing to satisfy the external financial analysts.

Lessons

This chapter has covered three very different topics, mergers, visual identity, and influencing minor but important stakeholder views. There are specific lessons within each area, but there are some general ones too that we should point to. One is the benefit of measurement. Reputation, image, visual identity, the perceptions of staff, are all intangible, open to interpretation and inherently difficult to nail down. A major benefit to us of having a quantitative scale is that you can 'nail things'. There will be areas of controversy as with any metaphorical approach but 'what gets measured gets done' is a useful and relevant saying. Even though the corporate reputation scale can never be more than a proxy for reality, it is easy to interpret into meaningful action. To date, Reputation Management has lacked analytical tools that provide direction.

---

11 Managing the personality of the organization

The different personalities of organizations, how they manifest their effects upon staff and customers and other stakeholders, what to do, the organization of the future.

In our work we have, at the time of writing this book, looked in depth at the personality of fifteen organizations. We have looked at the way reputation is managed in fourteen other commercial organizations. We have undertaken small-scale studies in a number of other organizations. The sectors we have worked in and with range from small not for profit organizations to global leaders in both services and manufacturing. Our work has been mainly in the services sector (where corporate branding tends to be the norm) where we believe our approach will be of most value. Between us we have individual experience of many more organizations as researchers, customers, and as employees. The purpose of this chapter is to paint a picture of the characteristics of organizations we have known, loved, hated using the personality framework that forms our main contribution to the study of corporate reputation. We emphasize that a main tenet in the reputation paradigm is that the way customer facing employees see their organization will influence the way customers see it. We end with an overview of how we feel every organization should manage its reputation.

We have shown how perceptions of corporate personality can drive the satisfaction of staff and employees and how this links to sales growth or decline. But how can any management recognize aspects of one or more personality dimensions within their own organization and what typically they can do about it? We will try to paint a picture of what it feels like to work within each main type of personality and what it feels like to be their customer.

The agreeable organization

Agreeableness with its three traits of warmth, empathy, and integrity is the most important dimension of corporate personality. It explains more variation between the way people see organizations and the perceptions people hold of them than any other dimension. It is highly likely to correlate with the satisfaction of both employees and customers and is matched only by *competence* in explaining both staff and customer satisfaction. On its own, it explains more than 40 per cent of the variation in staff satisfaction and more than 30 per cent of customer satisfaction. In other words improving on *agreeableness* is the easiest way to improve both staff and customer satisfaction. As satisfaction usually drives financial performance, it is often the easiest way to improve business performance.

First impressions count and the *agreeable* organization has this off to a T. They know intuitively that you are anxious as a new customer, that their performance may reflect on you for choosing them as a supplier, that your money was hard earned, and that you want to be assured that spending it with them is going to be a good decision. The *agreeable* company are confident enough in their products and services to know that the experience will be satisfactory but they also realize that quality of service or product is not enough. A new customer needs reassurance. You, the customer, want to believe that they are on their side, that you will not be ripped off, that what it said in the glossy brochure will be fulfilled in delivery.

But you want some sign of that *now*, even before you have parted with your money. You know that the doctor cannot guarantee that the operation will be totally successful. You know that the price of stocks and shares can fall as well as rise. But you do not want to be constantly warned about the possible dangers of what you are about to decide upon. You want to know that the doctor or broker are going to do their best, and that they are confident in their own abilities to produce a positive result if at all possible. Right from that first moment you need to believe as a customer that staff are concerned for your well-being and that they see things through their eyes as well as through their own. The *agreeable* organization delivers an initial feeling of confidence in the prospective customer.

As the relationship develops and you buy more from the organization some things might change. Something might even go wrong. Always concerned, the *agreeable* company employee will phone you to warn you that delivery will be late, not on the day before you are expecting what you paid for to arrive, but as soon as they know themselves. Yes, given enough notice, you may now decide to go elsewhere and the *agreeable* company may be risking one lost sale. But without evidence of concern they will risk losing a customer, and with you many lost sales in the future.

After delivery of an expensive piece of furniture there is a follow-up to see whether you are satisfied and a quick response if you say no. You are not asked to sign a delivery note that says, within a myriad of small print, that you have examined the goods and that they are in perfect order, only to find that there is a fault. In an expensive restaurant you are not asked whether 'everything is all right' half way through your meal. You are asked whether you are enjoying yourself, because that is the main reason why you are spending time and money with them. The hotel you are staying in overnight prior to an important meeting does not ask you to complete a questionnaire about whether the bed sheets were turned down, when what you wanted, and did not get, was a good night's sleep, because a security door in the corridor was banging all night. The *agreeable* organization's employees are as concerned that you are satisfied as they are that you bought from them in the first place. They treat you as they would like to be treated themselves.

Their customer handling skills are excellent. They take the initiative, approaching you not in a way that implies that they have been through, and suffered from, a highly packaged training programme (one that produces automatons not real people) but because they like dealing with people; they are people minded. The *agreeable* dimension of corporate personality is close to the dimension of the same name in human personality. *Agreeable* individuals see the best in others. They prefer to be in a group, and their hobbies indicate a preference for activities that require team effort. Agreeableness in human beings can be identified by a straightforward personality test and the *agreeable* company will look to recruit those who score highly on this personality dimension.

The *agreeable* organization scores highly on integrity. *Trust* is a key word here, but many organizations aspire to do better than this. Trust requires evidence and if one experience falls below our expectations then we are more wary the next time. Above trust are feelings such as belief and faith. While trust demands evidence to reinforce it, organizations in which we believe or that we have faith in can afford an occasional lapse in performance, because we are willing to give them the benefit of the doubt. We are convinced that they are doing their best.

This story used to be told of one of Britains' leading retailers Marks and Spencer. The retailer sells only own-brand products and pioneered what became known as 'ready meals', precooked meals such as Chinese pork in black bean sauce. Such dishes can be prepared by warming or briefly cooking them in the oven or more usually in the microwave, typically by microwaving for three to four minutes. The story goes like this: a customer purchased a ready meal from Marks and Spencer, took it home, and followed the instructions on microwaving the food carefully. 'Remove outer packaging. Pierce film. Place in microwave. Set timer for four minutes. Stir and serve'. However the dish was disappointing; the taste and texture were poor. The following day the customer phoned Marks and Spencer asking what *he* had done wrong in preparing the meal, in the belief that the company could not be at fault themselves. The story illustrates perfectly what faith and belief in a company can mean. In the late 1990s the retailer lost the faith the British consumer once had in them. They were still trusted, but customers now wanted evidence. They were more likely to question what the retailer did, to compare value for money elsewhere and not to accept that because 'it came from Marks it must be OK'.

Social responsibility is a feature of *agreeable* organizations. They, or rather their employees are concerned about social issues, the environment, about society as a whole and their impact upon it as an organization. They want to use their power to give back something to the community that has provided them with a living. This is not about adopting a 'company charity'. It is about whether the spirit inside the company means that employees want to feel part of the community they sell into. Too often a company will use its sponsorship of a good cause in its publicity, trumpeting its benevolence. Next year a new cause is found, one that is more likely to make headlines for the business. The corporate communications department will identify a cause that is 'compatible with our market position'. Compare this to the examples of corporate leaders who give their personal time to a good cause, to the establishment by some companies of permanent trusts to benefit society, such as that by sugar company

Tate or by bankers Rockefeller. Volunteerism is a current buzzword representing a significant attempt to link organizations to their communities, but the following example illustrates the cynical way in which staff can be exploited.

Staff in an educational establishment (not one associated with any of the authors) had been treated shabbily in their opinion by the senior management. Contracts of employment had been changed unilaterally. The working week was extended and holidays cut. Management believed that this would allow them to teach the same number of students but at a lower cost. Staff had to reapply for their own jobs but under the new terms and conditions of employment. Job titles were changed from lecturer to 'trainer', implying a lower level of skill, but the work required was no different. Staff knew that if they were not successful in their application that they would be made redundant and that most would have difficulty finding a similar job without moving from the area. Many of the staff were married women and it would be difficult to find equivalent work.

Even when the new contracts arrived for those fortunate enough to come through their interviews successfully, the contracts were not as attractive as many had believed they would be. Some staff left. Others were recruited to replace them but many of these lacked any of the formal qualifications normally expected of educators. Some had problems spelling common words. Staff turnover increased as many new arrivals left within a short time of joining.

About a year after changing the contracts, senior management sent around a memorandum asking, or rather instructing staff, to list their outside activities with voluntary groups, so that the college could boast about the contribution they were making to the community. Staff were advised that they should volunteer for roles such as members of the governing body of their local school. At no time was any support offered to staff who might wish to spend their spare time in a voluntary role. Staff felt that what they did in their diminishing free time was no concern of their employer.

A second memorandum came round voicing management concern at the poor response of staff to the first memorandum.

When staff volunteer for something, their employer can only expect to associate itself with their efforts if they offer tangible support to encourage staff to participate.

Social responsibility is a major issue for very different reasons for those who manufacture cigarettes or armaments. Values change in society and as smoking has become less and less socially acceptable, so the reputations of tobacco companies have suffered. With weapons manufacturers, we tend to forget the times when, without weapons, democracy would have been overrun by the less socially responsible dictatorships of the world. At the same time it is right that mass shootings in various countries call into question the ethics of those who market arms that land up being used by individuals who are clearly incapable of knowing right from wrong.

Being responsible does not just mean that you stay within the law. It means more than that. You need to think beyond what your products are used for and consider what happens to them once they are discarded. Car manufacturers will have to make their vehicles recyclable. Each component will need to be labelled such that the metals in the alloy can be identified and that the plastic monomers can be identified in each plastic part. Some car companies began the necessary processes of redesign and re-specification well before the legislators decided to introduce any legal requirement. Cynics might argue that the initiative, by two German car manufacturers, was more self interest than social responsibility, that having a ten year start and then convincing the EU that recycling of cars was the way forward, was just business acumen. Whatever the real reason, they caught the mood at the time in Europe that the environment needed to be protected, that natural resources must be conserved and that recycling is a core, not a peripheral, issue for any manufacturer.

Being responsible means thinking for your customer. Years ago the story of the woman who sued the manufacturer of her microwave oven because it burnt her pet dog when she used it to dry the animal, was a commonly told joke. She claimed that the manufacturer had failed to inform her about improper use. Now companies have to think the unthinkable and to put common sense advice on the product packaging or in their instructions to ensure that they cannot be accused of putting customers at risk.

Compare this with the traditional adage of *caveat emptor*, 'let the buyer beware'. Customers had to inspect a purchase before leaving the store. Once outside, any fault became their problem. Generations of consumer legislation ensured that those who sold to the public took their responsibilities more seriously and that responsibility was clearly identified with the seller. Times move on again and now social responsibility is something that companies seek to lead on, and not just follow the legislation.

Social responsibility is associated with *honesty, trust,* and *sincerity* in our Corporate Personality Scale. This means that being seen as being socially responsible contributes with these three traits to being seen as having integrity. Put another way if an organization is seen as socially irresponsible it will be judged as lacking integrity.

The *agreeable* organization treats its employees and suppliers with *integrity*. If a promise is given it is kept. Employees do not have rewards dangled in front of them, only for others, more politically adept but less hard working, to be seen to benefit in the next round of promotions. It is highly likely that the company has an appraisal scheme where manager and managed are both trained in how to give and receive constructive comment on the employee's work and to agree the main objectives for the coming period. Suppliers to the *agreeable* company feel trusted to do what has been agreed and in turn can trust that their customer will consider their perspective. Relationships are rarely transactional and are normally relational. Supplier and buyer do not sit down to haggle over a small price reduction but work together to improve each other's profits by increasing overall sales and lowering the costs of doing so in the long term.

The agreeable organization is honest. Few companies would want to be seen as dishonest but many are. They hide behind a façade of integrity. One British company markets products for the elderly. They use the image of a well-known British hero in their self-promotion but have no apparent links to the individual. One 93-year-old was keen to buy an electrically operated, reclining chair, following a minor stroke. She contacted the company and a salesman called and demonstrated a chair. He recommended a number of changes to the model he demonstrated to suit her size and shape. A discount was offered for immediate payment and for the part exchange of her existing chair.

The new chair arrived but was clearly the wrong size and shape and was uncomfortable. After a number of phone calls and letters a director of the company visited the customer's home and recommended various changes for which he suggested the company would charge, as the choice of chair size and design 'had been the customer's' – which was untrue. Eventually the company agreed to build a new chair. When it arrived it was little different from the first one. The company offered to amend the new chair, but not in a way that appeared to the customer to have a chance of giving her what she wanted. Frustrated by the months of delay and discomfort, the customer demanded her money back and the return of her original chair. Both requests were ignored. It took a court order before the company gave a refund. The original chair was never returned. An alternative chair with the same functionality was purchased from another supplier at one third of the price paid to the dishonest organization.

Agreeable organizations care for their employees, but they are not a soft touch as, for example, ignoring persistent absence for no good cause means that other employees carry an unfair burden. Compassion is often embedded in acts such as 'compassionate leave' in any company, but is it always present in the way employees treat each other? Do employees treat each other with respect? There will be in any organization certain codes of behaviour in the way employees treat each other and what is considered good or bad in these will vary by culture, but a greeting at the beginning of the day would probably be expected, something to acknowledge a colleague as a human being. A few minutes to enquire after a colleague's well-being is another way of showing concern and respect. If a fellow employee suffers a set back or has a problem they are struggling with, is the reaction of others one of relief that they are not in the same situation, or does everyone 'muck in' to help, in the certain knowledge that when they need help it will be freely given to them?

There is a clear role here for an induction programme for new employees to contain not only facts and figures but also guidance on appropriate behaviour. Managers will often be seen as role models and younger employees will pick up their good as well as their bad habits. Body language is a topic familiar to most managers today. Of the issues associated with non-verbal communication, listening skills are possibly the most important. We need to receive feedback when we are trying to say something important. This could be a nod of the head or a repetition back to us of one or more of the points at issue. Employees and managers can be trained to be sensitive to non-verbal communication and it is likely that the *agreeable* organization offers training to its employees in both skills and sensitivity.

One area where we would question the use of the word 'training' is that of customer care. Training can imply the opportunity to develop skills through practice, or it can imply forcing something to go in a direction it really does not want to go, as in training a rose up a trellis. Too many training programmes appear to have been designed by frustrated gardeners, keen to force employees into behaviour patterns that the trainer has predetermined to be desirable. Training videos tend to spell out what customer facing staff 'must do' in certain circumstances. Conversations with customers are often recorded or monitored to ensure compliance with predetermined response patterns. If you are training roses or circus animals then such a didactic approach is fine. If there are certain legal requirements to fulfil, such as ensuring staff working for a financial services company do not give inappropriate advice, then fine. But if you wish to win hearts and minds and bring out the latent humanity within us all in dealing with other human beings, then such an approach does not work, beyond the point of training in certain responses. Yes every customer facing employee needs to absorb the basics of serving the customer, how to place a hamburger in a box hygienically and attractively, how to measure a customer for a suit, how to use an overhead projector in making a presentation. But can you apply the same to training to promoting *warmth* and *empathy*? Companies have tried. Edicts such as 'smile within the first 30 seconds of meeting the customer', 'place the change into a customer's palm so as to bond with her', and 'always end the customer contact with the words "have a nice day"' have left us all with memories of being served by apparently mindless robots. Leave acting to actors. Theatre audiences know that they are entering a world of make believe. They accept the exaggerated gestures and speech of thespians performing a role. Customers in a service business want to meet real human beings, not actors, and the best training programmes recognize this by appealing to employees as human beings.

The most outstanding training video we have ever seen is this context is from the retailer profiled in Chapter 7. The dominant theme in the training video is a checkout operator who gradually realizes that her customers have had just as bad a day as she has, that the poor service she gets herself in other shops is a reason for giving better service in her own work. There are no specific training messages. There are no words, no instructions, the only sound is a backing track from the hit song by Irish pop group the Corrs, 'What can I do to make you love me?' The video is totally and unashamedly emotional in its appeal to the feelings of the checkout operator. It is perhaps incredible but true that people watching it can often barely hold back their tears, such is the emotive style of the film. The video is one of few examples of attempts to engage the customer facing employee emotionally. It is the equivalent of the emotional appeal of the television advertisement. If companies accept that customers can be influenced by emotional rather than purely rational presentation of their products, why do they not appear to accept that employees can be influenced by a similar emotional appeal in their training?

The competent organization

Competence is the second most important driver of satisfaction for both staff and customers. Interestingly it is not quite as important as *agreeableness*, but it should be remembered that our work has been solely concerned with actual employees and customers of the organizations we have worked with and not lapsed or potential ones. The respondents to our surveys would not be customers if they thought the company we were asking them about was incompetent.

There are three facets to *competence: conscientiousness, drive,* and *technocracy.* *Conscientiousness* is the easiest to explain. Customers in particular want to feel that the company is *reliable.* They are accurate in their work, careful in what they do, meticulous even. Their approach is probably underpinned by a strong sense of moral principle, a sense of what is right. Employees are serious about their work. Organizations such as consultancies, educational establishments and engineering companies will place particular emphasis on this dimension. Employees will pride themselves on their hard work and long hours. They will be persistent in their search for a technical solution to a customer's problem, eager even zealous in their pursuit of the answer. In dealing with the customer they will be dutiful and sometimes too keen to provide what is wanted at the expense of cost considerations.

We would expect most professional organizations, lawyers, teachers, doctors to be motivated by a feeling of *conscientiousness.* A feeling of professionalism will stem from being authoritative, in mastering the complex. Occasionally customers will feel that this concern for precision gets in the way of producing results that are as useful as they need them to be. Things will be presented to them as black and white with no room for alternative interpretation unless the customer has the courage and the specialist knowledge to challenge what is being said to them. At its worst *conscientiousness* will manifest itself in appearing to be rigid, overly strict, and finicky. Budgets will be exceeded, as will timescales, as the conscientious professional assiduously ensures that their work is beyond challenge. The notion that getting it 90 per cent right and moving on to the next problem will be an anathema.

Not surprisingly *conscientious* organizations will seek to employ those who score highly on the equivalent human personality trait. Conscientiousness correlates with superior job performance in a number of studies, but not in all. In some roles, blind adherence to the rules, irrespective of what the customer wants, is counterproductive.

Balancing the dangers of over emphasizing points of detail is the *drive* facet of the *competent* organization. The company and its employees are *ambitious* and *achievement oriented.* They want to be first, to be seen as winning. Employees are enthusiastic about their work but could be seen as too ambitious and too pushy. If this trait dominates there may be too many leaders in the company and perhaps too few 'completer finishers' wanting to sort out the detail. Companies probably need a balance between *drive* and *conscientiousness.*

Working for such an organization can be exciting. The senior management are goal oriented, aggressive in wanting success, and totally competitive. They are not afraid to take decisions and their moves will often be seen by the media and the business press as being bold, even audacious. The traits they seek in their employees mirror this. Such a company is perhaps no place for the faint hearted.

The third facet within *competence* mirrors the existence in many companies of a strong *technocracy*. In many markets a technocratic orientation is essential and we would expect to find this trait within most manufacturing organizations and especially in those involved in product areas such as electronics and pharmaceuticals. Twinned with the word 'technical' in this facet is the word 'corporate' indicating that technocracy is not just about matters technical. The word 'corporate' evokes pictures of corporate man, personified in the 1980s by the stereotyping of IBM employees as always wearing a white shirt, dark blue suit and tie to match. It also suggests bureaucracy and management structures. At its best a *technocracy* is highly organized, divided into functional areas to promote specialism, with each component having a clear view of what it does and what the other parts of the corporate machine are doing. At its worst it suggests too bureaucratic a business which has become inflexible and which is losing market focus. For example, new products are designed inside the company with little reference to the marketplace. Firms counter this possibility by introducing cross-functional teams, breaking down hierarchies, making organizations flatter, or even doing away with formal structures.

The *competent* organization is nevertheless just what the label implies. It is good at what it does. It produces and markets quality products and services. Not too surprisingly the *competence* dimension correlates strongly with financial performance. It is also the dimension most likely to be featured in the content of company mission and vision statements, Chapter 8.

Organizations can demonstrate competence but they can also infer it in the way they present themselves to potential customers. A bank will have a strong looking stone façade, implying reliability. An advertising agency can have examples of its work and testimonials from 'blue chip' clients. A small company can pay the fees for one of the larger accountancy practices because it wishes to infer a certain standard. A consultancy can move to a new address to imply that it is a leading player.

Competence is the most rational of our dimensions. Small wonder that it features strongly in the communication strategies of organizations and in their attempts to 'tangibilize' service quality. Product manufacturers can boast about independent tests, about making to international standards. Service companies can join professional organizations whose responsibility it is to monitor the quality of their members.

Training rather than development is a more obvious strategy to use to improve upon basic competencies. Firms will be concerned to ensure that they meet minimum standards for their sector in terms of formal qualification. One issue is whether academic qualifications required by many professions are indications of competence. Governments have moved to introduce competence based qualifications but in general these have failed to match the acceptance or prestige of traditional academic, examination based qualifications.

The enterprising organization

The third most important predictor of customer and staff satisfaction is *enterprise*. Staff often like to work for enterprising organizations and customers like to buy from them. *Enterprise* consists of three facets, *modernity, adventure,* and *boldness*. In markets such as fashion and the arts this dimension is one of the keys to success. *Modernity* is characterized by being seen as *cool*. Not that this means being chilly or off hand, far from it. *Cool* here means aplomb, poise, very much the modern interpretation of the word. Certain things are *cool* to do and being employed by such an organization or buying from them is the *cool* thing to do. *Cool* companies are seen as sophisticated and *trendy*, fashionable to be associated with, part of the contemporary scene. There is a freshness about their way of doing things that attracts.

On the down side *modernity* may imply 'here today but gone tomorrow'. Companies lack tradition and solidity. They are *young*, full of energy but perhaps as yet unproven. If you are seen as too *young* you risk being thought of as immature or even juvenile and brash, too audacious and presumptuous. This facet is also a problem for a more established company. Take for example an advertising agency that might have attracted attention in its early days because its ideas were different, outrageous even. As it matures does it continue to present itself in the same way or does it now present a calmer image so as to attract more interest from the mainstream of the market that are more risk averse? Many such companies have to re-invent themselves from time to time, bring in new blood, return to their roots. Without such actions what was once seen as trendy will be seen as staid. The retailer Laura Ashley became a shorthand for out of date 1970s fashion in the 1990s. It needed refreshing and rejuvenation but successive managing directors failed to breathe new life into an ageing brand.

An image for being *enterprising* is not one that every organization should aspire to. Combining *competence* with *enterprise* may be a mistake if say, you are a bank, yet one analysis indicated that the MBNA bank was trying to do just this in its self-presentation on its website, Chapter 8.

The second facet within *enterprise* is *adventure*. This is the creative facet. Companies scoring highly here are likely to be those customers go to for original ideas, advertising and design companies, interior decorators, television production companies. They have an image for being talented and ingenious, quick witted and resourceful. They could be regarded as the seminal source for a particular expertise, courted by the media for a comment on a topical issue. We would also expect certain consultancies, think tanks, research organizations and arts organizations to score highly on this dimension. The dimension might also be essential in publishing and in the media generally. The down side to this trait would become clear when the company's ideas are seen as too fanciful or their approach too slick and potentially shallow. An image combined with *competence* might be useful here to assure the less confident customer.

The same facet contains the item *up to date* implying that the organization is at the leading edge in its field. It is a source of whatever is new fangled and *innovative*. Their knowledge is current. Their solutions to problems are forward looking. They are not afraid of standing out from the crowd and are regarded as being independent in their stance. Customers with a choice of supplier between an *enterprising* or a *competent* organization would look to the former for more radical ideas, more *innovation* and creativity. Such suppliers or distributors only carry the more fashionable and innovative lines, the latest models.

The third item in this facet, *exciting*, tells you what it is like to work with or deal with such a company. It is stimulating and galvanizing, if a little wearing after a while. The experience is memorable and, if it is positive, potentially momentous for the customer. One good idea, one new perspective can transform a business and this is the organization that might be the source of such inspiration. The ideas will have to be sold well. Novelty is not enough, the ideas will have to be seen as powerful, compelling, and inspirational.

The *enterprising* organization is seen as *innovative*. It is not satisfied with the status quo. It spends time and resources on new product development and on new ideas. Management may appear to neglect established products, the cash cows of the company, and spend too much time on new ventures. The new ideas will rarely result in successful new business and this can be frustrating to those working on the cash cows, yet the need to innovate is a cultural one, a constant search for improvement. The organization benefits from its image in the marketplace but some customers will be reluctant to adopt the new idea or the new product. An image for innovation does not mean that customers will always buy the latest products, preferring instead the idea that their supplier is forward thinking and that this reassures them that the supplier is not stuck in the past.

The final facet is *boldness* and here there is a warning about some of the dangers of dealing with the enterprising company. Their audacity may veer towards insolence in their dealings with you. *Boldness* might be manifest in bluster, what is presented as new and exciting might have too little underpinning it. On the other hand they will have the courage to tell you what they think and if their reasoning is sound it will pay to listen, even if the way it is put is verging on the insensitive. *Boldness* consists of *extroversion* and *daring*. *Extroversion* is one of the main human personality characteristics and it is likely that the *enterprising* organization will employ its share of people who are outgoing and self-confident, people who have an inner confidence, who are relaxed in dealing with others in an affable style.

The business class carriage on a train is often a somewhat formal environment. There is some noise, but of mobile phones and the clatter of laptop keyboards. Few people engage in conversation unless they have to. Longer journeys can be boring. Time creeps by, as there is little to fill it with. Staff serve meals competently and the ticket collector is polite and informative, but they do little to entertain, that is not their role.

One journey was enlivened by a new, relatively young employee, who made sure that her customers noticed her. As she pushed the coffee trolley down the carriage she shouted, 'Is anyone alive in here? Goodness there is'. Similar comments and repartee followed.

She survived in her role about a month.

Fun was the third most frequently cited 'value' in the survey reported in Chapter 2. It is unfortunately not always valued by employers or even by other employees and the odd customer who may think the type of behaviour exhibited by the young employee mentioned in this example to be 'inappropriate'. 'Fun' days are introduced where employees are told that fun is now appropriate. Staff Christmas parties are often less than fun affairs. Try asking your own staff whether you are fun to work for and then you might discover whether you are part of any problem. You might enjoy coming to work but do they? Fun people can make an organization. Others like to be associated with them. They may have a fund of jokes. They will certainly see the funny side of life and ensure that the organization does not take itself too seriously. Some customers may appear to see funsters as acting inappropriately, but these are the ones that customers will talk about when they remember your company, not the more conscientious.

The chic organization

Chic is the overall label for the dimension of corporate personality that is most concerned with a deliberate attempt to manage external image. *Chic* has the facets of *elegance, prestige,* and *snobbery*. The *chic* organization is inherently attractive. It presents an image of being up-market, while companies who score poorly on this dimension may be seen as down-market and probably low cost/low price in their overall positioning. Being *chic* does not mean that you will be profitable. In fact being un-chic and low price/low cost is probably a better strategy for making money. However employees will be reluctant to admit that they work for an 'un-chic' employer.

The dimension evokes pictures of a luxury hotel chain, a manufacturer of *haute couture*, an elegant department store, a French wine chateau, an island resort in the Caribbean. There is an aura of exclusiveness, of appealing to the upper echelons of society or to the companies who regard themselves as being similarly placed at the elite end of the business hierarchy. The media have a fascination with such companies and with the personalities that run them. They include the fashion house of Dior and heavily branded companies such as Gucci. Companies involved in horse racing or motor racing will combine elements of *chic* and the *adventure* dimension of the *enterprising* organization. Organizations that will inevitably score low on this dimension will be those involved in primary goods production, mining, steel making, most of agriculture, but such companies should not be concerned. If they were to be seen as *chic* then they should start to worry! If the organization scores high on this dimension then it will be difficult for competitors to emulate it. The product or services it offers may not be unique but its imagery will be. There is only one Rolls Royce car, only one Rolex watch, one DeBeer diamond, one Rothschild bank.

The *elegance* facet of being *chic* contains the items *charming, stylish,* and *elegant*; words that are almost synonyms. Only the most discerning of customers need to bother to shop here if we are talking about the retail sector. If we are thinking of a bank then it is one where you would not expect to see a queue. Your own personal banker may even come to visit you. If you have to ask the price in the *chic* business then you probably cannot afford the tariff.

'Good manners' is a phrase that probably appears in the staff manual of how to deal with customers. Civility and ceremony are important. We are talking Ivy League not state owned, breeding not training. A business lunch here will be in surroundings that many of us are unused to. Double-barrelled surnames litter the list of employees. A private education is valuable and family connections important in gaining employment. Customers are managed with tact and diplomacy.

The second facet is *prestige*. Suppliers will boast about you in their list of customers, sorry, list of clients. The built environment is likely to be used to position these organizations to their stakeholders. The carpet will be of a certain quality, not functionality. This is a Marriott hotel not a Holiday Inn. Lighting will illuminate in two ways, the *prestige* of being and working there and the general stylishness of the décor. There will be a certain cachet in being a stakeholder. The company will give its customers a sense of being a member of an exclusive group. Celebrity names will be prominent among the customer base.

Working for the *prestigious* organization does not necessarily mean high salaries. The privilege of working there is part of the remuneration package. It offers in itself a certain social standing. Certain roles in society will benefit from the positive associations of the kudos or admiration that working in this or that profession affords. Once upon a time being a teacher or a nurse were two professions that were rarely well paid, but which carried a social status and respect that compensated for the poor financial rewards. As society became more demanding of education and healthcare and more questioning of standards, as professional management replaced trust as their method of getting things done, then both teachers and nurses have sought higher tangible rewards.

The *prestigious* organization will often be well connected. It will have influence in high places reflecting the status of its clientele. Staff might benefit from the same contacts in furthering their own careers. Their own personal image is likely to matter to them: urbane, cosmopolitan, and polished may be words that would be used to describe them. They, the employees, will form a key part of their employer's image. Some might see the employees as being too genteel, too sophisticated, putting on airs and graces rather than being themselves. Here the negative trait within chicness is relevant, that of *snobbery*. Self-importance and pomposity might take over in dealing with both customers and staff who might not fit with the self-image of the established staff. Some potential customers may be made to feel awkward and will leave without buying. Self-importance and over confidence leads to a loss of market focus. Others offer better value for money. Yet the attractiveness to some of the final item, *elitist* is undeniable. The elite are the best, the top, *la crème de la crème*, and for many of us that is where we want to be.

What is *chic* changes over time. Many restaurants aim to be seen as *chic* only to find that their opinion forming clientele have moved on almost as soon as they have arrived. It is *chic* to do one thing one year and *passé* to repeat it the next. The *chic* organization needs to be quick to identify trends, to change itself frequently.

The ruthless organization

At first sight the *ruthless* organization is one that cannot succeed. It is true that this dimension is the only one consistently co-related negatively with satisfaction. However in one company we have worked with *ruthlessness*, as seen by customers, co-related positively with financial performance.

Staff appear to be more negatively affected in their satisfaction by *ruthlessness* than are customers. Nevertheless, *ruthlessness* should be an area of concern to all organizations. Its two traits are labelled *egotism* and *dominance*. *Egotism* extends the negative trait of *snobbery* within *chic*. Its first item, *arrogance* implies that the organization is seen as conceited, pompous and pretentious. However in our experience the real issue here is how people are treated. The *arrogant* organization 'tells' its employees what to do and how to do it. The management model is essentially top down. There is little in the way of empowerment of customer facing employees. Employees have no say in how the customer is treated, which can be frustrating if employees can see all too clearly how customer satisfaction can be improved. Employees are treated much as part of the machinery and not necessarily as sentient beings. For many this is fine. If you come to work with the attitude that you are not paid enough to think and you are there just for the money, then an arrogant environment will suit. The problems are not then with such employees. The problems are those that such a culture creates with customers. Customers are dealt with in an impersonal and off-hand manner.

One of us was interested in buying a new Mercedes car. An hour spent in the showroom narrowed the choice down to one particular model. The salesman promised to phone back to arrange a test drive. Two days later another salesman phoned with the news that his colleague 'had moved on to better things'. A test drive was possible but now only on the payment of £90, a charge to hire the car for the day, refundable if the car was purchased. The only alternative was to drive a secondhand car but, unfortunately, the only vehicle available was an older model. The showroom had contained a number of versions of the new model but apparently none that could be taken for a test drive.

It may not explain the actions of the dealership but a week or so after this incident the *Financial Times* carried an article about a dispute between Mercedes and its dealerships. Apparently the manufacturer planned to replace its UK network of 156 agencies with fewer dealerships and many under its own control. Dealers had been told that their franchisees would terminate at the end of the year. A hundred Mercedes dealerships had joined forces to fight the proposal. Mercedes planned to own some of the new 'experience centres' replacing existing dealerships and to invite a (limited) number of dealers to manage the rest. The problem was that Mercedes planned to have only 35 sales sites compared with the 156 agencies it had at the time. If the parent company treated its agents in a certain way, is it not totally surprising to see potential customers treated in a similar way?

A week or two later a consumer affairs programme on BBC television, *Watchdog*, ran a piece on Mercedes and posted an article on to its associated website. During the year 2000 car manufacturers had been accused generally of charging overly high prices in the British market. Typically, it was claimed, the British paid 20 to 30 per cent more for the same vehicle than consumers in other EU countries. The British drive on the left side of the road while the rest of the EU drive on the right. Cars for the British market are then right-hand drive and this difference gives suppliers the excuse to charge more for the same model of car. While it is EU policy that the price of products should be similar throughout all member states, having a different configuration made it easy for manufacturers to charge more in the UK, as consumers could not easily source appropriate vehicles from another country. Car companies were accused of 'ripping off Britain' and seeing the country as a 'treasure island'. Under pressure from the British government and consumer organizations, car manufacturers reduced their prices in the UK by around 10 per cent in 2000.

However in 2001 Mercedes increased their prices. The price rise itself was not the main issue for *Watchdog*, it was that customers who had already placed an order for a Mercedes had been told the price rise applied to them. It was normal practice at the time in the motor trade for the price to be fixed once the car was ordered. Interviews with Mercedes' customers indicated they would be paying between £400 to £1700 extra. A spokesperson from the Mercedes Benz Dealers Action Group was quoted as saying, 'We didn't believe they'd be so crass as to do this now. Prices have been a big issue over the last few months and everyone's been deliberately trying to soften the blow for customers, because we need to win their confidence back. And here are they, putting them up after they were forced to drop them with the "rip off Britain" fiasco.'

A corporate reputation results from the cumulative effect of all contacts we have personally with an organization, both directly and secondhand via the media, other customers, and in this case the agents of the organization. The *Watchdog* article implied that Mercedes' actions were linked to financial problems in its parent company, Daimler Chrysler, and that the price rise in the UK was only possible due to the popularity of its cars there. The problem with reputation is that it is easier to lose one than to gain one. And Mercedes risked being seen as arrogant in the British marketplace.

Coupled with *arrogance* within this trait is the item *aggressive*. There can be some positive aspects of being *aggressive* as an organization. The marketplace is competitive and a hard driving style is sometimes necessary. Customers can be difficult and sometimes too demanding. An assertive style can be useful here, with clear norms on the replacement of goods outside of warranty, of rebates for cancelled orders and payment terms. Too frequently an *aggressive* stance with customers and other stakeholders will be self-defeating in the longer term. The *aggressive* organization is not to be trifled with. If they feel that their interests are threatened they will resort to the courts. 'Attack as the best form of defence' will be their maxim.

They may not be the best of companies with whom to form strategic alliances. They will tend to have difficulties coping with organizations with softer, more egalitarian cultures. That is not to say that the typical company here is likely to have strong links with the Mafia, but they will certainly be seen as strong in their dealings with others. Relationships with the *aggressive* organization are likely to be 'interesting'.

The final item in the trait is *selfish*. This implies a greedy, grasping, self-seeking, culture that appears to outsiders at least as self-serving, mean, and mercenary. They are unlikely to be known for their support of social causes, unlikely to see charity even beginning at home with their own staff, who will regard them as tight-fisted and inconsiderate. In dealing with them suppliers had better get everything in writing first, be careful not to open themselves up so that the *selfish* company's buyers can identify ways of demanding ever greater concessions. These buyers do not subscribe to a relational model of buyer–seller interaction. They are certainly predictable in their ability to switch from one supplier to another for a small short-term win and relaxed about seeing a long-standing supplier go out of business if they cannot keep up with their demands.

Coupled with an egotistical approach is a focus on *dominance*, the second of the two facets of *ruthlessness*. Within *dominance*, the first item is *inward looking*. This is not the same as the human personality factor of introversion. The inward looking company is not shy, reserved, and modest. However it does share one aspect of the human characteristic, and that is an antipathy to assimilate external perspectives. Customers are not listened to as much as they should be. There is no method of feeding back from customer facing employees into the strategy of the organization, other than the formal research that takes place that is sponsored by a central marketing department. The richness of information that could be available to the company is lost, but then the centralized marketing function is arrogant enough to believe that theirs is the only perspective worth considering.

Sometimes being *inward looking* can pay dividends. There have been many examples of new product ideas that barely made it to market or did not make it at all, because market research indicated that the new idea would never sell. The *inward looking* company is blissfully unaware of the lack of appreciation of their latest innovation and they plough on regardless. The new idea is a storming success and this is used to deprecate any formal attempts in future to use market research to improve an idea, thus ensuring the company remains *inward looking*.

The second item *authoritarian*, implies a company that is dictatorial, and autocratic in dealing with its staff and perhaps even its customers. Managers can be seen as strict even despotic in the way they command. There are some positive aspects to this approach. Employees will always know where they stand because management are clear, positive, and certain in what they want. But they can be too prescriptive, inflexible, and closed to new ideas. This implies that managers would score low on the human personality trait of openness to ideas, a dimension that is promoted by education, but which is frustrated within an environment where creativity is discouraged. The final item *controlling* emphasizes the same point. The company has a system. It is more systematic than its competitors and this is a strength. But it can also be a weakness if those who are managing the system get it wrong. Customer facing employees are not empowered to adapt the system to something that might work better. Indeed any attempt to do so will be greeted with accusations of inadequate compliance, and blame for poor implementation of the original thinking when it does go wrong. It does not matter that the original thinking was flawed. Its creators are too *arrogant* to listen to such nonsense. It was in their view poor implementation by others of their excellent ideas that was the cause of the problem.

In our experience *ruthlessness* co-relates negatively with financial performance in most instances. However in one company, involved with the marketing of construction services and the management of construction projects, this was not the case. It appeared that regions where customers claimed the company were more ruthless outperformed regions where this dimension was not so strong. We believe that some element of *ruthlessness* could be necessary for many organizations and that in some sectors where the culture is particularly *macho* (see later) the ruthless dimension may be more tolerated. In the construction sector, *ruthlessness* appears positive to performance, and cost control is paramount. If the organization we were working with made money, it did so because it could keep its costs below the bid price that it had been squeezed into by the tendering process that dominated its industry. It would appear this reality made it important to be ruthless with the client over costs and led to the need to squeeze every possible concession from them. However the client was not in a position to complain or retaliate, as the next project would still have to be open to a sealed bid process. Our company could well be the winner despite the way it was almost inevitably ruthless with the client historically.

Many senior managers are more ruthless themselves than they would wish their front line employees to be with their customers. In one organization we have worked with *ruthlessness* was a common trait within the hierarchy. Senior managers came and went. Middle managers were afraid to take initiatives. *Ruthlessness* was starting to be an issue with customers. One middle manager suggested that it would be acceptable for him to be treated with *ruthlessness*. After all he was paid enough. It would be wrong though for him to pass this on to his team and then on to front line employees. His role included that of acting as a filter, blocking whatever came down from above to him in the way of behaviours that would damage relationships with customers if they were passed on. In reality this meant absorbing the *ruthlessness* and instead re-emphasizing the *agreeableness* that motivated staff and customers.

Managing identity can be likened to the children's game of pass the parcel.

The parcel represents the package of behaviours that is being passed on down the organization, normally 'increase sales or else' type messages. The trick for middle managers is to stop the game by holding the parcel and start a new one with their own more positive message, 'We need to increase sales and so we have to be nicer to customers. What can I do to support you in achieving better results?'

The macho organization

The last two dimensions in our framework are the weakest in the sense that they account for relatively little of the variation in perception of the organizational identities and images that we have researched thus far. However we retained both in our framework as they do appear to us to be potentially useful.

The *machismo* dimension identifies an organization that is *masculine, tough,* and *rugged.* It is in some ways the reverse of *chic,* the more feminine side of an organization's characteristics. This is the trait associated with the stereotype of maleness, both its good and bad aspects. It evokes a picture of Malboro man, of the armed forces, of traditionally male oriented work such as mining, construction, and other heavy industry. It could also be relevant to sports companies, as commercial sport is male dominated. Companies such as Nike, Reebok, and Adidas might score highly here. The stereotypical male attributes involve bravery and determination on the one hand and bravado on the other.

Masculine also implies virility, chivalry, an heroic company. Its external communication will probably use symbols of being a winner, gaining the approbation of peers. Car manufacturers often appear to evoke such imagery in their advertising, 'Reach for the hero inside yourself' if you drive a Renault.

The item *tough* implies strength and power, an organization that you can trust to take the difficult decisions, a turnaround consultancy, a security firm. We have also seen this word used frequently in the presentation of political parties, who want us to believe that they will be 'tough on crime', 'tough on tax dodgers', and 'tough on illegal immigrants'. On the negative side a *tough* organization will risk being seen as callous, uncaring, and hard, as austere and uncompromising. Countries often turn to strong leaders at a time of crisis, closing their eyes to the negative aspects of toughness in a leader.

Ruggedness is a word that probably works better in an American context than in a British one. Yet it is still useful in suggesting another aspect of *machismo.* A *rugged* organization would be one that appears to be hardy and durable, an oil exploration company, a manufacturer of earth moving equipment. It suggests strength and solidity but with a certain lack of sophistication, an organization that is perhaps too indurate and adamant at times.

The informal organization

Although *informality* is the weakest of the seven dimensions that we suggest an organization can use to understand itself, we have retained it as it appears to us to be an evolving or emerging dimension in corporate personality. *Informality* consists of three items, *casual, simple,* and *easy going.* The word *casual* may imply being unpredictable, unsystematic, and erratic, even apathetic. But the strength of such companies lies in their abilities to be natural, relaxed, and unconstrained in their thinking and in the way they deal with customers and employees. The word says a lot about the style of the organization. Formal suits are not in evidence. First names and nicknames are used to refer to colleagues. Things get done but in a calm and unhurried manner. To many their culture will appear over familiar even disrespectful. Do not think that you as a customer will be referred to as 'Sir' or 'Madam' here; that is unless they are taking the rise out of you. They will be cordial but unceremonious.

The next item, *simple*, does not imply that the employees are retarded. It suggests that their approach is uncluttered by irrelevant detail. It is straightforward and clear, easily understood and lucid. The work environment is likely to be basic, plain, and unadorned, unassuming, and unpretentious. To some it will appear stark, even austere and spartan. Perhaps the company should embellish its work more, appear more sophisticated; but that is not its style. A business lunch could be in a snack bar or in the home of one of the employees. If you want to be put on a pedestal by your supplier, do not bother with the *simple* organization. If you want an up-market company car, look elsewhere for your employment.

The last item says it all. The organization is *easy going*. They appear relaxed and even-tempered. They can appear too lenient and over-tolerant and thus lax and weak, but a laid back approach is what typifies them generally. This dimension will be seen as highly undesirable by some management teams, but not by some of the emergent companies in the high-tech industries that we have seen. Here life is not about corporatism, work and leisure blur into a seamless week. Some small family businesses and agricultural organizations would also fit this dimension.

Reputation clusters

In our experience organizations tend not to have one outstanding association with a particular dimension of corporate personality. If they are seen as strong or weak on one dimension then they are seen as the same on some others. Figure 11.1 shows the way the dimensions cluster together as seen by staff. The three clusters are *competence* and *agreeableness*; *machismo* and *ruthlessness* and *chic*, *enterprise*, and *informality*. This means that in practice companies tend to be seen as both *competent* and *agreeable*, or both *macho* and *ruthless*, or *chic*, *enterprising*, and *informal*, or not as the case may be. The picture is similar for customers, with *informality* not quite as close to *chic* and *enterprise*.

Improving reputation and performance

There is no such thing as a single, 'ideal' organization when it comes to reputation. That is why global measures such as *Fortune*'s most admired survey can only skim the surface and cannot provide much in the way of corporate guidance as to what to do (if anything) if you fall down their rankings. Reputation is multi-faceted, what is good in one context will drive customers away in another. What follows is an overview of what we have identified in this book on what companies can and should do to improve reputation and performance.

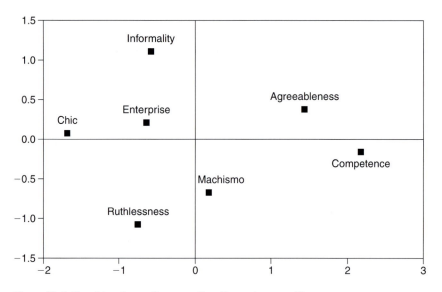

Figure 11.1 Combinations of personality dimensions: staff.

Step 1 Recognize that reputation is a strategic issue, because it connects image, identity, culture, employee and customer satisfaction, recruitment, customer loyalty, supplier relations, revenue growth and sales productivity. It is not something that can be left to the public relations department to 'manage'. It is in many ways the core and heart of the business. In a service business it is likely that reputation is the main asset that the organization possesses. Recognize too that managing reputation is about managing the way people feel and that emotions are difficult things to assess, let alone manage.

Step 2 Check that your organization's structure reflects the significance of reputation to your organization. Structure is not strategy but thus far we have not seen a structure in a large organization that is capable of managing reputation coherently. Reputation functions where they exist have evolved from PR into corporate communications functions. They need to move on to the next stage in their evolution so that they can manage the many facets of a business that contribute to reputation. For a smaller organization it may be possible to create an interdisciplinary team to be responsible for Reputation Management and to put someone in charge who has enough political clout in the organization or even give the role to the CEO. The team will represent human relations, corporate communications, training, business operations, marketing and finance. The team will be responsible for crisis management. Make sure they are trained in this role and that everyone knows that they are the focus as and when a crisis hits. Charge the team with identifying early warnings of potential crises.

Step 3 Measure the image you have with customers and your identity (particularly the view your customer facing employees have of the organization). If you wish, assess your image with other stakeholders.

Step 4 Identify what co-relates with, co-varies with, or drives (choose your own jargon here), stakeholder satisfaction, and your (commercial) performance.

Step 5 Identify those dimensions of reputation where you need to improve.

Step 6 Ask your employees and customers how they think you should make these improvements and what *specific* actions you should take, what changes in micro-behaviour need to be addressed. Consider also any changes in tangibles such as the built environment, visual identity, and other symbols such as uniforms that need to change.

Step 7 Support the ideas identified in the way employees need to feel about the organization through training, the selection and induction of new employees, and internal and external communications. Use emotion in training and communications. Reputation is about the actual quality of products and services but it is more about the way stakeholders feel about them. You cannot manage people's feelings using only rational methods.

Step 8 Once the internal view identity has been improved is it time to communicate to customers that things have changed? Tell them that things are now different and should they find out they are not, you will be back at a worse point from the one you started from.

Step 9 Check in a year or two whether you have changed your reputation for the good by surveying staff and customers. It will take time to change the way people feel about an organization.

Of these nine steps the most controversial in our experience is Step 6. Managers see their role as deciding how things should be changed. Asking employees and customers is seen as abrogating responsibility, not delegating it. Yet we are dealing here with feelings, how people see organizations, about the management of emotions. Trusting your employees and customers to be rational about the personality of the organization is a step too far for managers trained to manage from the top downwards. We can only conclude with one story, about one of the companies that are included in this book. Not every organization will be able to do as this one. Employees have to be willing to take responsibility for their own organization for what happened here to be possible. The organization is the same as one featured in Chapter 10 and we repeat some of the same material here to provide a complete picture.

The company had just merged with a rival. The two technologies they had been previously marketing separately were quite different and sales people from each were used to making claims that their technology was superior to that from the competitor. Now they were the same organization. To make matters worse the two cultures were different, one sales oriented, the other systems oriented. When we arrived the labour turnover was high. Employee satisfaction scores were the lowest we had ever measured. We surveyed every employee and presented the results to their national and international management. They decided to allow us to close the business down for half a day, to give every employee the chance to have their say. Some 90 per cent of employees attended the meeting, some giving up their free time to do so.

Using the personality data we repeated the same presentation we gave to the management team. We then divided them up into groups of about eight to ten. We gave each group one of the dimensions to work on, to suggest ways to improve their own ratings.

One at a time each group sent up a spokesperson to summarize the suggestions of the group. Some were senior managers, but many were young, junior employees unused to speaking in public. That did not hold them back. This was something they felt strongly about. It mattered little that their directors were in the front row and that much of what they had to say might be considered too bold. Shouts of encouragement from the floor greeted some points; strongly put counter-arguments followed other points.

Our role was to summarize their ideas and to present them back to the directors, who had promised in their turn to respond to every point. They did, and the company could move ahead.

In management we talk a lot about benchmarking, comparing ourselves to leading edge companies. Sometimes it is easier to learn from companies in trouble. We certainly learnt how to manage one aspect of reputation from these employees. If you think you have good employees, try trusting them in the same way. OK here was a company in crisis. So what were the risks in trying something radical? But most employees come to work for more than just the money. They form an affinity with their organization, an attachment that is as strong as any affinity we might have as customers for a brand. We might put on a designer branded jacket only once a week. We might spend more time inside our branded vehicle and in polishing it every weekend. But we spend eight hours a day at work, two hours more in travelling there and back and much more thinking and talking about what we did today. Our employer is the brand we are most closely associated with and most of us have strong feelings about that particular brand. What we value or do not value about our organization will affect the way we work. It will also affect the way we treat our colleagues. Most important it will affect the way we treat customers.

Managers, manage the way your employees feel about your organization and you are half way to managing how your customers feel about you too.

Issues that remain

Ours has been a research driven approach to managing reputation. Little in this book, particularly in the second half, has been based upon anecdotal comment. We have tried to base all our advice upon large scale surveys. But we have also checked our thinking with the managers, staff, and customers of the organizations we have worked with and those we have met in the classroom on executive and MBA classes over the last few years. We have also based our thinking where we can on the research of others in those centres around the world that see reputation in the same way as we do.

Not all of our ideas are uncontroversial. Here are some of the issues.

How do identity and image interact?

We have argued that customers obtain at least part of their image of an organization through their interaction with the customer facing staff they meet, see, or talk to. It is also possible that both staff and customers are affected by the atmosphere and therefore the built environment (design, colour, sounds, smell) of the premises they interact within. But we also believe that the micro-behaviours exhibited by customer facing employees are equally and often more important. How else can companies justify their customer service training programmes? Why should one employee be more successful with customers than another? The problem with many training programmes is that they address the logical way employees should behave and rarely the feelings they have towards their organization.

We may be as human beings the most advanced species on earth, but we are still animals that rely upon our senses as well as on our brains. We judge from quite remarkable distances whether someone looks friendly or threatening. Many of the signals we look for are in body language rather than in actual speech. Training employees to act in a certain way will not have the same impact on employees as when they are well disposed to act in that way because they have a particular personality or they have the emotional attachment we keep emphasizing.

Culture and identity

In the academic research on identity there is a debate as to whether identity and culture can be managed, in other words changed. Some argue that identity is more tractable than culture, which is deeper rooted in an organization. Much depends on what we mean by each of the two terms. If we stick with the simple definitions of both, that culture is the way we do things around here and identity is the way we see ourselves, then it should be possible to change both. The two will be related and changing one would be impossible at times without changing the other.

If we see identity as more akin to human personality, then identity will be more enduring, but seeing identity through the lens of corporate personality, which we have done, does not imply that the two are the same. We have used the metaphor of personality to try to understand identity and image. We know that image can be changed but we also know that improving upon a poor image will take time. There is no reason to believe that identity cannot be changed over a similar time span. It is not as difficult to change as human personality.

We would argue that identity is far from enduring and to emphasize the point we would argue for a different definition of the term. Identity is better seen as concerning the way we feel about ourselves, but even this does not take into account the links to culture. Therefore identity should be seen as 'the way we feel about our culture, what we value and do not value in the way we do things, our emotional attachment to the way we do things'.

Identity defined this way will have two levels. We talk about a business having a paradigm, a set of beliefs as to how the business works, and how it meets its objectives. Such beliefs are deep rooted and form the core identity of an organization. They cannot be changed easily. Universities must do research. Oil companies should not enter the fuel cell business. Marketing tobacco is ethical. Each of these are examples of fundamental beliefs about organizations that are open to challenge but which are so embedded in their respective cultures that it would be impossible to change them without changing the organization at its heart. Surrounding these fundamental aspects of identity are more tractable matters. Our research should be linked to teaching. Our oil company can invest in developing alternative technologies. Marketing tobacco to those aged 16 and under is unacceptable for us. These are examples of how aspects of identity related to the fundamentals (that are non-negotiable) can be changed.

The micro-behaviours of customer facing employees are examples of matters that can be modified, without challenging or threatening the core values of an organization. So are changes in visual identity. So are changes in recruitment policy and so on to most aspects of corporate personality.

Organizations of the future

Certain changes in the way organizations are and in the way they act are implied by our work. *Agreeableness* and *competence* are the two most important dimensions of corporate personality. *Competence* appears to be recognized in the way organizations talk about themselves in their vision and mission statements; *agreeableness* less so. We would expect to see organizations being less coy about such aspects of their personalities, certainly once it is realized that being seen as *agreeable* appears to be generally the quickest way to improve reputation. Some will go too far, not realizing that reputation has to be built upon foundations inside the organization. Image in our context is not the same as product brand image where what is created in the imagination of the customer is a marketable asset. If companies claim to be socially responsible they will have to be seen to be so.

We also expect a change in the structure of the service companies that organizations can look to help change their reputations. The role of advertising will decline and that of public relations will increase. This will threaten companies that rely upon advertising revenues to sustain them, especially the television media. There is already a role for reputation agencies that are able to go inside the organization to help change identity. And not just visual identity. The game should be up for those who claim that a change of name or logo on their own will evoke a fundamental change in an organization's identity or image.

References

Foreword

Gardberg, N. (2001) 'How do individuals construct corporate reputations? Examining the effects of stakeholder status and firm strategy on cognitive elaboration and schema complexity about firm performance', unpublished PhD dissertation, Stern School of Business, New York University.

1 A brief history of strategic thought

Barber, L., Hayday, S. and Bevan, S. (1999) 'From people to profits', Institute for Employment Studies Report 355, IES, Brighton.

Beauchamp, T. L. and Bowie, N. E. (1993) *Ethical Theory and Business*, 4th edn, Englewood Cliffs, NJ: Prentice Hall.

Buzzell, R. D. and Gale, B. T. (1987) *The PIMS Principles*, New York: Macmillan.

Campbell, A. and Tawaday, K. (1990) *Mission and Business Philosophy*, Oxford: Heinemann.

Drucker, P. F. (1973) *Management: Task, Responsibilities and Practices*, New York: Harper and Row.

Frederick, W. C. (1997) 'Business and society', in P. H. Werhane and R. E. Freeman (eds), *The Blackwell Dictionary of Business Ethics*, Cambridge, MA: Blackwell Business.

Heskett, J. L., Jones, T. O., Loveman, G. W., Sasser, W. E. and Sclesinger, L. A. (1994) 'Putting the service profit chain to work', *Harvard Business Review*, March/April: 164–74.

Hogan, S. (1998) 'Positioning brand in the market place', articles from Lippincott-Margulies website; http://www.lippincottmargulies.com/sense/index.html

Klemm, M., Sanderson, S. and Luffman, G. (1991) 'Mission statements: selling corporate values to employees', *Long Range Planning* 24 (3): 73–8.

Kotter, J. P. (1996) 'Leading change', Boston, MA: Harvard Business School Press.

Lynch, R. (1997) *Corporate Strategy*, London: Pitman.

Mintzberg, H. (1987) 'Crafting strategy', *Harvard Business Review* July/August: 66–75.

Opinion Research Corporation International (1999) *Global 100: Attitudes to Corporate Branding Report*, April.

Porter, M. (1998) *Competitive Strategy*, New York: Simon and Schuster.

Rucci, A. J., Kirn, S. P. and Quinn, R. T. (1998) 'The employee customer profit chain at Sears', *Harvard Business Review*, Jan/Feb: 83–97.

Schultz, H. (1998) *Pour Your Heart into it*, New York: Hyperion.

Slater, S. F. and Narver, J. C. (1995) 'Market orientation and the learning organisation', *Journal of Marketing* 59 (1): 5–16.

Want, J. H. (1986) 'Corporate mission', *Management Review*, August: 46–50.

Zeithaml, V., Berry, L. L. and Parasuraman, A. (1990) *Delivering Service Quality*, New York: Free Press.

2 The traditional approach to Reputation Management

Aaker, J. L. (1997) 'Dimensions of brand personality', *Journal of Marketing Research*, 24: 347–56.

Abratt, R. (1989) 'A new approach to the corporate image management process', *Journal of Marketing Management* 5 (1): 63–76.

Allan, G. (1992) *Brands as Mental Connections, in People, Brands and Advertising*, Basingstoke: Millward Brown International.

Alvesson, M. (1990) 'Organisation: from substance to image?' *Organisation Studies* 11 (3): 373–94.

Balmer, J. M. T. (1995) 'Corporate branding and connoisseurship', *Journal of Global Management* 21 (1): 24–46.

Bennet, R. and Gabriel, H. (2001) 'Corporate reputation, trait covariation and the averaging principle: the case of the UK pensions mis-selling scandal', in J. Balmer (ed), 'Corporate identity and corporate marketing', *European Journal of Marketing*, Special Edition 35 (3/4): 387–413.

Bernstein, D. (1985) *Company Image and Reality*, Eastbourne: Holt, Reinhart, Winston.

Berry, L. L., Lefkowith, E. E. and Clark, T. (1988) 'In services, what's in a name?', *Harvard Business Review*, Sept/Oct: 28–30.

Brown, T. J. and Dacin, P. A. (1997) 'The company and the product: corporate associations and consumer product responses', *Journal of Marketing* 61, Jan: 68–84.

Carter, S. M. and Dukerich, J. M. (1997) 'Corporate reputation and its effect on organisational actions: how reputations are managed', *Corporate Reputation Review* 1 (1): 152–6.

Davies, G. and Itoh, H. (2001) 'Legislation and retail structure – the Japanese example, International Review of Retail Distribution and Consumer Research 11 (1): 83–95.

Davies, G. and Miles, L. (1998) *Reputation management: theory versus practice, Corporate Reputation Review* 2 (1): 16–27.

Davies, G. and Whitehead, M. (1995) 'The legislative environment as a measure of attractiveness for internationalisation', in P. J. McGoldrick and G. Davies (eds), *International Retailing, Trends and Strategies*, London: Pitman, pp. 117–32.

Dowling, G. R. (1993) 'Developing your company image into a corporate asset', *Long Range Planning* 26 (2): 101–9.

Dutton, J. E., Dukerich, J. M. and Harquail, C. V. (1994) 'Organisational images and member identification', *Administrative Science Quarterly* 39: 239–63.

Fink, S. (1986) *Crisis Management, Planning for the Inevitable*, Amacom.

Fombrun, C. (1996) *Reputation, Realising Value from the Corporate Image*, Cambridge, MA: Harvard Business School.

Fombrun, C. and Shanley, M. (1990) 'What's in a name? Reputation building and corporate strategy', *Academy of Management Journal* 33 (2): 233–58.

Fryxell, G. E. and Wang, J. (1994) 'The fortune corporate reputation index, reputation for what?', *Journal of Management* 20 (1): 1–14.

Giles, R. (2001) 'The art of agenda setting', *World and I*, 16 (5): 62.

Hatch, M. J. and Schultz, M. (1997) 'Relations between organisational culture, identity and image', *European Journal of Marketing* 31 (5/6): 356–65.

Kitchen, P. and Proctor, T. (1991) 'The increasing importance of public relations in fast moving consumer goods firms', *Journal of Marketing Management* 7: 357–70.

Kotler, P. and Barich, H. (1991) 'Framework for marketing image management', *Sloan Management Review*, Winter, 94–104.

Kruskal, J. V. and Wish, M. (1978) *Multi-Dimensional Scaling*, Thousand Oaks, CA: Sage.

Margulies, W. P. (1977) 'Make the most of your corporate identity', *Harvard Business Review*, July/Aug: 66–74.

McGuire, J. B., Sundgren, A. and Schneeweis, T. (1988) 'Corporate social responsibility and firm financial performance', *Academy of Management Journal* 31 (4): 854–72.

Meyers, W. (1984) *The Image Makers*, London: Orbis.

Miles, L. and Davies, G. (1997) *What Price Reputation?* London: Haymarket Business Publications.

Morella, G. and Boerema, E. (1989) 'Made in and communication' paper given at Esomar Conference, Milan.

Morley, M. (1998) 'Corporate communications: a benchmark study of the current state of the art and practice', *Corporate Reputation Review* 2 (1): 78–86.

Olins, W. (1978) *The Corporate Personality*, London: Design Council.

Post, J. E. and Griffin, J. J. (1997) 'Corporate reputation and external affairs management', *Corporate Reputation Review* 1 (1): 165–71.

Reese, J. (1993) 'America's most admired corporations', *Fortune*, February 8: 16–32.

Sauerhaft, S. and Atkins, C. (1989) *Image Wars*, New York: John Wiley.

Selame, E. and Selame, J. (1988) *The Company Image*, New York: John Wiley.

Siomkis, G. J. and Malliaris, P. G. (1992) 'Consumer response to company communications during a product harm crisis', *Journal of Applied Business Research* 8 (4): 54–65.

Smythe, J., Dorward, C. and Reback, J. (1992) *Corporate Reputation*, London: Century Business.

Sobol, M. and Farrelly, G. (1988) 'Corporate reputation, a function of relative size or financial performance', *Review of Business and Economic Research* 26 (1): 45–59.

Strauss, G. (1964) 'A case study of purchasing agents', *Human Organisation* 23 (2): 53–69.

Wartick, S. (1992) 'The relationship between intense media exposure and change in corporate reputation', *Business and Society* 31 (1): 33–49.

Weigelt, K. and Camerer, C. (1988) 'Reputation and corporate strategy: a review of recent theory and applications', *Strategic Management Journal* 9: 443–54.

3 The reputation paradigm

Albert, S. and Whetten, D. A. (1985) 'Organisational identity', in L. L. Cummings and B. M. Staw (eds), *Research in Organisational Behaviour* 7: 263–95.

Anon (1986) 'The very best of British marketing', *Marketing Week*, 3 October: 53–72.

Balmer, J. M. T. (1998) 'Corporate identity and the advent of corporate marketing', *Journal of Marketing Management* 14: 963–96.

Barish, H. and Kotler, P. (1991) 'A framework for marketing image management', *Sloan Management Review*, Winter: 94–104.

Beauchamp, T. L. and Bowie, N. E. (1993) *Ethical Theory and Business*, 4th edn, Englewood Cliffs, NJ: Prentice Hall.

Bernstein, D. (1984) *Company Image and Reality*, Eastbourne: Holt, Rinehart and Winston.

Bevis, J. C. (1967) 'How corporate image is used', ESOMAR Wapor Conference, Vienna.

Davies, G. and Miles, L. (1998) 'Reputation management: theory versus practice', *Corporate Reputation Review* 2 (1) Winter: 16–28.

Dowling, C. R. (1993) 'Developing your company image into a corporate asset', *Long Range Planning* 26 (2): 101–9.

Doyle, P. (1998) *Marketing Management and Strategy*, 2nd edn, London: Prentice Hall.

Fombrun, C. J. (1998a) *Reputation, Realizing Value from the Corporate Image*, Boston, MA: Harvard Business School Press.

Fombrun, C. J. (1998b) 'Indices of corporate reputation: an analysis of media rankings and social monitors' ranking', *Corporate Reputation Review* 1 (4): 327–40.

Fombrun, C. J., Gardberg, N. A. and Sever, J. M. (2000) 'The reputation quotient: a multi-stakeholder measure of corporate reputation', *The Journal of Brand Management* 7 (4): 241–55.

Fryxell, G. E. and Wang, J. (1994) 'The Fortune corporate "reputation" index, reputation for what?', *Journal of Management* 20 (1): 1–14.

Hatch, M. J. and Schultz, M. (1997) 'Relation between organisational culture, identity and image', *European Journal of Marketing* 31 (5–6): 356–65.

Herbig, H., Milewicz, J. and Golden, J. (1994) 'A model of reputation building and destruction', *Journal of Business Research* 31: 23–31.

Ind, I. (1992) *The Corporate Image*, London: Kogan Page.

Kumar, S. (1999) *Valuing Corporate Reputation in Reputation Management*, London: IOD and Kogan Page.

Marwick, N. and Fill, C. (1997) 'Towards a framework for managing corporate identity', *European Journal of Marketing* 31 (5/6): 396–409.

McGuire, J. *et al.* (1988) 'Corporate social responsibility and firm financial performance', *Academy of Management Journal* 31 (4): 854–72.

Miles, L. and Davies, G. (1997) *What Price Reputation?*, London: Haymarket Business Publications.

Sobol, M. and Farrelly, G. (1988) 'Corporate reputation, a function of relative size or financial performance', *Review of Business and Economic Research* 26 (1): 45–59.

Topalian, A. (1984) 'Beyond the visual overstatement', *International Journal of Advertising* 3: 55–62.

van Riel, C. B. M. and Balmer, J. M. T. (1997) 'Corporate identity: the concept, its measurement and management', *European Journal of Marketing* 31 (5/6): 340–55.

4 The company as a brand

Ambler, T. and Barwise, P. (1998) 'The trouble with brand valuation', *The Journal of Brand Management* 5 (5): 367–77.

Arnold, J., Egginton, D., Kirkham, L., Macve, R. and Peasnell, K. (1992) 'Goodwill and other intangibles', *The Institute of Chartered Accountants of England and Wales*, London.

Bannister, J. P. and Saunders, J. A. (1978) 'UK consumers' attitudes towards imports: the measurement of national stereotype image', *European Journal of Marketing*, 19 November: 562–84.

Berry, L. L., Lefkowith, E. E. and Clark, T. (1988) 'In services, what's in a name?', *Harvard Business Review*, September/October: 28–30.

Black, M. (1962) *Models and Metaphors*, New York: Cornell University Press.

Collins, E. (1977) 'A name to conjure with', *European Journal of Marketing* 11 (5): 339–63.

Da Silva, R. V., Davies, G. J. and Naude, P. (2001) 'Country of origin and destination effects in buyer decision making', *Journal of Business to Business Marketing*, forthcoming.

Davies, G. (1992) 'The two ways in which retailers can be brands', *International Journal of Retail and Distribution Management* 20 (2): 24–31.

Davies, G. (1998) 'Retail brands and the theft of identity', *International Journal of Retail and Distribution Management* 26 (4): 140–6.

Davies, G. and Brito, E. (1996) 'The relative cost structures of competing grocery supply chains', *The International Journal of Logistics Management* 7 (1): 49–60.

Davies, G. and Brooks, J. (1989) *Positioning Strategy in Retailing*, London: Paul Chapman.

Davies, G. and Chun, R. (2002) 'The use of metaphor in the exploration of the brand concept', *Journal of Marketing Management*, forthcoming.

DeChernatony, L. and McWilliam, G. (1989) 'The varying nature of brands as assets', *International Journal of Advertising* 8: 339–46.

Dentsu Inc (1994) 'Images of Europe', Report for the European Commission quoted in M. Solomon *et al. Consumer Behaviour* (1999), Englewood Cliffs: Prentice Hall, 229.

Doyle, P. (1990) 'Building successful brands: the strategic options', *Journal of Consumer Marketing* 7 (2): 60.

Durgee, J. F. (1988) 'Understanding brand personality', *Journal of Consumer Marketing* 5 (3): 21–5.

Erickson, G., Johansson, J. and Chao, P. (1984) 'Image variables in multiattribute product evaluations: country of origin effects', *Journal of Consumer Research* 11 (2): September: 694–9.

Fournier, S. (1998) 'Consumers and their brands: developing relationship theory in consumer research', *Journal of Consumer Research* 24 (4): 343–73.

Gaedeke, R. (1973) 'Consumer attitudes toward products "made in developing countries"', *Journal of Retailing* 49, Summer: 13–24.

Gardner, B. B. and Levy, S. J. (1955) 'The product and the brand', *Harvard Business Review*, March/April: 33–9.

Halfhill, D. S. (1980) 'Multinational marketing strategy: implication of attitudes toward country of origin', *Management International Review* 20 (4): 26–30.

Hampton, G. M. (1977) 'Perceived risks in buying products made abroad by American firms', *Baylor Business Studies*, October: 53–64.

Han, C. and Terpstra, V. (1987) 'Country of origin effects for uni-national and bi-national products', *Journal of International Business Studies* 19 (2): Summer: 235–55.

Hanby, T. (1999) 'Brands – dead or alive?: qualitative research for the twenty-first century: the changing conception of brands', *Journal of The Market Research Society* 41 (1): 1–8.

Johansson, J. and Nebenzahl, I. (1987) 'Country of origin, social norms and behavioural intentions', *Advances in International Marketing* 2: 65–79.

Johansson, J., Douglas, S. P. and Nonaka, I. (1985) 'Assessing the impact of country of origin on product evaluations: a new methodological perspective', *Journal of Marketing Research*, 22 November: 388–96.

Jones, J. P. (1990) 'Ad spending: maintaining market share', *Harvard Business Review*, Jan/Feb: 38–42.

Kaynak, E. and Cavusgil, S. T. (1983) 'Consumer attitudes towards products of foreign origin: do they vary across product classes?', *International Journal of Advertising* 2: 147–57.

Keeble, G. (1991) 'Creativity and the brand', in D. Cowley (ed), *Understanding Brands* (2nd edn).

Kerin, R. A. and Sethuraman, R. (1998) 'Exploring the brand value–shareholder value nexus for consumer goods companies', *Journal of The Academy of Marketing Science* 26 (4): 260–73.

King, S. (1973) *Developing New Brands*, London: Pitman.

Kotler, P. and Armstrong, G. (2000) *Principles of Marketing*, 9th edn, Englewood Cliffs, NJ: Prentice Hall.

Kotler, P. (1988) *Marketing Management*, 6th edn, Englewood Cliffs, NJ: Prentice Hall, p. 463.

Laurent, G. and Kapferer, J.-L. (1985) 'Measuring consumer involvement profiles', *Journal of Marketing Research*, February (22): 41–53.

Lillis, C. and Narayana, C. N. (1974) 'Analysis of "made-in" product images – an exploratory study', *Journal of International Business Studies* 5 Spring: 119–27.

Lumpkin, J. R., Crawford, J. C. and Kim, G. (1985) 'Perceived risk as a factor in buying foreign clothes implications for marketing strategy', *International Journal of Advertising* 4: 157–71.

Martineau, P. (1958) 'The personality of the retail store', *Harvard Business Review* 36: 47–55.

Mintel (1998) *Corporate Identity, Special Report*, London: Mintel.

Morello, G. (1984) 'The "made in" issue: a comparative research on the image of domestic and foreign products', *European Research* 12 (1): January: 4–21.

Murphy, J. M. (1990) *Brand Strategy*, Cambridge: Director Books, p. 65.

Olins, W. (1978) *The Corporate Personality*, London: Design Council.

Perrier, R. (1989) Valuation and licensing, in J. Murphy (ed), *Brand Valuation*, Basingstoke: Hutchinson, pp. 105–14.

Porter, M. (1998) *The Competitive Advantage of Nations*, Basingstoke: Macmillan Business.

Reierson, C. (1966) 'Are foreign products seen as national stereotypes?', *Journal of Retailing*, Fall: 33–40.

Schooler, R. D. (1971) 'Bias phenomena attendant to the marketing of foreign goods in the U.S.', *Journal of International Business Studies*, Spring: 71–80.

Schooler, R. D., Wildt, A. R. and Jones, J. M. (1987) 'Strategy development for manufactured exports of Third World countries to developed countries', *Journal of Global Marketing*, 1 (1–2): Fall–Winter: 53–68.

Selame, E. and Selame, J. (1988) 'The company image', New York: John Wiley.

Shostack, G. L. (1977) 'Breaking free from product marketing', *Journal of Marketing*, April: 73–81.

Smiddy, P. (1983) 'Brands – an asset to be ignored?', *Accountancy*, July: 95–6.

Tongberg, R. C. (1972) 'An empirical study of relationships between dogmatism and consumer attitudes toward foreign products', PhD thesis, Pennsylvania State University.

van Riel, C. B. M. (1997) 'Protecting the corporate brand by orchestrated communication', *The Journal of Brand Management* 4 (6): 409–18.

Ward, R. and Perrier, R. (1998) 'Brand valuation, the times are a changing', *The Journal of Brand Management* 5 (4): 283–9.

White, P. D. (1979) 'Attitudes of U.S. purchasing managers toward industrial products manufactured in selected European nations', *Journal of International Business Studies* 10 (2): Winter: 81–90.

Zajonc, R. and Markus, H. (1982) 'Affective and cognitive factors in preferences', *Journal of Consumer Research* 9: 123–31.

5 Defending a reputation

Downing, S. J. (1997) 'Learning the plot: emotional momentum in search of dramatic logic', *Management Learning* 28 (1).

Gwyther, M. (1999) 'King Richard: a tragedy in three acts', *Management Today*, April: 78–86.

Mitroff, I. I. (1988) 'Crisis management: cutting through the confusion', *Sloan Management Review*, Winter: 15–20.

Murray, E. and Shohen, S. (1992) 'Lessons from the Tylenol tragedy on surviving a corporate crisis', *Medical Marketing and Media*, February: 14–19.

Shrivastava, P. and Mitroff, I. I. (1987) 'Strategic management of corporate crises', *Columbia Journal of World Business*, Spring: 5–11.

6 Measuring reputation: the Corporate Personality Scale

Aaker, J. L. (1997) 'Dimensions of brand personality', *Journal of Marketing Research* 34 August: 347–56.

Aaker, J. L., Benet-Martinez, V. and Garolera, J. (2000) 'Consumption symbols as carriers of culture: a study of Japanese and Spanish brand personality constructs', Research Working Paper 1668, Stanford University, School of Business.

Albert, S. and Whetten, D. (1985) 'Organizational identity', in L. C. Cumming and B. M. Staw (eds), *Research in Organizational Behavior*, Greenwich, CT: JAI Press, pp. 263–95.

Anderson, E. W. and Fornell, C (1994) 'A customer satisfaction research prospectus', in R. Rust and R. Oliver (eds), *Service Quality: New Direction in Theory and Practice*. Thousand Oaks, CA: Sage Publications, pp. 241–68.

Anderson, E. W. and Sullivan, M. W. (1993) 'The antecedents and consequences of customer satisfaction for firms', *Marketing Science* 12 (2) Spring: 125–43.

Anderson, N. H. (1968) 'Likableness ratings of 555 personality-trait words', *Journal of Personality and Social Psychology* 9 (3): 272–9.

Andreassen, T. W. and Lindestad, B. (1998) 'The effect of corporate image in the formation of customer loyalty', *Journal of Service Research*, 1 (1) August: 82–92.

Barrick. M. R. and Mount, M. K. (1991) 'The big five personality dimensions and job performance: a meta-analysis', *Personnel Psychology* 44: 1–26.

Barrick, M. R. and Mount, M. K. (1993) 'Autonomy as a moderator of the relationships between the big five personality dimensions and job performance', *Journal of Applied Psychology* 78 (1): 111–18.

Batra, R., Lehamann, D. R. and Singh, D. (1993) 'The brand personality component of brand goodwill: some antecedents and consequences', in D. A. Aaker and A. (eds), *Brand Equity and Advertising.*

Bernstein, D. (1986) *Company Image and Reality*, Eastbourne: Holt, Rinehart and Winston.

Berry, L. L. (1969) 'The components of department store image', *Journal of Retailing* 52: 17–32.

Biel, A. L. (1993) 'Converting image into equity', in D. A. Aaker and A. Biel, (eds), *Brand Equity and Advertising: Advertising's Role in Building Strong Brands*, Hillsdale, NJ: Lawrence Erlbaum Associates, pp. 67–82.

Chatman, J. A. and Jaln, K. A. (1994) 'Assessing the relationship between industry characteristics and organisation culture: how different can you be?', *Academy of Management Journal* 37 (3): 522–53.

Costa, P. T. and McCrae, R. R. (1992) 'Revised NEO personality (NEO-PI-R) and NEO five-factor inventory (NEO-FFI) professional manual', Odessa, FL: Psychological Assessment Resources.

Costa, P. T. and McCrae, R. R. (1995) 'Domains and facets: hierarchical personality assessment using the revised NEO personality inventory', *Journal of Personality Assessment* 64 (1): 21–50.

Daneke, G. A. (1983) 'Regulation and the sociopathic firm', *Academy of Management Review* 10 (1): 15–20.

Davies, G. and Brooks, J. (1989) *Positioning Strategy in Retailing*, London: Paul Chapman.

Davies, G., Chun, R., da Silva, R. V. and Roper, S. (2001) 'A Corporate Personality Scale to assess internal and external views of corporate reputation', MBS Working Paper 431.

Digman, J. M. (1990) 'Personality structure: emergence of the five-factor model', *Annual Review of Psychology* 57: 195–214.

Flatt, S. J. and Kowalczyk, S. J. (2000) 'Do corporate reputations partly reflect external perceptions of organizational culture?', *Corporate Reputation Review* 3 (4) Fall: 351–8.

Fombrun, C. J. (1998) 'Indices of corporate reputation: an analysis of media rankings and social monitors' ranking', *Corporate Reputation Review* 1 (4): 327–40.

Fombrun, C. J., Gardberg, N. A. and Sever, J. M. (2000) 'The reputation quotient: a multi-stakeholder measure of corporate reputation', *The Journal of Brand Management* 7 (4): 241–55.

Ford, D. (ed.) (1997) 'Understanding business markets', 2nd edn, London: Dryden Press.

Friedman, M. (1970) 'The role of social responsibility is to increase its profits', in T. L. Beauchamp and N. E. Bowie (eds), *Ethical Theory and Business,* 4th edn, Englewood Cliffs, NJ: Prentice Hall.

Guilford, J. P. (1973) 'On personality', in H. N. Mischel and W. Mischel, (eds), *Readings in Personality*, New York: Holt, Rinehart and Winston, pp. 22–3.

Hakansson, H. (1982) *International Marketing and Purchasing of Industrial Goods*, Chichester: John Wiley.

Hanby, T. (1999) 'Brands – dead or alive? Qualitative research for the twenty-first century: the changing conception of brands', *Journal of the Market Research Society* 41 (1): 1–8.

Hogan, R. T. (1986) *Manual for the Hogan Personality Inventory*, Minneapolis: National Computer Systems.

Hulland, J., Yiu Ho, C. and Shunyin, L. (1996) 'Use of causal models in marketing research: a review', *International Journal of Research in Marketing* 13 (2) April: 181–97.

Jaccard, J. and Wan, C. K. (1996) *Lisrel Approaches to Interaction Effects in Multiple Regression*, Thousand Oaks, CA: Sage Publications.

Kaptein, M. (1998) 'The ethics thermometer', *Corporate Reputation Review* 2 (1): 0–15.

Keller, K. L. (1998) *Strategic Brand Management*, Englewood Cliffs, NJ: Prentice Hall.

Kets de Vries, M. F. R. and Miller, D. (1984) 'Neurotic style and organisational pathology', *Strategic Management Journal* 5: 35–55.

King, S. (1973) *Developing New Brands*, London: Pitman.

Kumar, N., Scheer, L. K. and Steenkamp, J. E. M. (1995) 'The effects of supplier fairness on vulnerable resellers', *Journal of Marketing Research*, 32 February: 54–65.

Lindquist, J. D. (1974) 'Meaning of image', *Journal of Retailing*, 50: 29–38.

Lloyd, T. (1990) *The Nice Company*, London: Bloomsbury.

Markham, V. (1972) *Planning the Corporate Reputation*, London: George Allen and Unwin.

Martineau, P. (1958) 'The personality of the retail store', *Harvard Business Review*, 36: Jan/Feb.

Marwick, N. and Fill, C. (1995) 'Towards a framework of managing corporate identity', *European Journal of Marketing* 31 (5/6): 396–409.

McCrae, R. R. and John, O. P. (1992) 'An introduction to the five-factor model and its applications', *Journal of Personality* 60 (2): June: 175–215.

Mulligan, T. M. (1992) 'The moral mission of business', in T. L. Beauchamp and N. E. Bowie (eds), *Ethical Theory and Business*, 4th edn, Englewood Cliffs, NJ: Prentice Hall.

Naumann, E. and Giel, K. (1995) *Customer Satisfaction Measurement and Management*, London: Thompson Executive Press.

Nielson, C. C. (1998) 'An empirical examination of the role of closeness in industrial buyer–seller relationships', *European Journal of Marketing* 32 (5/6): 441–63.

Nunally, J. C. (1978) *Psychometric Theory*, 2nd edn, New York: McGraw-Hill.

O'Reilly, C. A., Chatman, J. and Caldwell, D. F. (1991) 'People and organisational culture: a profile comparison approach to assessing person–organisation fit', *Academy of Management Journal* 34 (3): 487–516.

Oliver, R. L. (1997) *Satisfaction: A Behavioural Perspective on the Consumer*, Boston, MA: McGraw-Hill.

Samiee, S. and Jeong, I. (1994) 'Cross-cultural research in advertising: an assessment of methodologies', *Journal of The Academy of Marketing Science* 22 (3): 205–17.

Schumacker, R. E. and Lomax, R. G. (1996) *A Beginner's Guide to Structural Equation Modeling*, Mahwah, NJ: Lawrence Erlbaum Associates.

Schwartz, H. S. (1987) 'On the psychodynamics of organisational totalitarianism', *Journal of Management* 13 (1): 41–54.

van Riel, C. B. M. and Balmer, J. M. T. (1997) 'Corporate identity: the concept, its measurement and management', *European Journal of Marketing* 31 (5/6): 340–55.

Wanous, J. P. and Lawler, E. E. (1972) 'Measurement and meaning of job satisfaction', *Journal of Applied Psychology* 56 (2): 95–105.

Winkleman, M. (1999) 'The right stuff: survey on corporate reputation', *Chief Executive* (US), 143 April: 80–1.

Xenikou, A. and Furnham, A. (1996) 'A co-relational and factor analytic study of four questionnaire measures of organisational culture', *Human Relations* 49 (3): 349–71.

7 The management of image and identity

Chun, R. (2001) 'The strategic management of corporate reputation, aligning image and identity, PhD dissertation, Manchester Business School, University of Manchester.

Davies, G. and Miles, L. (1998) 'Reputation management: theory versus practice', *Corporate Reputation Review* 2 (1): 16–27.

Fombrun, C. J. (1996) *Reputation: Realizing Value from the Corporate Image*, Boston, MA: Harvard Business School.

Hatch, M. J. and Schultz, M. (1997) 'Relation between organisational culture, identity and image', *European Journal of Marketing* 31 (5/6): 356–65.

Heskett, J. L., Jones, T. O., Loveman, G. W., Sasser, W. E. and Sclesinger, L. A. (1994) 'Putting the service profit chain to work', *Harvard Business Review*, March/April: 164–74.

Kohli, A. K. and Jaworski, B. J. (1990) Market orientation, the construct, research propositions and managerial implications', *Journal of Marketing*, April: 1–18.

Liu, H. and Davies, G. (1995) 'The retailer's marketing mix and commercial performance', *International Review of Retail Distribution and Consumer Research* 5 (2): 147–65.

Lynch, R. (1997) *Corporate Strategy*, London: Pitman.

Narver, J. C. and Slater, S. F. (1990) 'The effect of a market orientation on business profitability', *Journal of Marketing*, October: 20–35.

Slater, S. F. and Narver, J. C. (1994) 'Market orientation, customer value and superior
performance', *Business Horizons*, 22–7.

Smircich, L. (1983) 'Concepts of culture and organizational analysis', *Administrative
Science Quarterly* 28: 339–58.

Srivastava, R. K., McInish, T. H., Wood, R. A. and Capraro, A. J. (1997) 'The value of
corporate reputation: evaluation from the equity markets', *Corporate Reputation Review*
1 (1/2): 62–8.

Weick, K. (1995) *Sense-Making in Organizations*, Thousand Oaks, CA: Sage.

Whetten, D. (2001) 'In corporate history and reputation formation, a panel' proposed
to the fifth International Conference on Corporate Reputations, Identity and Competitiveness, Paris.

Whetten, D. A. and Godfrey, P. C. (eds) (1998) *Identity in Organizations: Building Theory
Through Conversations*, Thousand Oaks, CA: Sage.

8 Managing the Reputation Chain

Aaker, J. L. (1997) 'Dimensions of brand personality', *Journal of Marketing Research* 34
August: 347–56.

Andaleeb, S. S. (1996) 'An experimental investigation of satisfaction and commitment in
marketing channels: the role of trust and dependence', *Journal of Retailing* 72 (1):
77–93.

Anderson, J. C. and Narus, J. A. (1990) 'A model of distributor firm and manufacturer
firm working partnerships', *Journal of Marketing* 54 January: 42–58.

Anderson, E. W., Fornell, C. and Lehmann, D. R. (1994) 'Customer satisfaction,
market share, and profitability: findings from Sweden', *Journal of Marketing* 58 July:
53–66.

Bradley, K. and Taylor, S. (1992) *Business Performance in the Retail Sector, the Experience of
the John Lewis Partnership*, Oxford: Clarendon Press.

Brown, J. R. and Frazier, G. L. (1978) 'The application of channel power: its effects and
connotations', in S. C. Jain (ed.), *AMA Educators' Conference Proceedings*, Chicago:
American Marketing Association, pp. 266–70.

Campbell, A. and Tawaday, K. (1990) 'Mission and business philosophy', Oxford: Heinemann.

Carr-Saunders, A. M., Sargant, F. P. and Peers, R. (1938) *Consumer Co-operation in Great
Britain*, London: George Allen and Unwin.

Chun, R. and Davies, G. (2001) 'E-reputation: the role of mission and vision statements
in positioning strategy', *Journal of Brand Management* 8 (4/5): 315–33.

Cole, J. (1994) *Conflict and Cooperation*, Littleborough: George Kelsall.

David, F. R. (1989) 'How companies define their mission', *Long Range Planning* 22 (1):
90–7.

Davies, G. (1993) *Trade Marketing Strategy*, London: Paul Chapman.

Davies, S. W. and Glaister, K. W. (1997) 'Business school mission statements – the bland
leading the bland?', *Long Range Planning*, 30 (4).

Doyle, S. X. and Shapiro, B. P. (1980) 'What counts most in motivating your sales force',
Harvard Business Review 58 (3): 133–40.

Gaski, J. F. and Nevin, J. R. (1985) 'The differential effects of exercised and unexercised
power sources in a marketing channel', *Journal of Marketing Research*, 22 May: 130–42.

Gassenheimer, J. B., Calantone, R. J., Schmitz, J. M. and Robicheaux, R. A. (1994)
'Models of channel maintenance: what is the weaker party to do', *Journal of Business
Research* 30 (3) July: 225–36.

Geyskens, I., Steenkamp, J. E. M. and Kumar, N. (1999) 'A meta-analysis of satisfaction in marketing channel relationships', *Journal of Marketing Research* 36 (2) May: 223–38.

Geyskens, I. and Steenkamp, J. B. (2000) 'Economic and social satisfaction: measurement and relevance to marketing channel relationships', *Journal of Retailing* 76 (1): 11–32.

Hatch, M. J. and Schultz, M. (2001) 'Are the strategic stars aligned for your corporate brand?', *Harvard Business Review*, Feb: 129–34.

Heskett, J. L., Jones, T. O., Loveman, G. W., Sasser, W. E. and Schlesinger, L. A. (1994) 'Putting the service profit chain to work', *Harvard Business Review*, March/April: 164–74.

Hogan, S. (1998) 'Positioning brand in the market place', articles from Lippincott-Margulies website; http://www.lippincottmargulies.com/sense/index.html

Johnson, J. L. and Raven, P. V. (1996) 'Relationship quality, satisfaction and performance in export marketing channels', *Journal of Marketing Channels* 5 (3/4): 19–48.

Klemm, M., Sanderson, S. and Luffman, G. (1991) 'Mission statements: selling corporate values to employees', *Long Range Planning* 24 (3): 73–8.

Larzelere, R. E. and Huston, T. L. (1980) 'The dyadic trust scale: toward understanding interpersonal trust in close relationships', *Journal of Marriage and the Family*, 42 August: 595–604.

Lazo, H. (1937) *Retailer Cooperatives*, New York: Harper and Bros.

Muckian, M. and Arnold, M. A. (1989) 'CEO network '89', *Credit Union Management* 12 (12): Dec: 21.

Oliver, R. L. (1997) *Satisfaction: A Behavioral Perspective on the Consumer*, Boston, MA: McGraw-Hill.

Opinion Research Corporation International (1999) 'Global 100: attitudes to corporate branding report', April.

Pearce, J. A. and David, F. R. (1987) 'Corporate mission statements: the bottom line' *Academy of Management Executive* 1 (2): 109–16.

Ruekert, R. W. and Churchill, G. A. (1984) 'Reliability and validity of alternative measures of channel member satisfaction', *Journal of Marketing Research*, 21 May: 226–33.

Shoham, A., Rose, G. M. and Kropp, F. (1997) 'Conflict in international channels of distribution', *Journal of Global Marketing* 11 (2): 5–22.

Simpson, J. T. and Mayo, D. T. (1997) 'Relationship management: a call for fewer influence attempts?', *Journal of Business Research* 39 (3) July: 209–18.

Want, J. H. (1986) 'Corporate mission', *Management Review*, August: 46–50.

Williams, A., Dobson, P. and Walters, M. (1993) *Changing Culture*, 2nd edn, London: Institute of Personnel Management.

Zeithaml, V., Berry, L. L. and Parasuraman, A. (1990) *Delivering Service Quality*, New York: Free Press.

9 Reputation and business performance

Liu, H. and Davies, G. (1995) 'The retailer's marketing mix and commercial performance', *International Review of Retail Distribution and Consumer Research* 5 (2): 147–65.

10 Challenges in Reputation Management

Aldersey-Williams, H. (1994) *Corporate Identity*, London: Lund Humphries.

Carter, D. (ed.) (1978) *Corporate Identity Manuals*, New York: Art Direction Book Company.

Munari, B. (1999) *Made in Italia*, Milan: Istituto Nazionale Editoriale Italiano.

Olins, W. (1989) *Corporate Identity*, London: Thames and Hudson.

Index